A Walk Along the Ganges

A Walk Along the Ganges

Dennison Berwick

'It is trite that one half the world knows not how the other half lives. Who can say what sores might be healed, what hurts solved, were the doings of each half of the world's inhabitants understood and appreciated by the other?'

Mahatma Gandhi
1869–1948

Century Hutchinson Ltd
London Melbourne Auckland Johannesburg

© Dennison Berwick 1986
First published in 1986 by Century Hutchinson Ltd,
Brookmount House, 62–65 Chandos Place, London, WC2N 4NW

Century Hutchinson Publishing Group (Australia) Pty Ltd
PO Box 496, 16–22 Church Street, Hawthorn, Melbourne, Victoria 3122

Century Hutchinson Group (NZ) Ltd
PO Box 40–086, 32–34 View Road, Glenfield, Auckland 10

Century Hutchinson Group (SA) Pty Ltd
PO Box 337, Berglvei 2012, South Africa

Printed and bound in Great Britain by
Anchor Brendan Ltd, Tiptree, Essex

British Library Cataloguing in Publication Data
Berwick, Dennison
A walk along the Ganges.
1. Ganges River Region (India) —Description and travel
I. Title
915'.4'10452   DS485.G25

ISBN 0–09–163760–0

To family and friends who have put up with a lot

Contents

Acknowledgements

This solo journey was made possible by the hospitality and enthusiasm of hundreds of people, many of them anonymous. Especially, I thank the many families and individuals in India who unstintingly shared the comforts of their homes. They include: Gunadhar Bera; Father Boniface and the fathers at the Franciscan Ashram in Bhagalpur; Cyril; Bhagwan Das; Gopal Das; Professor A. Deb and family; Onkar Dubey; Raj and Adarsh Dutt; Dr and Mrs Dutta; Miss Hardless Kennedy; Daya Shankar Keshai; Father Josey Kunnunkal and fathers in Patna; Lakshman Menon, his mother and sister; Brijesh Kumar Misra; S. K. Mortoja; Prakasha Thakur; Miss Gudrun Saether; Swapan Saha; the Jesuit fathers and brother at Sahibganj; the Saran family; Geoffrey and Kusum Seager; Diptish Sen; the Madem Sharma family; Balram Singh; Gulab Singh; Lakbir Singh; Prakasha Nand Singh; Prem Singh; Surendra Singh; Novshad Ali and family. And my special thanks to Joe Collins.

I am indebted to Professor C. P. Varma for his patience and generosity in teaching me the rudiments of Hindi and to the ladies of St Mary's, Old Delhi for their hospitality in having me to stay for six weeks following the walk. My thanks also to Dr K. R. Ranganathan who willingly provided a report on water pollution in the Ganga and to the customs officer at New Delhi airport who released me from bureaucratic idiocy as I was leaving the country. My thanks also to Jamie Campbell, SCF field director in India, and his staff.

Veteran travellers Wilfred Thesiger and Eric Newby were both generous with advice, encouragement and introductions. I am deeply grateful.

In Canada, I thank Ann Garneau for literally keeping the home fire burning and tirelessly performing a hundred errands; Dr David Baird; Jack and Laura Bales, Bruce Elniski, Terry Holliss, Linda Krause, and Joanne Lavkulich for their active, generous support and patient listening. I thank my parents and friends, to whom this book is dedicated, for helping me through this project.

I also thank Horst Schaefer for providing a knapsack and camera bags.

Author's Note

The idea of walking the length of the Ganga fixed itself in my mind suddenly one morning while gazing over the Nile, but it was several years before I felt myself ready to undertake the journey. My motives and ambitions were mixed. I wanted to make a great walk, to set off with no prospect of ending for months. I wanted to see the land that had fired the British imagination for generations. I wanted to travel at the pace of rural India, where four out of five Indians live, and to walk in the footsteps of the peasants.

And why the Ganga? I was searching for answers to one question: How could a river also be a goddess? For millions of Hindus, the river Ganga is the physical expression of the goddess Ganga; bathing in her waters is both spiritual ritual and necessary ablution. We have learned so well in the West to separate sacred from secular that the very notion of their being indivisible, like the Ganga, seems absurd. However, the Native Indians of Canada have a saying, 'Never judge a man until you've walked a mile in his moccasins,' and this was something I took literally. I was determined to wear village clothes, eat local foods, adopt local customs for washing and toilet and as much as possible speak the language. I felt that meeting India's people and walking through her villages and beside her most sacred river was the only way to learn about the country. Perhaps then, I thought, I might begin to understand something of the relationship between the Ganga and her devotees and might find answers to my question. My walk beside the Ganga was also being used as a money-raiser by Save the Children Fund in England. 'If you're crazy enough to make the walk, can we use it to raise money for our work in India?' the Fund's head of public relations had asked. Project Ganges was thus born under the direction of my mother, who was vice-chairman of the Fund's United Kingdom Committee at the time. This aspect of the journey was to become more and more important to me as the walk continued and I saw the conditions of some of the poorest people in India. It was with immense gratitude to the people who donated to Project Ganges that I had the honour to present the final cheque to HRH The Princess Anne, President of Save the Children Fund, when she visited Bradford, West Yorkshire in November 1984. The walk along the Ganges was made between November 1983 and June 1984. At that time, the foreign exchange rates were: Fifteen Indian rupees (R15) = £1; R8 = Canadian $1. Ten million rupees equals one crore rupees.

Finding My Feet

My mind returned to the first morning of the walk, to the tepid sea water, pale brown before sunrise, when I went out for a solitary swim where the holy Ganga merged with the Indian Ocean in the Bay of Bengal. I had hoped that the rising sun would burst portentously through the billowy grey clouds in shafts of brilliant light, for Hindus honour the sun as the Divine, represented by warmth and light. But the sun did not shine; instead, the empty beach at Ganga Sagar stretched dully for miles and all along the water's edge families with pink or blue fishing nets, set up like wind-breaks at right angles to the shore, were catching fry on the retreating tide. These near-transparent fish were being trapped in small bags at the narrow end of the conical nets and strained into earthen bowls by women and children wrapped in shawls against the cold morning wind. Later, the fish would be released into freshwater village ponds to grow or to be eaten by the larger fish already living there.

Up behind the beach, on a stretch of flat, white sand, stood the lonely, sky-blue temple of Kapil Muni. I passed a man taking down the bamboo shutter of one of the dozen stalls that sold prayer beads, brass idols, boiled sweets and coconuts for pilgrims to offer in the temple, and three holy men in their bright orange robes peered at me from a row of bamboo cubicles, raised from the sand on stilts, and scratched their grey beards when I took off my sandals and followed three civil servants from Calcutta up the steps into the temple.

A man with a grey stubbled chin and dark complexion was sitting cross-legged on the dirty marble floor in front of a stone statue thickly daubed in orange paint. The statue was of the seer Kapila in whose honour the temple was named and whose eyes seemed to glare angrily at all visitors. He was flanked by the goddess Ganga on his left, whose features were all but obliterated by the orange paint, and by one of the famous holy men from Hindu mythology, called Bhagirathi. The first visitor knelt in front of Kapila and I looked on before taking my turn.

The priest gave him flower petals to offer at the base of the statue and poured a teaspoon of holy water into his right hand, which he drank while the priest gabbled a sacred poem with the speed of an auctioneer before reaching out for his 50 paise offering. The civil servant got up, bowed and stood beside the temple door waiting for his companions. I was then invited forward.

As many as half a million pilgrims come to this temple and to bathe in the sea during the great Ganga Sagar fair which is held in late January. Unfortunately, I was twelve weeks too early.

After leaving the temple, I went to the tea-stall across the lane from the *ashram* where I had been staying in a small room with bed and table, like a monk's cell. I was received at the tea-stall with friendly smiles, as if the men sitting at the wooden benches already knew me, which in one way they did. The whole village of Ganga Sagar had had to endure my toneless singing at evening prayers the night before.

'Do you have fear of God?' I had been asked in the *ashram*.

'Yes', had been my innocent but correct response, and I was then ushered into a room crowded with monks dressed in white. A gallery of portraits of a dozen gods and goddesses hung round the walls and a group of young monks were sitting at a box harmonium, *tabla* (drums), cymbals and microphone in front of a dais on which stood a large portrait of the founder of the *ashram*, decorated with a garland of orange marigolds. Enthusiastic hand-clapping accompanied their devotional songs which were being broadcast by loudspeakers throughout Ganga Sagar and across the empty beaches. I am no musician, or singer, and I sat cross-legged and silent on the hard floor with a silly smile on my face. The smile vanished when the microphone was passed to me and I was urged to sing. I declined the invitation but after the next song the microphone came back again. It was obvious that I would have to perform but my mind had gone blank. With a little longer to prepare myself, I would have sung William Blake's 'Jerusalem', but the only song I could think of at the time was 'Evergreen'. I had no idea of the words, and nor had anyone else, so I mumbled through the song out of key, and this murder of music and devotion was received with good humour. I was not asked to sing again, but my performance did serve to introduce me to the community and the men in the tea-stall were welcoming the next morning when I sat down to enjoy sweet, milky tea and a final moment of rest.

There were no well-wishers or fanfare on 23 November when I strapped the little knapsack to my back and started out alone along the empty lane heading north. After three hundred yards, a man stopped me to ask where I was going. It sounded preposterous to say 'to the source of the holy river', so I just smiled and pointed up the lane. To the next person who asked, I gave the name of the next town and he suggested I should take the bus. I pointed to my feet and he gaped at me in disbelief.

I started out with four blisters inflicted by a pair of brand new sandals bought in Calcutta and quickly gained two more. I wore a skirt called a *lungi* of green-check cotton cloth that reached my ankles and a beige shirt (or *kurta*) down to my thighs, having decided not to wear my *sahib* uniform of Western shirt and trousers, as although I felt self-conscious in these village clothes and continually had to remind myself to take small steps to avoid tripping, it removed one barrier between myself and the people I met. My long, confident stride marked me as a foreigner, but villagers were not quite sure what to make of a foreigner who wore ordinary village clothes and in the initial moment of hesitation allowed their humanity to shine through.

To my relief, after eight miles a group of school children accosted me at a tea-stall by the roadside and their teacher came to invite me to stay at his house overnight. This augured well because I had no idea where I would be sleeping each night. I carried no tent, there were no hotels outside cities, and I did not want to have to request shelter from village leaders. The first two weeks of the walk, from the Bay of Bengal upstream to Calcutta, were to give me the chance to reconnoitre conditions in the countryside and to decide how little equipment would be necessary and what I might need to buy in Calcutta.

'Now you will take your bath', said Gunadhar Bera, my host, in English. I duly stripped off shirt, sandals and money belt and stood half naked outside the front door with a bucket of cold water. Light drizzle began to fall as three boys stopped to stare at me lathering soap over my flabby, lily-white body, shivering in the cold rain and attempting to wash under the *lungi* and maintain public modesty, which forbade standing in underpants. Having rinsed off the soap and dried as well as possible in the drizzle, I changed into horse-shoe shaped pyjama trousers and regretted not having practised this manoeuvre before my public debut. I had rehearsed putting on and knotting the *lungi* but still lived in fear of it falling down at any moment.

Gunadhar lived with his young wife and 18-month old son in a small adobe house that looked like a loaf of brown bread with a small door and red roof tiles. The five little rooms were sparsely furnished and neat and clean. An incense burner and framed picture of a god stood in a small alcove in the living room but Gunadhar could not remember the god's name when I asked him.

The deputy headmaster from Gunadhar's school was also invited for the meal of fish, rice and pieces of potato in a sour sauce which we ate sitting cross-legged on mats on the earth floor of the living-room. I declined the offer of a spoon, being determined to master the art of eating with the right hand, and sat hunched over the bowls with an aching back spilling food incompetently through my fingers. Gunadhar's wife busied herself in the kitchen while the men ate and a ten-year-old girl fetched extra rice and potato to us. I was told that she came from a poor family in the village to help with cooking, cleaning and with the baby in return for food, shelter and schoolbooks. She was speechless and shy but often smiled at me from behind the chattering adults.

After lunch, while the women ate, I was put to bed on a low table, the size of a double bed, made up with quilt and blanket, to sleep off the enormous plate of chunky rice that I had just consumed. Gunadhar lit three incense sticks to keep off mosquitoes and I fell asleep to the sound of heavy rain clattering on the roof tiles over my head. When I woke, a *tiffin* of sweet, milky tea and freshly shredded coconut with sugar and warm milk was served, which I washed down with lots of water. Then at dusk Gunadhar and I went off with umbrellas to Hospital Bazaar, one mile up the road, to buy vegetables and fish. These were laid out on jute matting in the mud at the roadside and Gunadhar quickly bought on credit the only *hilsa* and sent the fish home with a bicycle rickshaw-*wallah* to be cooked for our dinner while we visited his friends in Hospital Bazaar, named after the 25-bed hospital that served Sagar Island's 20,000 inhabitants.

Hilsa is a strong-flavoured fish, similar to herring, and considered a delicacy by the people of Bengal, despite its abundance of tiny, forked bones. I did not know its cost, though it was certainly high. I had been warned about eating food offered by poor people and of the need to do my own cooking to ensure good nutrition. Consequently, I carried a small kerosene stove, pressure cooker and supplies of lentils, peas and dried vegetables, but after walking eight miles on this first day I had already realised that cooking was completely impractical, and would attract crowds of curious onlookers. I also carried Indian rupees and travellers' cheques and intended to pay for my food whenever possible. However, it would have been very offensive to offer to pay for food given to me as a friend. Once before, in Africa, I had fallen foul of this—instantly converting my friend into just a servant. I had no intention of scrounging, but I wanted to avoid an arrogant, patronising attitude and felt that people, poor or rich, would know their own affairs best, especially whether they wanted or could afford to offer hospitality to a stranger. If Gunadhar wanted to splash out to buy a *hilsa*, which both he and his wife would also enjoy greatly, then it was my responsibility to be an appreciative and grateful guest.

The market was deserted and the night silent when we left the bazaar to return home for dinner. Pinpricks of light from oil lamps shone in the darkness on either side of the road and we passed a group of men in a room rehearsing for a forthcoming village play. Gunadhar and I walked side by side and he told me of his desire to visit many of the places I would be seeing beside the Ganga. It was not possible for him to do so, he said, with a wife and son to support on an income of 900 rupees per month. Only at government expense would there ever be a chance of seeing his own country, and he commented: 'You know, life here is very monotonous.' His words were to stay with me for months.

Early next morning, I took another public bath and a *tiffin* of banana, shredded coconut, boiled egg and two white balls of milk solids saturated in syrup. This was a popular sweet in Bengal and one on which I gagged each time and had to chew quickly and swallow. We took a second *tiffin* of fresh fruit and tea with the friends of the previous night in Hospital Bazaar. More than 30 people gathered in the street with Gunadhar to see me off with good wishes and a short bow executed with the palms of the hands pressed together as if in prayer. After a final wave, I settled into a steady stride along the lane that ran up the middle of the island between palm trees and fields of ripening rice. The local single-decker bus trundled by once an hour scattering flocks of goats and men on bicycles into the ditches and I walked with a quick pace delighting in the freedom of walking.

'I speak no Bengali. Very little Hindi', I said in hesitant Hindi to each crowd of faces and eyes that gathered whenever I stopped at a tea-stall. I fetched out a Hindi picturebook with mangoes, goats, pens and sugarcane and when people saw my children's book they smiled and relaxed and glasses of sweet, milky tea were brought to me. Always there were questions, in Bengali, repeated so often that I eventually understood: Where are you coming from? Where are you going? What is your educational qualification? What is your age? Where is your wife? What is your good name? Which country are you from?

'Canada', I usually said, although born and educated in Britain. The pageant of the British Raj, the eccentric English architecture of the sub-continent, the dedication of District Commissioners, the snobbery of the gymkhana clubs and the fussing of English *memsahibs* all seem to be bizarre and inappropriate now. India has many memories of the British Raj, both good and bad, but being a citizen of both Canada and Britain, I wanted to travel under a neutral flag and avoid being associated with the British in India.

I was to hear many times: 'Before the English came we were not poor. They are the reason for our poverty. They took our riches, the wealth from our people. They squeezed them like juice from a lemon.'

In the late morning under a blue sky, a man selling betel nut at a small stall stopped me on the road wanting to buy the kerosene stove protruding from my knapsack. Having decided it was a useless piece of equipment I was happy to extol its virtues with a great deal of mime and salesman's chatter in English and Hindi, praising its solid brass construction, its toughness, its ideal size. I pumped up the pressure and let the blue flames burn with a loud roar. He offered me 70 rupees, I wanted R85, the price I had paid in Calcutta, and we compromised at R75. I was glad to be rid of the stove and container of kerosene and happy to be soon walking again with a lighter load.

Wild orchards of palm trees shaded the adobe houses in each village I passed, arranged around the innumerable ponds of green water that were used for bathing, dish-washing, laundry, and fishing with small circular nets thrown spinning into the water. Black water buffaloes wallowed up to their big necks amid the pale-purple water hyacinth flowers, munching on the succulent leaves. Brown myna birds, with yellow beaks and yellow mascaraed eyes, flew between palm trees and buildings, pecking at insects and seeds on the earthen patios outside people's homes. These yards were outdoor extensions of the houses where cattle were tethered at night, rice and wheat could be threshed in their seasons, children played with marbles and women gossiped while knitting or shelling peas.

I was always met by staring brown eyes, silence and sometimes laughter from children. Women pulled up the veils of their saris making hoods to hide their faces or turned away. Only dogs, cows and ducks preening themselves beside the ponds carried on without a second look.

I reached the northern end of the island on the second day at about 2 p.m. after an 11-mile walk and sat down tired and a bit giddy on a bench outside a tea-stall, to wait an hour for the sun to sink in the sky. After a shave by a local barber who operated next to a radio repair stall, I boarded the wooden ferry to cross a mile-wide stretch of the Ganga to the mainland. This channel was a minor branch of the huge Ganga delta that covers an area of 22,000 square miles in India and neighbouring Bangladesh.

The ferry chugged away from the pier, out into the flat, brown river. An old man with a cream-coloured shawl hanging over drooping shoulders, grasping a bamboo staff in his brown, sinewy hand moved along the deck with his begging bowl. He elicited little response from the eight passengers, who continued talking, ignoring him while he stood silently in front of them before slowly looking round for somebody else to approach and shuffling away empty-handed on legs as thin as his walking stick. When he reached me, I could not look in his eyes but dropped a 25-paise coin into his bowl. I had never before seen any man look so pleased to receive so little money, but not wanting to dwell on this, I turned away to gaze at the orange sun setting over the line of trees across the water on Sagar Island.

I thought of the story of this mighty river's descent to earth from heaven. It is a story known throughout the country by every Hindu and told in poetry, drama, comic books and in the lullabies which old men sing their grandchildren:

Once upon a time there was a king called Sagara, a mighty and just ruler with 60,000 sons. In the traditional manner, to expand his kingdom he released a horse and claimed lands wherever the animal wandered for one year. Neighbouring rulers had either to submit or fight. The horse visited so many lands that the gods feared that Sagara's territories would reach heaven itself and the horse was therefore kidnapped by the goddess Indra. Sagara was angry when he heard of the theft, though he did not know the identity of the thief, and sent out his sons to recover the animal. They looked throughout the world and even went into the underworld to seek out their father's horse. At last, they found the animal in an *ashram* beside the sea. Nearby sat the seer called Kapila (actually he was the great god Vishnu) deep in meditation. Believing they had found the thief, all 60,000 sons rushed forward to Kapila. He was not pleased and he reduced them all to ashes by the fiery look in his eyes.

When his sons did not return, King Sagara sent out his grandson who found the ashes in heaps on the foreshore where Kapila lived and he returned home with the sad news that their souls would not rest in peace until the goddess Ganga flowed from heaven to earth to purify their ashes. This was an impossible condition and Sagara died of a broken heart; though according to one legend, he lived to be 30,000 years old.

At length, Sagara's great-great-grandson Bhagirathi became ruler. He was a valiant king, an honest seeker of Truth, but childless. Desiring an heir, he entrusted his kingdom to ministers and went off to the Himalayas to spend years in prayer and austerities, eating only once a month. After years and years, Brahma (the four-headed Creator and another great god with Shiva and Vishnu) was pleased by Bhagirathi's perseverance and granted him both an heir and that the goddess Ganga would flow to earth to purify his ancestors' ashes.

The young goddess Ganga was not pleased to be told what to do and Bhagirathi had to petition the Lord Shiva to receive the impetuous goddess in his hair and to release her slowly, otherwise her fall from heaven would smash the earth. Ganga decided to show off to Shiva and she came at him in a great flood intending to wash him away. Shiva remained calm and took the goddess in his hair, not allowing one drop of her water to spill, in order to teach her good manners. Bhagirathi had to ask Shiva to release Ganga and he did this in seven streams, the seven sources of the river in the Himalayas.

Then Bhagirathi led Ganga—in the form of the river—towards the ashes of his 60,000 ancestors at Kapila's *ashram*, said to be on the site of the Kapil

Muni temple in Ganga Sagar. All did not go well on the journey across the dry plain of north India because Ganga had a mishap. Her flood damaged the prayer platform of a young ascetic who was so annoyed that he swallowed up the whole river. This perplexed Bhagirathi. Yet again the gods intervened and the ascetic released Ganga out of his ear. Ganga followed Bhagirathi once again towards Kapila's *ashram* without further accident and Bhagirathi performed the necessary funeral rites for his ancestors at Ganga Sagar, securing their entry into heaven.

This was how Mother Ganga came to earth to purify the souls of mankind. It seemed an unlikely story, as I gazed across the two-mile-wide river as we neared the landing on the mainland.

On reaching the mainland, I went quickly to Kakdwep (pronounced Kaakdeep), the nearest village along a brick road to look for accommodation before dark. There was no room at the government bungalow (intended to accommodate visiting civil servants), there was no hotel, and I paced up and down the congested market street as night fell, hoping that something would happen, though I was not quite sure what. Eventually, nothing did happen and I went into the Bharat Petroleum office clutching my Hindi exercise-book, pointing to the appropriate phrase that I couldn't hope to pronounce; 'I am looking for a place to sleep.'

The man at the desk called an ancient messenger to take me to a noisy, dusty shop four doors along the cobbled street where a great machine was stripping husks off the rice brought in by people from surrounding villages. Dry, brown rice went in at the top and white, de-husked rice came out at the bottom. The husks, the most nutritious part of the rice, were either taken home to be fed to cattle, burnt as fuel or occasionally used in making concrete. People eat white rice because they prefer its taste and because brown rice takes too long to cook and the extra fuel is expensive.

An empty warehouse adjoined the rice dehusking machine and an old man laid out a bamboo mat on the grimy concrete floor. Relieved at having found shelter, I put down my bags and went in search of supper.

I had taken daily Hindi lessons with a tutor in Bengali-speaking Calcutta for two weeks before beginning my walk and could now read and write the 45 letters of the Hindi alphabet like a three-year-old child and knew such useful phrases as, 'I don't speak Hindi'. My tutor, Professor Varma, was from Allahabad, in the heart of the Hindi-speaking region of India. Private tutoring is common in India and several schoolchildren came to him for lessons. On our third session, I asked the fee for my tutorials and he dismissed the question with a wave of his hand. 'God has given me enough', he said. 'Let those others pay. Your enthusiasm and sincerity for Mother Ganga are enough for me.'

I had been anxious to learn Hindi as this is the language most widely spoken in northern India, but it is hardly spoken at all along the first 300 miles of my journey through West Bengal. Efforts by the Central Government in New Delhi to impose Hindi as the national language, to replace English, have been strongly resented in Bengal and southern India.

'I am a Bengali. My mother tongue is Bengali, then I know English. What is Hindi? It is the language of New Delhi', was a view I was to hear many, many times.

So my few words of Hindi were of little use to me in Kakdwep when I went in search of supper. A woman took me to a neighbouring shopkeeper who relayed to her in Bengali my desire for rice, *dal*, fish and vegetables. She smiled, nodded her head and took me back to sit at one of the tables next door. The serving of rice was enormous and twenty minutes later I paid the bill of six rupees and fifty paise (R6-50) and waddled back among the bright lights of the fruit market to the concrete floor of the empty rice warehouse. An hour later, a frail, elderly man came in with a big, black book for guests to register and pay R1 for the floor space. Three men already asleep under mosquito nets, set up like see-through shoe boxes over their mats, were woken from their groaning and snoring to complete these formalities, and then two young men, with plastic shopping bags and blankets, came into the warehouse and settled against the brick pillars that supported the bamboo rafters and tiled roof.

Now no one was in a mood for sleep and I passed round *beedis* to keep away the mosquitoes. *Beedis* are poor men's cigarettes, consisting of a noxious combination of dried leaf rolled with a few shreds of tobacco and tied with a pink thread at one end. A spell of questioning ensued and was only concluded when everyone knew the caste, birthplace and occupation of his neighbour.

We finally lay down to sleep at 9.30, after the market had been closed for over an hour, and the streets were deserted, with shop shutters down and padlocked, stalls abandoned, the last bus gone and only the footfalls and chatter of half a dozen stragglers going home in the dark to be heard. The front doorway of the warehouse was closed with a fence of bamboo and bolted, and two calves were led inside from the back-yard and tethered. A frog began croaking beside me in the dark, then hopped away, and I lay waiting for the scurrying of rats but was probably too sleepy to hear them. Having foolishly not brought a mosquito net, I wrapped my shawl around my feet, tucked in the sides with care and pulled the top over my head in the way I had seen so many people doing when sleeping on the streets. But each toss and turn in the night exposed me to loud, hungry mosquitoes. I woke hourly throughout the night either maddened by the bloodsuckers or sweating beneath the blanket. I was impatient for dawn to come and arose with a face grotesquely puffed out from numerous bites.

I set out along the top of an embankment beside the river, leaving behind the yawning, shivering tea-*wallahs* of Kakdwep fanning their fires into life. I was uncertain whether I would be able to keep close to the river on my walk north to Calcutta because I had now hit the edge of the forested swamps called the Sunderbans, which stretch 120 miles across the southern fringe of the Ganga delta. Sluggish rivers, sand-banks, tidal channels and mudflats criss-cross the forests of mangrove trees where the last Royal Bengal tigers, estuarine crocodiles, leopards, pythons and wild hogs survive despite the steady encroachment of Man.

The Ganga delta covers an area almost twice the size of Belgium and even 175 miles from the Indian Ocean the land never reaches 60 feet above sea level. Calcutta is 80 miles from the sea and only 20 feet above sea level. During the monsoon, the river's torrential water backs up behind high tides, flooding the honeycomb of delta channels, submerging the rice fields, making millions of people homeless and disrupting their lives for months. High embankments such as I was walking along have been built to protect the low-lying fields wherever the Sunderbans have been cleared. I had no idea where the embankment path would lead and I might yet reach impassable mudflats or a tributary river too deep to wade.

It was Day Three of the journey from Ganga Sagar and I was walking alongside the holy river for the first time. Its choppy, grey water glistened with the morning sunshine and thick, white mist concealed the opposite shore that was at least seven miles away. The estuary did not seem like a river at all and it was more like walking along a seashore, where the ebbing tide had stranded black fishing boats on broad mudflats and where men had pitched their nets to fish for fry on the retreating water.

It was the beginning of the rice harvest and men and women were crouched out in the fields cutting the crop with their hand-held sickles, bundling each handful into stooks that would be carried home on their heads at sunset. Wages were low—at most R7 for men and R6 for women, well below the legal minimum wages of R11 and R9 per day, but without land to grow their own food, families were grateful for the opportunity to earn even this at harvest and planting times, and sometimes I would hear women singing as they laboured.

The embankment either circled villages or ran through the middle and I walked elevated like a model on a catwalk, visible to all, being alternately greeted with friendly laughter and a pointing finger, or by a sudden fearful silence. I encountered children playing with marbles and shy girls mixing chopped straw with cow dung and patting the mixture into discs with their hands, to be dried in the sunshine and burned as cooking fuel. Boys called brothers and sisters to look at the approaching spectacle; others raced away to hide behind their mothers' saris or to vanish through dark doorways into their homes. Some would come up to the edges of their gardens to stare with brown eyes at the stranger, and then to chatter and to nudge each other, giggling.

Sometimes an older boy, perhaps aged ten, would call out in Bengali, 'Where are you going? Where have you come from? Which is your country?' I was by now so familiar with those questions that I had picked up the meaning and was able to reply in Hindi. If I smiled, the children smiled back and this form of communication relieved them from having to stare at me. Occasionally, a group of children—almost always only boys—would follow me happily along the path up to the invisible boundary line of their village. Then they could go no further and we would part with hand waves and laughter.

At mid-morning, I arrived at a small tributary river with a V-bank of grey, slimy mud. There was no way to get across and I walked half a mile inland looking for a bridge before coming to two boats, shaped like crescent moons, where a couple of youths were mending fishing nets. They watched me stepping barefoot towards them across the cold mud, which oozed up between my toes, presumably expecting me to fall on my back at any moment and to slither down the mud into the grey water. After a brief exchange of sign language, they obligingly punted me across the *nullah*. On the other side was a bank of mud that was like soft clay, and I climbed up by digging my feet firmly into this, making deep steps, watched all the while by the youths and several men standing at the top. I completed the ascent without mishap, to the good-natured disappointment of this audience, and with mud plastered up to my ankles like thick winter socks. There was no water to wash my feet, so I walked several miles barefoot and carried my sandals until the mud dried, cracked and fell off. But it would still be several months before my feet were sufficiently hardened to be able to walk like this comfortably.

At midday I stopped at the first tea-stall I had seen that day to eat *muri* (rice roasted in hot sand and resembling Rice Krispies) with milk and sugar, and to answer the inevitable string of questions.

'Is this Kulpi?' I asked in a moment of lunacy.

'Yes, yes,' came the helpful reply.

If this was Kulpi, a place marked on my map, then I was not far from the town of Diamond Harbour, where I could find accommodation, and this simple delusion made enthusiasm overcome common sense.

I drank water at the village handpump and although it was still hot started on my way again. My feet began to ache after a couple of miles. The sensible action would have been to return to the fishing village and take my chances on accommodation and food for the night, but instead, I compounded a mistake with stupidity. I sat down under a tree to rest, allowing the burning sensation to spread across the soles of my feet. I waited five minutes and then decided to keep walking. I walked and walked and walked, deliberately outweighing the pain in my feet by the pleasure of striding beside the river on such a bright afternoon.

The estuary was narrower and the morning mist had burnt off to reveal the opposite shore as a blur, half-hidden by haze on the horizon. I could distinguish cranes, warehouses and the oil refinery of a new port rising above the fringe of palm trees several miles away across the calm water. This was the port of Haldia which will one day replace Calcutta as the major harbour of north-east India. Calcutta's port is slowly dying, due to the river silting up and the difficulty and danger encountered by big modern ships in reaching a port that is 80 miles from the sea around tight bends and up narrow channels. The port's life has been extended 20 years by a barrage built 193 miles upstream of the harbour, which diverts water into the left arm of the delta, but Calcutta will eventually join the long list of silted-up ports along the Ganga.

By late afternoon, when my shadow stretched out across the foot-path, I was walking slowly, with both shoulders aching from the unaccustomed weight of the knapsack, and my feet burning. The setting sun glistened on the river and shone across the chequer-board of golden stubble and pale yellow rice. Men were carrying home the heavy stooks of rice either hanging from yokes across their shoulders or on their heads by the time I reached a tea-stall, limping, exhausted and aware that I had foolishly walked too far.

'This village, what is the name?' I asked, proudly reciting one of the Hindi phrases I had mastered.

'Kulpi,' said the tea-*wallah*.

I had walked 19 miles on Day Three of the journey and made a bloody mess of my feet. In three days I had covered 37 miles from the start of my walk at Ganga Sagar and was now 1520 miles from the source of the Ganga in the Himalayas. There was apparently nowhere to stay in Kulpi and my mutilated feet rendered me incapable of seeking somewhere out. So I boarded a local bus and travelled eight miles north to be welcomed by the monks into a Hindu *ashram* after evening prayers.

Rice, *dal* (thick lentil soup) and vegetables were brought to where I sat on the bed in one of the rooms, with burning feet. I felt sick and irritated with myself, and had little appetite. The light of a single bulb shone from the green gloss walls of the room that contained only the metal bed on which I was sitting and a table beneath the shuttered, glassless window. One of the novice monks, dressed in white, had fetched a metal bucket to be filled in the morning with cold water for washing both myself and my clothes, and it stood now at the foot of the table beside my knapsack.

I woke after a long sleep to find both feet were swollen and throbbing and my back and thighs aching. I cut open, drained and cleaned half a dozen blisters—evidence that my feet could not yet support my enthusiasm—and slept most of the day, or sat cross-legged on the bed, reflecting on my stupidity in walking too far too quickly. However, I did not doubt my ability to walk to the source of the river nor the sanity of such an undertaking. Already the Ganga had claimed me and I was determined to see the journey through whatever the cost.

The next day I laid out my six-foot map of the Ganga along the length of the bed. This was a US Government aviation map showing targets of military importance, not religious centres, and although the river altered its course every year the map was to prove remarkably accurate. The width of three fingers covered the distance I had so far walked and I realised for the first time just how far I was planning to go. Even without ever pausing in Calcutta, Benares or other cities, or in the villages along the way, it would take three months, and I had sore feet after only three days.

2

By the Banks of the Hooghly

Prayers and worship (*puja*) were offered at 4 a.m., 11 a.m. and 7 p.m. in the temple of the *ashram* in Diamond Harbour eight miles up the road from Kulpi where I was recuperating from my over-enthusiastic start to the journey. I sat each evening with 20 people on the wooden floor of the hall, singing devotional songs for half an hour before moving into a small room to stand respectfully in front of a portrait of the *ashram*'s founder, Swami Pranavanandaji Maharaj. He was sitting cross-legged, dressed in an orange toga, and looked to have been a plump man in his forties, who gazed at us with neither smile nor closed lips, neither speaking nor listening, but in that expressionless pose beloved by the painters of chocolate boxes. I cannot recount the details of our *puja*, nor give the words, nor the meaning of each symbolic act. It was all alien to me and I felt as a Martian might feel attending the Catholic Mass for the first time.

After finishing our devotions to the *swami*, we crammed into a smaller adjoining room and stood round a marble *linga* of Shiva. This thick, smooth, 14-inch pillar represents the phallus. The carved stone in which the *linga* stands represents the vulva, for Shiva is both male and female, and destroyer and reproducer.

The Brahmin leading the *puja* rocked back and forth with fan in hand over the *linga* then switched to violently shaking a brass handbell. Musicians with box harmonium, conch shell, drum, cymbals and handbells played as fiercely and as loudly as possible, shaking the room with an ear-splitting clangour. A young white-robed monk handed out flower petals and dotted our foreheads with a mark of white powder. A second monk came to each man and woman, holding a brass candelabrum that looked like a knuckleduster with five birthday candles. I watched to learn what to do and when my turn came, extended my right hand over the flames to receive their warmth and passed my hand over my forehead and hair. The music crescendoed to a climax and suddenly, mercifully, stopped. The Brahmin *pujari* knelt in the silence before the *linga* and offered pink petals to Shiva, placing them on top of the shaft and receiving a spoonful of Ganga water in the palm of his right hand to sip and wipe over his hair. One by one, everyone came forward to make their offering of flowers and to receive the spoonful of holy water from a monk, and although I hesitated, I too was invited forward to the *linga*. Here was none of the awkward reserve between people of different religions; it was a happy start to the long journey and struggle ahead.

Afterwards, the *pujari* and the doctor from *ashram*'s clinic sat outside on the verandah so that anyone who wanted to could touch their feet in veneration and receive their blessing. I was asked to sit with the grey-haired doctor, but did not presume to touch his feet. His voice was slow and soft and pleasing to the ear. He asked about my journey and, perhaps sensing my uncertainties, leaned towards me to tell a story about Dr R. S. Radhakrishnan, former president of India and one of her foremost modern philosophers.

'He was once in Moscow at a scientific convention. They asked him why he was so much concerned with religion. "We do not believe in God" they told him. "We believe in science."

"What is the purpose of your science?" asked Doctor Radhakrishnan.

"To seek truth for the good of people and for prosperity," came the reply.

"Then there is no difference between us. We too seek truth, good and prosperity in our religion" said the doctor.'

Truth, good and prosperity—these were standards, acceptable to Hindus, against which I might test the unusual, the bizarre and the sublime of Hinduism in the months ahead while living beside Mother Ganga.

The doctor asked my reasons for wanting to make the walk and commented in his gentle voice, 'I am in wonder that someone of your age and from your country should come to face such dangers, such hardship, such difficulties. It is a wonderful thing.'

The following evening, I strolled on my feeble feet past the brightly-lit stalls heaped with fruits and vegetables to buy tangerines which were in season and selling at six for R2. I also bought a small, rectangular mosquito net and paid a tailor to cut off twelve inches round the bottom, wanting to save space and not needing to be able to sit up under the net. I paused at a tea-stall and almost immediately a student introduced himself and thus I instantly became his friend. He took me to a glass-fronted shop selling the paraphernalia of consumer India—pressure cookers, electric fans, kerosene stoves and electric light bulbs—where another friend worked. Both were about 22 years old, with black moustaches and tan-brown faces and dressed in the western trousers and T-shirts which are the uniform of the modern in India. Teas were ordered and we sat at a table on the wide pavement outside the shop.

'This is my god, Lord Shiva', said the shopkeeper, producing a silvery bust made of shiny plastic. Shiva's hair was coiled in a bun on top of his head and his face was feminine and smooth, with small lips and a straight, slender nose.

'Why did you choose Shiva?' I asked.

My companions did not understand, so I began a pantomime of English, sign language and Hindi, and after much guesswork on both sides we went into the brightly-lit shop, where I carefully put down Shiva on the counter. My companions pointed to rows of framed pictures of different gods hanging above the top shelves of electric irons and boxes of light bulbs. I recognised the fun-loving Krishna and Kali and Durga, who rides a tiger. Then I was led through a tiny, dark passage behind the shop, where a man was cross-legged on the floor repairing a brass stove, and emerged into a small, oblong courtyard. Several doors opened into the courtyard where the shopkeeper's family of ten lived. One door was open and I looked into a narrow room crowded with miniature stone and brass sculptures of gods and goddesses. There must have been over a hundred figures set out on the floor and coloured posters of other deities hung in neat rows on the white-washed walls. The young man's widowed mother was kneeling on the stone floor presenting red flowers to a deity in front of her.

I realised that I had already seen many of the figures in that small room, without noticing them. Images of the most popular of India's 330 million gods are to be seen in alcoves and shelves or hanging on walls as calendars in almost every tea-stall, shop, taxi or bus and as medallions around people's necks. Deities often stand in pairs, the favourite deity shoulder-to-shoulder with the ubiquitous elephant-headed Ganesh, remover of obstacles and god of prosperity, who will be decorated with a few yellow or orange marigolds to match his fat yellow belly. Moslem shopkeepers compete with posters of Mecca, Medina or the Taj Mahal.

In India, there is no divorce of the supernatural from daily life. There is no word for 'religion'. The supernatural controls all things—whether by the action of invisible gods or by the movement of a person's soul. Sins are punished in this world and the righteous are blessed in this world. God brings both good and bad. God contains all things. The Ganga, both goddess and river, brings moisture and fertile soil and she also sweeps away villages and fields, causing despairing peasants to feud over whatever parcels of land remain.

On my last evening in Diamond Harbour, I was summoned while strolling in the market to a man sitting in the shop of a homeopathic doctor.

'I have wanted to see you. We shall talk tomorrow. Where is your home? Why have you come to India?' asked this stranger in a high-pitched nasal voice.

'No,' I said, 'I am leaving tomorrow.'

He was annoyed at this and gazed in silence at his gold wristwatch. He looked up after a minute and asked what I thought of Indian philosophy.

'I don't know anything,' I replied and he embarked on a long monologue on reincarnation and the law of Karma, the belief that actions and inactions in this life have consequences in future lives. When I asked why God allowed so much suffering he informed me:

'It is the punishment for wrong doing. No one is innocent.' The man talked at length, with punctilious pronunciation of English, about the mechanism of cause and effect that places Brahmins (the spiritual good-guys) at the top of the caste system and Untouchables at the bottom, just ahead of India's tribal peoples.

'What on earth has a month-old baby done wrong to die from diarrhoea?' I asked.

'The baby sinned in its previous life,' the man said, telling me that the consequences of every deed and misdeed were explained in the scriptures.

I asked my next question when I got the chance to interrupt him. 'If illness is punishment from God for previous crimes, then surely a doctor giving medicines to cure the illness is interfering with God's will?'

My host smiled at my ignorance and explained. 'It is not medicine that cures the patient, but God, when He is merciful.'

'Then why have medicines?' I asked, pointing to the rows of tiny bottles of homoeopathic remedies in a glass-fronted cabinet behind us.

'Yes, yes. They are just for the common people. They like to have them. Holy men have no need of medicines. It is God who cures, when he is merciful, you see. The West believes in material things. In India, we believe in the spiritual.'

I looked at his gold wristwatch, his high-fashion sandals and lambswool shawl and I nodded in silence. The law of Karma was a return to the fear, ignorance and superstition of the Dark Ages when people prayed to God to cure dysentery instead of digging deep latrines.

Before leaving Diamond Harbour after three days' rest and heading upstream to Calcutta, it was necessary first to return to Kulpi. I took the bus the eight miles south to there and dutifully walked back to Diamond Harbour. 'Earth Station Kulpi' declared a sign outside two big satellite dishes and a radio tower on the edge of the village. Across the road, a man and his son were goading two scrawny bullocks dragging a board across their ploughed field to break up clods of dry rice stubble!

Next morning at seven o'clock, I donated R100 to the head of the *ashram* for my five nights' stay, exchanged good wishes and set out north beside the estuary. A light dew covered the grass and white mist cloaked the opposite shore of the river, though the sun had been up for half an hour. It was peaceful, and it was marvellous to be walking again. I promised myself that I was going to be temperate and sensible. There was a long way to walk and pounding my feet for three days and recuperating for five days was plainly idiotic. This had the sound of a New Year's Resolution: made to be broken.

The tide was flooding and a line of four empty freighters heading for Calcutta—American, Russian and Indian—passed by after two hours. The 16 major sandbanks between the ocean and Calcutta could only be cleared at high tide and the ships moved slowly along the restricted navigable channel, guided by a pilot of the Bengal Pilot Service. The Portuguese founded the Bengal Pilot Service in 1661 and it was operated successively by the Dutch, French and English as their fortunes rose and fell in turn prior to Indian independence in 1947.

Ships going to Bengal's major port have not always followed the Hooghly. For almost a thousand years, the chief port was Tamralipti on a tributary of the Hooghly. This was flourishing two centuries before Christ and was famed throughout the civilised world from the Near East to China. But, by the time the Normans invaded England in 1066, the port of Tamralipti had died, its harbour and passage to the sea blocked by silt, and other ports along the Hooghly rose to prominence—Satgaon, Gaur, the town of Hooghly and Calcutta— only to silt up just as Tamralipti did.

Later in the afternoon, a young man on a bicycle stopped abruptly beside me on the footpath and asked who I was and where I was going.

'Calcutta,' I said.

'You must wait,' he said and cycled away.

I waited obediently on the footpath and he came back with three green coconuts and numerous spectators. One of these lopped off the top of the coconut with four swipes of his machete and this Nature's goblet was handed to me. The fresh juice was cool and tasted like weak mandarin orange juice.

Mortoja, the coconut provider, wanted me to ride to his home sitting on the parcel rack of his bicycle. Happily, I was walking! So he pushed his bike and we walked for two hours on the embankment footpath past several brickworks on the river bank. We questioned each other about many things, conversing amicably in a jumble of English, Hindi, Bengali, sign language and laughter.

'What is your caste?'

'I have no caste. In my country all men, one man,' I replied.

Mortoja was returning from his family's brickworks a few miles down river on the opposit bank, one of the many that transform Ganga's grey mud into bricks, flower pots and the disposable cups without handles used by tea-stalls and yoghurt sellers. I concluded that the many brick houses and adobe houses with tiled roofs were evidence of the rising prosperity of some Indians.

There are over 200 brickworks on the river banks between Diamond Harbour and the fringe of Calcutta (a distance of 48 miles) producing annually an estimated 80 million bricks. Each brick is hand made. Men dig the clay with shovels from pits beside the river and it is forced through a barrel-shaped puddling machine turned by a pair of bullocks goaded by a boy with a stick. One man lifts it out onto a stretcher from a small door at the base of the barrel, and two more carry it across to the moulders. These men work squatting on their haunches, their bare feet flat on the earth and their knees folded up into their armpits. They sprinkle the moulds with white sand, as if flouring bread tins, drop in the clay, cut off the top with a wire, dust the top with sand and knock out each brick with a sharp tap on the ground. I was told that on a good day a brick moulder produced a thousand bricks—that's one every 36 seconds for ten hours without stopping. The bricks dry in the sun and women then carry them 12 or 16 at a time on wooden boards on their heads into kilns. These are shaped like oblong fish boilers sunk into the ground, and the bricks are fired with wood and coal blazing through black funnels.

Mortoja told me the labourers received R35 for every 1000 bricks. When I checked later, this was about four times the daily wage of ploughmen and field labourers and seemed unbelievably high. Brickworks and stone quarries have a reputation as being amongst the most brutal and exploitative businesses in the country, where men, women and children are treated as slaves. The families lived in the worst conditions that I was to see during my journey. Their one-roomed homes were worse than the hovels inhabited by the rural destitute and far worse than sleeping, eating and raising families on Calcutta's pavements. After little over 50 miles on the walk, I was already learning to distinguish those minute gradings which mark the differences between the poor, the destitute and the slaves. I walked through several brickworks and families were always housed in single rooms varying in size between dog kennels and chicken coops. Their homes were constructed of loose bricks and built in terraced rows on bare earth in one corner of each brickworks. They were thatched with grasses or reject roof tiles if these were produced on site. Children played and families spent much of their time in the dirty alleys of mud or dust running between their homes. On most sites, water had to be fetched by bucket from the river, which also served as the latrine. There was no work for four months during the monsoon and no pay whenever work stopped because of rain, sickness or festivals.

We reached the tiny town of Falta late in the afternoon. This was a place that had slept since it had been a Dutch trading post in the eighteenth century, when the Dutch, French, Portuguese, Danes and English squabbled over the riches of Bengal. Mortoja cycled home to his village and I was left to look for a place to sleep. There was no *ashram* or hotel but the police suggested the little government bungalow two miles away, where after protracted negotiations I was allowed to sleep. I ate supper at a stall in the town, set up my newly-bought mosquito net on the hard bed and lay down inside.

Mortoja found me next morning resting under a banyan tree (Indian fig tree) watching an American ship coming up river. He and his friend, who had ridden out balancing on the parcel rack of Mortoja's bicycle, went down the path to attend to business and promised to catch up with me later.

Mortoja met up with me late in the morning and we walked to his family home which stood amid palm and banana trees beside a large pond. There were 45 people in his household: three mothers, three fathers, one sister-in-law, 18 girls and 20 boys (the children of the three couples and all calling one another sister or brother though, actually, they were cousins) aged between four and 45, and they were Moslems.

We stripped off shirts, sandals and money belt and plunged into the tepid pool of green water for a midday bath, watched and welcomed by half the household. I was inured to being a spectacle, having already found that it was impossible to do anything except defecate without an audience. We washed and splashed about in our *lungis* while dry *lungis* were fetched for us. Everyone laughed when they saw how I tied mine. Mortoja showed me how to tie the cloth both comfortably and securely. He made it look simple, but I found the technique hard to follow, and practised whenever I thought I was alone. Thereafter, I was at least confident that the *lungi* would not suddenly fall round my legs. But the advanced techniques of the rickshaw-*wallahs* who use one end of the cloth as a purse for coins, like the spare end of a knotted handkerchief, always eluded me.

Mortoja's father finished his prayers towards Mecca around 9 p.m.

and I was then called into the oblong compound of the abode house for supper. (There was another half-built brick house beside the pond but Mortoja said that they didn't yet have enough money to finish it.) The feast prepared by his mother was the spiciest I had ever eaten. I lost count of the glasses of water I gulped to rinse off the pain of burning lips, burning mouth and burning throat. *Hilsa* fish was served in a sauce so sharp it would have cut anyone's throat, along with curried chicken, fried eggs and bowls of rice. I ate with Mortoja, his father and six brothers (cousins) watching over my shoulder to make sure everything was perfect. They would eat after I had taken my fill and the women would eat after them.

The meal was delicious in its way but so hot that I was surprised not to vomit. It was probably the dessert that saved my stomach from exploding. The bowl of yoghurt, sweetened with molasses, had been bought specially for me and it was impossible to refuse taking at least a little. It was so disgustingly sweet that I thought I would gag on every mouthful and had to swallow quickly and rinse out with water.

I went to bed after the meal in a little room in the garden where the older children did school homework, and lay on the bed sweating and panting hard and desperately hoping not be sick. However, I slept well and was delighted to wake feeling refreshed to the sound of the Moslem call to prayer next morning at 4.45 a.m.

Allah Akbar, Allah Akbar . . . God is great, God is great.

The faces of a dozen children peered round the door at sunrise two hours later when they saw that I was awake: I was on stage again. After morning tea, Mortoja and a neighbour said they would walk with me to the Bata shoe factory four and a half hours' distance away and then ride home on the bus (a journey taking 40 minutes). The neighbour invited us to his home for tea, pastries and plantains (sweet bananas) before setting out, but I wanted to get moving. Thankfully Mortoja feigned not to understand and he led us to his neighbour's house, thus averting a breach of etiquette. Mortoja's friend described himself as a 'vagabond'. He was 26 years old and one of millions of university and college graduates without jobs who are considered, and consider themselves, too educated to take manual or clerical work, even if it were available.

We reached Batanagar (meaning Bata-port) at noon and the uniformed guards at the factory gates at first tried to turn us away. I insisted on seeing an officer to organise a tour so we went to eat at a *dhaba* while we waited. The ramshackle stall was in complete contrast to the neat, white workers' cottages set in the large park beside the factory. The Bata factory had been built by the multinational shoe company in 1934 and about 10,000 employees now produce over 23 million pairs of shoes, slippers and boots annually. Indeed, my own sandals were Bata made.

Wages at Batanagar are high (about R60 per working day), and the factory compound, which smells strongly of rubber, contains its own temple, schools, cinema, sports ground and 60-bed hospital, with single-storey homes for low grade employees and villas for senior management behind an additional wall and barbed wire. Jacaranda trees line one of the two broad avenues that lead across the park to the factory. Everything is modern, Western and conscious of Bata's advertising slogan:

'When You Buy Bata You Buy More Than Just A Pair Of Shoes.'

Cows and goats grazed beneath texts daubed in English on the high walls: 'Our Customer Our Master.' 'Our Shoes Our Pride.' Along with wristwatches and radios, shoes are promoted as symbols of a prosperous Modern India.

We were inside the visitors' room before the end of the factory's lunch hour, waiting in padded armchairs and our thigh-length shirts, *lungis* and sandals, incongruous beside salesmen from Bata's suppliers wearing sober Western suits. We sat near the door in one corner beside two washbasins and mirrors where these gentlemen could preen themselves, comb moustaches and readjust their ties. The self-confidence of my two companions began to wane under the scrutiny of these city slickers. They shifted uncomfortably from one foot to another, fidgeted with their hands and fumbled for the correct words of English when asked to sign the visitors' book.

'Can you write your name?' asked a security officer in English. Mortoja did not immediately reply in fluent English. The officer repeated his question with aggravated patience in Bengali, unconsciously marking the barrier between the English-speaking elite of industrialised India and the country to which all other Indians belong.

Here the fact that I was a white foreigner was to my advantage, and without the passport of my pale complexion, Mortoja and his friend would have been sent packing long ago. This reverence for the West was peculiar to the industrial cities where the ability to speak English marks one as a social superior.

We waited for three hours and I was eventually told that even a quick tour of the factory was impossible on a Friday. We were all disappointed, especially Mortoja and his friend, as without a high-caste companion, such as a foreigner, they would have no chance of seeing inside the factory. We went for tea, *samosas* (small pastries stuffed with spiced vegatables) and a smoke before parting.

It was too late for me to continue walking into Calcutta and there was no accommodation to be found locally. I did not want to impose on people's hospitality unnecessarily and I did have an invitation to stay from a young banker in Calcutta with whom I had stayed briefly before starting the walk. I decided to take the bus into the city and went immediately to the Fairlawn Hotel where I had sometimes eaten while taking my Hindi lessons and where my letters were being sent. The hotel had originally been a private house, built in the imposing colonial style in a garden secluded by high walls in the old Jewish quarter of the city. The foyer was open to the garden under a large, green portico, and the dining room, painted gloss white, was at the back of the foyer. It was all very British, with pictures of Prince Charles and Princess Diana and heaps of potted palms arranged just so, a gong to announce meals, and servants in white uniforms with turbans and white serving gloves. The hotel was owned by a Mr and Mrs Smith. Mr Smith was a tall, quiet, elderly man with white hair who ate luncheon with two white poodles sitting on his chair beside him. Mrs Smith was short, alert and had starched, brunette hair.

I reached the hotel after dark at about 5.30 p.m., tired, dusty and still wearing my *lungi*. I was checking through the box of letters on the glass-topped coffee table, which was piled high with women's magazines, when Mrs Smith noticed me from behind the counter and glared hostilely:

'And WHO are you? And WHAT are you doing?' she demanded.

'Hello,' I said, looking up cheerfully from the six letters in my hand. 'My name is Dennison Berwick. I'm the chap walking up the Ganga.'

'Oh! Ah!' exclaimed Mrs Smith, a smile quickly replacing her frown. 'How nice to see you.'

'May I have some tea?' I asked.

'Of course,' she said, and a servant was summoned forthwith.

3

Calcutta: A Hell Filled with Good Things

No visitor comes to Calcutta without preconceptions. It is a city that inevitably evokes an intense emotional response, and that has inspired many to unite about their responses.

'Dreadful, gruesome, frightening. The world's largest slum. A disastrously overcrowded place where tens of thousands sleep in the streets, a hell of degradation and squalor, the cesspool of the world. A dying city. A vision of the end of man,' wrote Peter T. White in *National Geographic* magazine in 1973.

The visitor is assaulted on arrival, as if entering a hectic laundry, by hot, humid air at the massive Howrah railway station or at Dum Dum airport (where the bullet of that name was invented). Drifting into the city on foot spared me this shock but instead I was engulfed by its strong, malodorous perfume which is a mixture of sweat, urine, rotting vegetables, coal and cow dung smoke, spices and traffic fumes all simmered together by Bengal's hot, humid climate. I gazed up at the crumbling stucco of the buildings, watched nursing mothers cook food by the roadside, was assaulted by blaring traffic and ever-moving crowds and very soon had a vision of Calcutta as being some kind of moving fungus.

'It all inspires anger, hatred, revulsion and pity,' wrote Trevor Fishlock, former India correspondent of *The Times*.

More than 12 million people live in the Calcutta Urban Agglomeration which stretches 50 miles along both sides of the Hooghly. The cities of Calcutta and Howrah lie at the southern end of this sprawl, facing each other across the black water. They officially contain over four milllion people but this count leaves out the tens of thousands of people who live on the pavements, rooftops and wherever there is space. It is a commonplace that the City is massively overcrowded, and that virtually non-existent sanitation fosters rampantly spreading disease. More than a century ago the *Statesman* observed: 'The masses of the people live in houses badly built, badly ventilated, and badly drained; and with all our costly machinery for educating them in other things, no attempt is made to impart popular education on the laws of health.'

Most people have always lived in wretched conditions because water, sewerage and street plans were provided only for the European quarter of the city. These Victorian services were overwhelmed long ago by a population which has constantly multiplied since the official population estimate of 300,000 in 1820. It is not surprising that many of India's own business executives shudder at the possibility of being transferred to Calcutta from Delhi, Bombay or Bangalore. But however bad the conditions in Calcutta, village people come to the city from Bihar and other states, and as illegal immigrants from Bangladesh, because there is at least the hope of work and survival.

I walked into a humble restaurant one evening to find a tall American woman with blonde hair standing near the entrance ordering plates of rice, *dal*, mutton curry and spinach for two boys whose chins touched the table top as they gobbled up the food. Customers and waiters watched with smiles as the self-assured lady instructed the owner to tell these ragged boys to be sure to return the next night for another meal. She paid for their food and departed, leaving her young guests still wide-eyed at their free feast.

My own response to the city was to walk instead of taking rides in the rickshaws hand-pulled by men like thin ponies. I could not participate in this appalling exploitation. It was only later that I realised the selfishness of denying a man the means of survival merely to avoid corrupting my own moral principles. The rickshaw-*wallahs* themselves have resisted the introduction of cycle rickshaws, which have small wheels. They rent their wooden machines for about R8 per day and can make R20 on a good day, but lose money when foreigners walk. Cycle rickshaws cannot operate when the city floods every year, whereas people are willing to pay handsomely to be pulled through waist-high water while keeping dry on the high seats. Most of the rickshaw-*wallahs* are men from the villages of Bihar, the state west up the river, who sleep communally on the streets, eat rice and spices, suppress their appetites with marijuana, drink moonshine beer, use prostitutes who have also come from villages to earn their living and send money to their villages.

Rudyard Kipling called Calcutta 'the city of dreadful night', but this is not at all the way people living in Calcutta regard their city, nor how millions of people in villages throughout the state of West Bengal regard their capital. A Bengali man said to me in a cafe one day, 'There is poverty, there is squalor in so many places in our country. It is our disgrace. At least in Calcutta we have also culture and poetry.' I stayed in Calcutta for five weeks altogether and tried during that time to break through the filth, stench, decay and crowds to find the city that the people of Bengal love so much.

Calcutta was founded for trade and profit in the middle of the rainy season in 1690 by Job Charnock, the local agent of the East India Company based in England. The Company had been founded by London tradesmen and merchants on the last day of 1599 and began trading in India in 1608. By 1690, the Company had already been expelled once from a town further up the Hooghly, and Charnock, who had been in India 35 years, was looking for a site to re-establish a trading post in wealthy Bengal. Charnock selected the site of three villages amid swamp and jungle. One of the villages was called Kalikata.

Thus the midday halt of Charnock—more's the pity!—
Grew a City.
As the fungus sprouts chaotic from its bed,
So it spread—
Chance-directed, chance-erected, laid and built
On the silt—
Palace, byre, hovel—poverty and pride—
Side by side;
And, above the packed and pestilential town,
Death looked down.

wrote Rudyard Kipling in 1887.

The 1,000 or more Europeans called the settlement Golgotha, the place of skulls. Golgotha was a deathtrap. Sickness, such as dysentery or malaria, killed almost three-quarters of the Europeans in the ten years up to 1756. No one kept records of the death-rate among the estimated 150,000 Indians encamped beside the foreigners. Despite the high risk of dying, there was no shortage of young men paying their passages from England to India in the hope of making fortunes in private trade. Officially, they worked as writers, or clerks, handling the Company's paperwork, and later became known as 'civil servants' to distinguish them from men bearing the Company's arms. India was one of several destinations in the growing list of English foreign interests suitable for young scoundrels cast out by their families. If the climate did not kill them, they might return home rich. One such cast-off was 18-year-old Robert Clive, son of an impoverished country gentleman, who returned for a visit to Shropshire in 1760 with a glorious reputation and a fortune exceeding £401,102, having made both in Bengal.

French and English rivalry in India was strong, and with the approach of the Seven Years' War in Europe in 1756 both sides began fortifying their stations. The Nawab of Bengal was uncertain of the intentions and power of the Europeans and he ordered them to stop, fearing a similar rivalry to that of the Afghans and Marathas who were seizing power from the Mughul emperor in Delhi. The French complied with the order. The English did not, and the 20-year-old ruler, who had been on the throne less than three months, attacked Calcutta. Its English governor deserted after four days and Seraja-daula captured the settlement on June 20, 1756. It was the eve of the breaking of the monsoon and probably the hottest and most oppressive night of the year. The Nawab locked the English prisoners in the only secure room in the fort. It was a room measuring 18 feet by 14 feet 10 inches, nicknamed the Black Hole. When the door was unlocked on June 21st, many of the prisoners had suffocated or died of heat exhaustion in the appalling conditions and through the callous neglect of their captors. The Black Hole's self-appointed hero, John Zephaniah Holwell, claimed that 123 people died and only 23 survived the tragedy, but these figures have since been proved a nonsense. The death-toll was more probably 43 out of 64 prisoners. Whatever the truth of the numbers and circumstances, the English were incensed and the Black Hole of Calcutta became the first of their many legends of English heroics in India.

Indians made no distinction between English, Scots, Welsh or Irish, who were all the 'English' as far as they were concerned. 'English' is still the word for 'foreigner' in the countryside.

Robert Clive sailed up the coast from Madras determined to avenge the English deaths and his forces easily retook the city. Having done so, he considered it imprudent to leave Calcutta open to attack again from the Nawab or the French by withdrawing south. On his own initiative and against orders to return to Madras, Clive decided to meet these challenges head on. He sailed up the Hooghly, sacked the French colony of Chandernagore, and six months thereafter defeated Seraja-daula at the battle of Plassey. Clive became temporary kingmaker in Bengal and received a fortune from the man he installed as the new Nawab. The French were eclipsed in Bengal and the East India Company could continue trading duty-free in Bengal and up river as far as Benares, encouraged by their puppet ruler. Permission to trade duty-free had been granted in 1717 by the Mughul emperor in Delhi, who was titular head of India though lacking the power to enforce his authority.

For the next forty years, 'trade' was the basis of the foreigners' riches while they secured and expanded territorial control. The Company's writers (clerks) took advantage of their unchallenged military power to trade duty-free for their own benefit and this practice became a flagrant abuse. The power of the British flag to avoid customs duty was such that Warren Hastings never saw any other flag when he sailed up the Ganga in 1762.

> The English merchants could undersell the Bengalis in the Bengali market. They could also undercut the local merchants in their purchase of goods for manufacture, resale or export. Moreover, by their methods of intimidation, and the supposed backing of the Company for their actions, they could make retailers in general afraid to deal with them. But this was not all. Buying commercial crops like opium and indigo or cotton at cut prices affected the land revenue as well, for the annual demand was related to the average price of the produce,

wrote historian Percival Spear in *Master of Bengal, Clive and His India.*

Profits in this trade were high, averaging between 20 and 30 per cent and up to 75 per cent on items such as salt and tobacco. It was during this period that the English language gained the word 'loot', Hindi for stolen goods.

'We are men of power, you say, and take advantage of it. Why, man, what is the use of station if we are not to benefit from it?' asked the East India Company's governor of Calcutta in 1761.

Indian and English merchants built splendid mansions for themselves and Calcutta became known as the city of palaces, though life was far from refined.

'Corruption, Licentiousness and a want of Principles seem to have possessed the Minds of all Civil Servants, by frequent bad examples they have grown Callous, Rapacious and Luxurious beyond Conception,' declared Robert Clive.

Many merchants opted to return home to England where they bought or built country mansions and lived like gentlemen. Jealousy in England spurred attacks on the new nabobs. There was also anger at the imbalance of trade between England and India. English gold and silver bullion were being shipped to India in return for Indian silks and cotton cloths. These flooded the market, undercut English manufactured goods and put English people out of work. The import of Indian cloths was banned in France, Venice and other European cities to protect jobs.

Other Indian imports to England included saltpetre for armaments and many spices. The East India Company enjoyed a monopoly on pepper imports, which was enough to make many jealous merchants sneeze. The East India Company and private merchants also shipped opium from India, not to the home country, but to China, where it was sold to buy tea. The latter was much in demand in Britain after its introduction in 1657. China tried hard to stop the opium trade and by the end of the eighteenth century the Company and merchants were resorting to smuggling the drug into the country in order to buy tea.

Tea was another monopoly of the East India Company, and even a tax of four shillings per pound did not halt its increasing popularity in England. However, 13 colonies in North America regarded the tax on tea as English repression and it was the East India Company's tea chests that they dumped in the harbour in what became known as the Boston Tea Party, 16 months before the start of the American War of Independence.

Despite all its trading, expenses were high and by 1772 the Company was almost bankrupt, and was forced to accept a Board of Governors nominated by the British Government in return for a £1.5 million loan. This regulation was the first of several that brought the Company under the control of the British Government. Warren Hastings was the first Governor-General and in the sixty years during and after his tenure the economic foundations were laid on which Calcutta was to rise. The most important was a revolution in the system of tax gathering.

After the battle of Plassey, Clive forced the Nawab of Bengal to surrender to the East India Company the power of tax-collecting in Bengal and a wide area along the Ganga, leaving the Nawab with only 'the name and shadow of authority', according to Clive. The Company proved an efficient tax collector, sending £1 million to the Mughul emperor and the Nawab while retaining a profit of £3–4 million. By the end of the eighteenth century, revenue from taxes exceeded revenue from trade, and it was then considered time to put affairs in proper order.

Traditionally, as much tax as possible had been extorted from the hereditary peasants by hereditary *zamindars* who then paid the Nawab as little as possible, with the difference making the middlemen's profit. The amount of money raised varied each year, according to the needs of the rulers and circumstances of the peasants. This was not a satisfactory arrangement according to Lord Cornwallis, the Governor-General in 1786, who wanted to regularise tax collection. He also dismissed all high-ranking Indian officials and made the Company's administration exclusively European.

'The *zamindar* would be treated like an English country gentleman, yielding the same taxes year by year, with no opportunity to belabour the poor peasant for more than was just and at no risk of being thrashed himself for failure to supply an inflated demand,' wrote Geoffrey Moorhouse in *India Britannica*.

What might work on Lord Cornwallis' estate in England could not automatically be applied to India. Under the Permanent Settlement, *zamindars* and peasants could not be terrorised for failing to pay taxes, as had been common under Mughul authority, but they could be dispossessed. For the first time, collection of land revenue (and hence control of peasants cultivating the land) became a commodity. It could be bought or sold by anyone with money. The hereditary ties between peasants, *zamindars* and the land were broken. Gradually, during the nineteenth century, the countryside came under the control of a rising class of city-based merchants who cared nothing for the land or its wretched people but who enjoyed lavish city living. The system was officially stopped soon after independence in 1947, but I was astounded to meet in Calcutta a man asserting that no one in his family had ever visited the villages which they had owned for generations.

The Permanent Settlement coincided with a reversal of trade between England and India at the start of the nineteenth century. Exports of Indian handloom textiles stopped and miles of cheap, machine-made cotton cloth from Lancashire mills began arriving at the ports of Calcutta and Bombay. Imports of British cloth increased from 818,208 yards in 1818 to 51,777,277 yards by 1835, and imports of Indian cloth into Britain declined from 1,266,608 yards to 306,086 yards in the same years, according to evidence given by the Chairman of the East India and China Association to a Select Committee of the British House of Commons in 1840. This was under the guise of free trade. It was 1887 before a fully-fledged cotton mill opened in the country. The cheap, machine-made cloth destroyed the livelihood of the handloom weavers in every village at just the same time as absentee landlords were gaining control under the Permanent Settlement. Both events greatly diminished self-sufficiency outside the money economy and increased the dependence of the villages on towns and cities. The countryside sank into a forsaken wretchedness. Famines and peasants' revolts broke out. It was no wonder that a century later Mahatma Gandhi selected the burning of imported cloth for a mass protest against British rule.

The East India Company lost its trading monopoly in India in 1813 and ceased trading in 1834 after yet more reforms in the British Parliament, where the Radicals and the Evangelists were championing the causes of free trade, Christian morality and popular education in Britain and the expanding British Empire. The Company settled down in Calcutta to administer India on behalf of the British Government, and the Company's shareholders received a guaranteed dividend. Governor-General Bentinck followed the new spirit of the age and encouraged and instituted many reforms and improvements, such as rebuilding and improving the Grand Trunk Road from Calcutta to Delhi, reducing land taxes, building irrigation canals and establishing a Medical College in Calcutta. His most important reform was to make English the medium of education and administration, replacing Persian which had been the language of the Mughul court.

'We must at present do our best to form a class who may be interpreters between us and the millions whom we govern; a class of persons, Indian in blood and colour, but English in taste, in opinions, in morals, and in intellect,' advised the Governor-General's Law Member, Lord Macaulay.

Macaulay's words were fulfilled. The sons of India's rising middle class produced an unintentionally hilarious mimicry of Englishness transplanted to Asia and were the enthusiastic beneficiaries of the new Western education. Calcutta's St Xavier's School is still known as 'Harrow on the Hooghly' and continues to educate the English-speaking elite of the city.

It is arguable that the introduction of the English language and Western, Christian education had the greatest impact and was the greatest legacy of British rule in India. English has continued as the unifying language of India, despite efforts by the Central Government in New Delhi to impose Hindi. The visitor is more likely to hear bankers, lawyers, Rotarians and senior civil servants chatting in English than in any of India's 15 official languages. Far from smothering Bengali or Indian culture, the foreign intrusion caused a vigorous reaction, regrowth and renaissance in Indian ideas and ideals which spread out like sunshine from Calcutta.

No man was both greater producer and greater product of the new circumstances than Raja Ram Mohan Roy, born in 1772 the son of a *zamindar* ruined by the Permanent Settlement, who traded as a moneylender to the English. Mohan Roy was the first of Hinduism's modern reformers, responding to the challenge of Christianity's stress on love and compassion by stressing the qualities and strengths of his own faith. His example was to be followed by many anglicised Indians, including Gandhi in the twentieth century. Mohan Roy's most famous campaign was against *suttee* which Lord Bentinck eventually outlawed. The English were reluctant to suppress widow-burning for fear of exciting Hindu religious sentiments, and a total of 983 widows were burned alive on their husbands' funeral pyres in Calcutta in 1815 and 1816.

By the middle of Queen Victoria's reign, Calcutta was no longer a city of palaces but the sprawling, bustling capital of India. Commerce was King and businessmen and managers from the Home Country lived and worked behind the high gates of their splendid homes, offices and social clubs attended by scores of servants. 'In the evening . . . the richer British *box-wallahs* emerged in top-hats and frock-coats to promenade the Maidan, driving steadily here and there in broughams, hansoms and victorias, exchanging bows and transient assessments,' wrote James Morris in *Pax Britannica*: The Climax of an Empire. The new, anglicised Indian middle class, whose interests were bound to those of the English, were tolerated but barred from high public office or the premises of such prestigious establishments as the Bengal Club on Chowringhee or the Tollygunge Club. By the time of the Queen-Empress Victoria's Diamond Jubilee in 1897, Calcutta was the second city of the British Empire; perhaps no one noticed the slums surrounding the White Man's mansions where a million people had congregated in order to work in mills and offices. The port of Calcutta was the biggest and busiest in the country, handling most of India's imports of manufactured goods and exports which were primarily jute, cotton and tea.

Jute cultivation was a gift of the Ganga delta where the hot, humid air, fertile soil and abundance of water made ideal conditions. Mechanised jute spinning started in 1855 following the interruption of flax supplies from Russia during the Crimean War, and powerloom weaving began in 1859, one year after the Indian Mutiny had been quelled. Soon the banks of the Hooghly were lined by big mills, half-hidden by palm trees, with names like Caledonian, Cheviot and Laidlow. Production surpassed Dundee's in 1908 and by the end of the 1930s over 300,000 people were employed in 110 mills and ten times as many peasants earned part of their living by growing jute as a cash crop. The mill owners were making so much money supplying sandbags during the First World War that they christened Armistice Day, on November 11th 1918, as Black Friday because of the profits they would lose.

Problems for the industry began in 1947 when Bengal was divided into East Pakistan (now Bangladesh) and West Bengal, belonging to India. Most of the jute mills were beside the Hooghly in India. The main growing areas were across the border in East Pakistan. Since then, West Bengal has dramatically increased jute cultivation as the main cash crop of the state's peasantry and Bangladesh has built its own mills.

Tea cultivation in India also began as a replacement for interrupted supplies when the East India Company lost its monopoly of tea from China in 1832 and needed a new source of supply to satisfy the demand from Britain's increasing working class. Experimental tea cultivation had already been started at the Botanical Gardens in Calcutta and by 1862 there were 160 tea gardens in the north-eastern state of Assam. Production in India reached 42.9 million pounds in 1880 and most of this was sold by auction in Calcutta or London and exported through Calcutta.

Today, Calcutta tea auctions are one of the few places in the world outside the United Nations where Iranians, Americans, Soviets, Chinese, Taiwanese, Japanese, Afghans and people from a dozen other nations congregate to select and purchase chests of tea.

Tea seems so synonymous with India that I was surprised to learn from Mr Rikhys, chairman of the Indian Tea Association and head of one of the big tea houses, that the Indian habit of drinking strong, sweet, milky tea only started during the First World War when Indian soldiers picked up a taste for the brew from British army canteens. A glass of tea costs 30–50 paise which is not cheap compared to a labourer's daily wage of R12 (enough to buy 24 cups), but consumption has increased so greatly in the past half-century that the Indian Government temporarily stopped exports in 1984 fearing the high world price might push up the domestic price during an election year. The increase in tea drinking is evidence of growing prosperity for many people, though it has not been welcome in all parts of India and coffee remains the popular drink of south India. Elders in one village in the state of Rajasthan imposed a vow of abstinence because they thought the youths of their district were wasting time and energy sipping tea instead of helping their families. Indians drink an estimated 187,500 million cups of tea each year, which is almost 825 million pounds (64 per cent of total production in 1984). It is also only 1.1 pounds per person per year compared to 7.5 pounds per person in Eire, 6.9 pounds in Britain and 0.26 pounds in France.

'The 24 carat feeling—Duncan's Gold Cup Tea' proclaims the advertisement in the glossy magazine *Eve's Weekly*. Tea drinking is taken seriously in India by anyone who can afford to buy more than tea dust and advertising is widespread in up-market magazines and on street billboards. Corner grocers stock Lipton's Green Label 100 per cent Darjeeling on their shelves beside Brooke Bond's distinctive red-trimmed orange packets which range in size from as large as shoeboxes to as small as matchboxes. The familiar names remain but the industry is now almost totally owned and operated by Indians.

Many of the tea companies are clustered in the area of Mission Row, a wide, noisy street of big, Victorian buildings each with cracked masonry, peeling faded paint and everywhere crammed with people. The concrete and glass office tower of Macneill & Magor at 4 Mango

Lane, just off Mission Row, is one exception to the dilapidation. It was here, in his mahogany-panelled office at the top of the building, that Mr Rikhys revealed some of the mysteries of the tea trade.

He unsealed small sample tins onto his leather-topped desk to show me the difference between 'orthodox' (what I had always called ordinary leaf tea) and CTC (Cut, Tear and Curl), looking like granules, which make stronger brews with less flavour. I'd never known that 'orange pekoe' was a grade, not a variety of tea, or that the experts pronounced 'pekoe' as peck-o not peek-o. There were also a confusing number of tea grades between full leaf and dust, including b.o.p. (broken orange pekoe) and g.f.b.o.p. (golden flowery broken orange pekoe). Darjeeling is the best tea in the world, said Mr Rikhys and bought by the Soviet Union. The United States buys the worst. Darjeeling tea was only 'orthodox', though three times more tea was sold as Darjeeling than was actually grown in the state. I was ready for a cup of tea when all this had been explained.

The offices of one of India's largest companies, operated by a single family, stand just up the street from Mango Lane in a tall, modern office tower.

'If it is possible to conceive of a London family which owned Imperial Chemical Industries, Shell, Unilever, British Leyland and half a dozen lesser concerns the size of Sainsbury's, it is just possible to grasp the position of the Birlas in the Indian order of things and their ridiculous hold on the national economy,' wrote Geoffrey Moorhouse in *Calcutta*.

The family business has grown from one jute mill 65 years ago into at least 200 companies with assets estimated at R2,500 crore (ten million) and an annual turnover of up to R3,000 crore. They don't smoke or eat meat and the men won't allow themselves to be photographed without wearing coat and tie. They are strict about religious observance and are well known for charitable donations and religious and cultural endowments, such as the Birla planetarium in Calcutta. The Birlas are the most successful of the Marwaris. They had been moneylenders to the former princely states such as Jaipur and Udaipur in the present-day state of Rajasthan. Marwaris first migrated from their homeland at the end of the nineteenth century and now seem to dominate business life in Calcutta, having taken over company positions vacated by the British. They have a reputation in Calcutta as business vultures.

The new Birla Building and the tea houses of Mission Row stand within a rickshaw ride of the paper heart of the city, where bankers, bureaucrats, lawyers, stockbrokers and businessmen work in grand, dilapidated Victorian buildings crammed with old, discarded ledgers each neatly tied with red ribbon and stacked floor to ceiling in offices, in long, dark corridors, in abandoned rooms, in locked steel boxes and heaped on top of every cabinet. They all remain forgotten in all these places until eaten by rats and worms.

As Bengalis never tire of explaining, it was the English who taught India all this red tape and confusion when the clerks of the East India Company scribbled records of business transactions in the vast Writers' Building in Dalhousie Square. The building still stands and their modern counterparts, the Bengali *babus* of the state government, carry on the tradition of clogging the world with letters, receipts and memoranda in triplicate.

It was in the grand buildings within half a mile of the East India Company's Dalhousie Square headquarters that British money, British management and British ambitions controlled the economy of India for 150 years, behind high colonnades, Early English façades, heavy wooden doors and brass nameplates. The Calcutta stock exchange is housed behind the classical pillars of the Royal Exchange building in Calcutta's Wall Street, adjacent to the offices of the Allahabad Bank, the reserve Bank of India, the Hongkong and Shanghai Corporation and Grindlay's Bank.

Long before the markets open each morning and business begins, the standpipe on the pavement outside Grindlay's great mahogany doors will have served as public bathroom for a long line of men and boys stripped to their shorts and lathered in white soap under the gushing brown water. There are thousands of such broken pipes and hand-pumps in the streets where people wash themselves and their clothes and where women and girls manage to change from wet, clinging saris into dry saris without losing their modesty. The discovery that the English actually washed in baths in their own dirty water caused disdain when revealed early in the long relationship between Indians and the English. In the hot, sticky climate of Asia, nothing could be more abhorrent than not bathing every day under running water. Yet people's private hygiene is in shocking contrast to the public squalor on the streets, in post offices and in many offices and banks.

Soon, men selling polyester shirts, fashionable and totally unsuited to the fetid climate, or selling jars of honey, plastic combs, trousers, plastic toys, mirrors or posters of gods will be crowding the pavement where the bathers have frolicked at the handpumps. Side streets will fill with chauffeur-driven Ambassador cars of the executive bankers and their chauffeurs will gossip at the row of tea-stalls until their services are required. There are less than 900,000 of these 1957 Morris Oxford cars in the country. They are made by the Birlas and until recently were the only model of car available in a land of many millions of scooters and bicycles. Most of the cars are owned by governments or big business and private ownership is very rare.

One million people commute into Calcutta every morning on hundreds of electric trains, trams, buses and minibuses. One morning, I saw a bus conductor climbing up the windscreen on the outside of his bus, with leather satchel of tickets and money dangling from his neck, to collect the fares of two dozen men crouched on the roof as the vehicle sped through the streets.

Construction of a 10-mile underground railway began in the city in 1973 but it is not yet complete and seems to have become another gravy train of government contracts. Its estimated cost has accelerated from R140 crore in 1972 to an estimated R800 crore in 1984 and is expected to exceed R1,000 crore before trains begin running. Only one-quarter of the work has yet been completed, though the project has provided work for thousands of men and women digging with shovels. The construction has disrupted traffic along the length of Chowringhee, Calcutta's main north–south road, but people accept the confusion and delays with the same shrug of shoulders and smile as they live with muddled telephones, erratic water service and fitful electric supply.

The exodus of *babus* and bank tellers from the heart of the city begins daily at five o'clock, when the movement of trucks is forbidden and every street clogs with bicycles, pedestrians, taxis, cows, cars and convoys of tin-plated buses and minibuses with screeching horns and youths hanging out of the doors touting for passengers. People pack into the buses and under giant fans in the antiquated trams so tightly that the rush-hour is one occasion when the rigours of Hinduism's untouchability must be ignored.

The fortunate few, including my generous host in Calcutta, Mr Lakshman Menon, are chauffeur-driven home in the company car. We drove south down Strand Road between the Maidan, the Hyde Park of Calcutta, and the promenade beside the Hooghly, where men sell cups of cinnamon tea from big kettles wired to buckets of hot coals.

We passed concrete legs being built for the second bridge across the river and through the grey gloom saw the tents of tarpaulin and plastic sheeting where construction workers and their families live amid cooking pots, firewood and drying cow-dung cakes. Parents and children sat round one fire, indifferent to the fumes of buses and cars and the clanging of passing trams. We crossed the tidal stream called Tolly's Nullah, passing hoardings which advertise in English superior banking services, softer soap and cigarettes—'Charms is the spirit of freedom. Charms is the way you are'—and entered white-washed Alipore. No one lives on the pavement here, nor begs from passers-by. It is not allowed, for this has always been the calmest and smartest part of the city, ever since Warren Hastings built a mansion here and imported tons of marble from Benares for the staircase.

The daywatchman welcomed us home and Lakshman's manservant, upstairs in the apartment, had the drinks trolley already set out with gin, whisky, tonic and soda waters and an ice-bucket. The bedsheets in the guest room were already turned down and there was hot water in the attached bathroom. After showering, we sat for a pleasant drink, with fan revolving overhead and a Barbra Streisand record on the record player.

The previous night we were guests at the annual prize-giving of the Calcutta Ladies' Golf Club, one of many private clubs built as enclaves on the Maidan. Drinks had been served on the lawn and after an hour's chit-chat we had picked at the splendid hot buffet of fresh fish, curried meats and vegetarian dishes served to a background of Bee Gees and Dolly Parton music outside the small Edwardian clubhouse and putting green, surrounded by thick bushes and wire fence like a stockade.

That night we were being taken to the Middleton Mansions for a dinner party of twenty people. Everyone knew everyone, making introduction easy. A bare-footed servant in white trousers, white jacket and white gloves brought drinks on a tray and we nibbled peanuts and smoked cigarettes offered on plates on the coffee table in a large room with white walls, high ceiling and shelving at one end for books, hi-fi, video and *objets d'art*. The ladies sat in a group on the large sofa and armchairs, each in a gold-bordered sari of stunning colours, explaining the doings of their children, their problems with servants and the latest diets to shed a few pounds of tummy fat. Well-nourished men, in sober suits and ties, stood outside on the balcony in the warm night air, talking business and banking and troubles with employees and unions. Like the stars of Indian films, everyone looked just a little tubby. In a country of thin, poorly nourished people, looking well-fed is a status symbol.

The mahogany doors into the dining room were opened after two hours of chatter and drinks, to reveal a dozen hot dishes and salads laid out on a large table. Glasses of filtered, boiled water were served with the meal and later coffee and liqueurs. The latter are obtained from bootleggers who smuggle liquor, tobacco and electronic goods into India in volume. *Paan* (betal nut and leaf) was served on a silver tray for the men and half an hour later the dinner party broke up and we descended in the polished mahogany lift to our drivers waiting outside.

Such is the social life of Calcutta's affluent population, with whom I ate and drank in smart restaurants and in whose luxurious houses I revelled for several weeks.

However, Calcutta is a city of poor and sick people synonymous for Westerners with Mother Theresa.

One morning I got up before the arrival of morning tea, to attend the 6 a.m. Mass at the Mother House of the Sisters of Charity at 54A Lower Chitpore Road. I rang the bell hesitantly and the door was opened by a smiling sister in a white, blue bordered sari who showed me upstairs to the chapel. The service had already started and over 200 novices and sisters were kneeling on the floor while a priest read the lesson. I left my sandals outside and sat down cross-legged just inside the door, alongside half a dozen other foreigners facing the altar and the statue of the Virgin Mary, which had been adorned with garlands of marigold and jasmine flowers. All windows and all the shutters were open and the sounds of the city awakening filled the room, so that the trundle and clanging of trams drowned out the priest's voice. Mother Theresa knelt at the back, her small body wrapped in a grey cardigan over a white cotton sari, and I was strangely moved by this frail old woman with her back bent double and her wrinkled face resting on clasped, stubby hands. For the first time I could understand why Hindus had flocked merely to *see* Gandhi. I could begin to understand what they meant by *darshan*—receiving a blessing by observing someone or something holy.

Mother Theresa started alone in 1948 in a Calcutta slum and since then the Missionary Sisters of Charity have grown to be more than 1000 strong and a separate Brotherhood has also been formed. The Order's Mother House was sold to Mother Teresa in 1950 by a Moslem man emigrating to Pakistan, who charged less than the value of the land for the large house. The Sisters and Brothers now operate over 81 schools, 335 mobile dispensaries serving 1,600,000 people annually, 28 family planning centres, 67 leprosy clinics with 43,000 lepers, 28 homes for 2000 abandoned children and 32 homes for 2000 dying destitute men and women.

Shishu Bhavan, two hundred yards up the road from the Mother House, is one of the Sisters' main centres in Calcutta. The large, grey building was donated by ICI (India) and serves as clinic, soup kitchen and children's home where orphans and the sick are nursed and loved until they are able to rejoin their families or find adopting parents. Five hundred men and women dressed in little more than rags congregate each afternoon with their sick children and babies outside the high gates waiting for the clinic and soup kitchen to open. I was surprised by the smiles and lack of suspicion with which they greeted the handful of curious foreigners pressing through the crowd towards the small door. The sisters greeted us with smiles and led us upstairs to the nursery for children too sick to be treated in the clinic with their mothers. There were only six children that day, sitting in a group on the floor. These three and four-year-olds were so malnourished that they looked like nine-month-old babies.

'How many children can you take?' I enthusiastically asked the sister.

She was silent for a moment then smiled. 'As many as need to come,' she replied, already knowing what Mother Theresa has said on the subject of numbers, 'We ourselves feel that what we are doing is just a drop in the ocean. But if that drop was not in the ocean, I think the ocean would be less because of the missing drop.'

The work and life of the Missionaries of Charity stands out as one of the pinpricks of light in squalid Calcutta. It is an illustration of the inscription on the plinth of the statue of Mahatma Gandhi in mid-stride on his famous salt march which stands on the Maidan:

In the midst of death life persists, in the midst of untruth truth persists, in the midst of darkness light persists, hence I gather that God is life, truth and love.

Outside on Lower Circular Road, bodies that had been shrouded by sheets all night were waking and men, women and children were getting up to begin another day. Buckets with coal fires were already smoking in the street adding to the haze that hangs over the city mornings and evenings. Roadside stalls were already serving hot tea to their first customers and green coconut and sugar-cane juice sellers were setting up their stands. Shafts of morning sunlight would soon penetrate the cathedral gloom of coal smoke from the fires in the backstreets where men and boys were preparing curried beans and dough for *chapatis* at filthy *dhabas*, often built over open drains.

Untouchable men all across the city were sweeping up garbage from the gutters, piling it into wheelbarrows and dumping these in vile-smelling heaps at street corners. Women and children were here beginning the revolting daily task of picking through the garbage by hand for anything reusable; half-burned coals among the ashes from the tea-stalls, waste paper and cardboard, old bottles, tin cans and metals to be sold; bones to be boiled for glue; coconut shells to be processed into coir matting. The women and children worked along-side cows nonchalantly chewing crushed sugar-cane stems while dogs and kites scavenged scraps and peelings from juice stands. Gangs of men would come later in the day to load whatever remained of the garbage onto Municipal trucks to take it away. Just down the street from one such garbage site, people would wait on Sundays for free rice and *dal* distributed by a Hindu welfare organisation, which they ate sitting together in the road.

One mile south, every Sunday, worshippers file into the pews of St Paul's Cathedral for services in Bengali, Hindi or English. This church was completed in 1847 and its combination of several Victorian architectural styles, including the steeple copied from Bell Harry Tower at Canterbury, possibly derives from the British travels of its architect, Major W.N. Forbes of the Bengal Engineers. The forty-six large fans suspended on a grid of wires beneath the high white roof are a local adaptation to the climate of Bengal. It struck me as a complacent anachronism, but I was cheered when I looked at the visitors' book and read the comments of a police inspector from Uttar Pradesh:

'It is a very divine place. I am very surprise because I am Hindu but when I find my mentally peace in this mandir, really this is a supreme house of god'.

I attended an 8 a.m. Sunday service of Holy Communion in English in the cathedral and thoroughly enjoyed singing from *Hymns Ancient and Modern*. About 14 million Indians are Christians, either Roman Catholic, Syrian Christian who claim conversion by St Thomas, or members of the Churches of South or North India formed by the amalgamation of Anglican, Methodist, Congregationalist, Presbyterian and Dutch Reformed Churches. Christians are an almost invisible minority (though outnumbering Sikhs by about four million) and most are either Anglo-Indians, low-caste Hindus or tribal peoples seeking to escape by conversion the economic and social slavery of their position in Indian society. In Bengal some high-caste families also became Christians when Calcutta was capital of the Christian rulers of the British Raj and an informal caste system divides the Christian community of the city. High caste men and women attend the English services of the cathedral in sober Western suits or gorgeous silk saris and have their chauffeurs collect them after services.

Despite good intentions to stay 'close to the people', I was surprised at how quickly I could become used to the convenience of servants to bring early morning tea and a breakfast tray to my bed, provide hot water for showers, ice for drinks, drive me wherever I wanted to go, buy stamps at the post office and manage one hundred other chores and luxuries. I could enjoy this comfort while it lasted but I was alarmed at how quickly and easily I separated myself from the hardships and struggle for survival on Calcutta's streets. After just a few weeks in the city, I could now understand the exasperation of the lady who had remarked to me as we were being driven past a band of five lepers playing drums and rattles and begging for money, 'when one goes shopping—you know—it's a little uncomfortable.'

I had arrived in India too late to attend Calcutta's annual jamboree during Durga *puja* but found preparations underway for Kali *puja* one month later. Durga and Kali are both different forms of Shiva's wife. Each day I saw a huge pavilion of bamboo and green cloth gradually being erected in a small park beside a congested market. This would be decorated with chandeliers and serve as Kali's palace during her four-day festival. The goddess herself, standing 20 feet above her mortal admirers, did not arrive until the eve of the celebrations.

Kali is the patron goddess of the city and her awful appearance matches that of the city. She holds a large machete in one of her four arms, the heads of some of her victims dangle on a string, her bright red tongue is thrust out to lick up the blood and she stands on the sprawling prostrate body of her husband Shiva. Kali is usually painted black, occasionally blue, and is terrible in appearance. 'Dripping with blood, encircled with snakes, hung round with skulls and human heads and in all respects resembling a fury rather than a goddess', recounts John Dowson in *A Classical Dictionary of Hindu Mythology*. About 3000 pavilions large and small, each with a model of Kali, were built throughout the city for Kali *puja*, on spare land, blocking side streets and in the courtyards of big buildings. The money for each pavilion is raised by voluntary and enforced donations from shopkeepers and well-wishers, collected by members of youth clubs. The festival is both religious and social, and clubs compete with each other to build the biggest, brightest pavilions with magnificent models of Kali, who may be wearing a wristwatch to show that she is modern.

Priests install each goddess in her pavilion and invoke the deity to be present in the statue for the duration of the festival. Musicians may give concerts each evening and men and women offer flowers, sweets, dried fruits and coconuts to the goddess. Kali enjoys noise and for a week the city reverberates to the bang of crackers and fireworks in the streets and the blare of Hindi disco music. To the young people, Kali has a modern outlook and must therefore enjoy the latest sounds from the film world. The festival ends with the statue from each pavilion being taken in procession to the river where the clay models are thrown away. I joined one procession that took five hours to march two miles to the river. The goddess was getting a good send-off with three bands (one of them playing bagpipes), a vintage car, several handcarts with generators and electric wires strung out to women paid to carry pink, green and white flashing fluorescent tubes on their heads, and gyrating youths dancing with as much pelvic thrust as Elvis Presley ever managed. Kali travelled to the river looking out from the back of a truck over the thousands of spectators. The procession, deity and palace cost R75,000, I was told, and issued from one of about 3,000 palaces, large and small, organised for the four-day festival. Another included over 150 vehicles and 50 music bands.

Kali is permanently resident on the site where one of 52 slices of her body fell when Vishnu chopped her up. He did this to save the world which the gods feared would be pounded to pieces if the mourning dance of the grief-stricken Shiva was not stopped following Kali's death. Tens of thousands of pilgrims throng to Kali Ghat through streets congested with people, cows, dogs and bicycles to make their *puja*, perhaps sacrifice a goat and bathe in the stinking Tolly's Nullah, which is an enfeebled branch of the Hooghly.

Nirmal Hriday, the Place of the Pure Heart, the most famous of Mother Theresa's homes for the dying, stands beside the Kali temple in a former pilgrim hostel. It is here that dying men and women with nothing and no one come to be loved by the Sisters before 'going home to God'.

'We help the poor to die with God. We help them to say sorry to God. To make peace with God according to their faith,' says Mother Theresa. There is no attempt at conversion and the initial hostility to having Christian women so near Kali's shrine softened after Mother Theresa took in two of the temple's priests who were destitute and near death.

Besides festivals such as Kali's, Calcutta's diverse population comes together at cricket matches, for cricket is undoubtedly India's 'national game'. The second largest cricket ground in the world stands in Calcutta, at the north end of the Maidan, and Test Matches draw large crowds and great attention. Test Matches are even used to promote family planning, with big posters advising, 'Declare After Two'. Cricket is India's passion, played at well-appointed grounds with full teams wearing white flannels watched by rows of spectators in deck-chairs, and also in the streets and wastelands of cities by groups of boys with bats and rubber balls and using bricks as stumps. There are more than a dozen cricket pitches on the Maidan in use at weekends.

The 1280-acre Maidan is also one of the main venues on Saturdays and Sundays for informal readings by poets of their work to groups of Westernised businessmen, bank clerks and rickshaw-*wallahs* sitting together in groups on the grass. More than 1600 poetry magazines are published regularly in Calcutta, and half the drama groups in the country are based here. Along with Arabic and Urdu, Bengali is said to be one of the most poetic languages in the world, and it was disappointing not to be able to understand the work of best-selling poet Shakti Chattopadhyay, for example, who has sold over 120,000 copies of his work and won a R10,000 Sahitya Akademi prize for outstanding literary achievement in Bengali.

The most famous Bengali poet was Rabindranath Tagore, whose

talents as poet, novelist, dramatist, philosopher, musician, painter and educator have continued to be celebrated since his death in 1941. Tagore won the Nobel Prize in 1913 for a collection of songs called 'Gitanjali', and though much of the force of his Bengali is lost in translation, the poems remain powerful even in English.

The day is no more, the shadow is upon the earth. It is time that I go to the stream to fill my pitcher.

The evening air is eager with the sad music of the water. Ah, it calls me out into the dusk. In the lonely lane there is no passer-by, the wind is up, the ripples are rampant in the river.

I know not if I shall come back home. I know not whom I shall chance to meet. There at the fording in the little boat the unknown man plays upon his lute.

After spending five weeks in Calcutta trying, and failing, to understand the city, it was time for me to be walking again; and to leave behind the beguiling comforts of regular and varied meals, soft bed, warm showers, marmalade, bookshops and films. I bought five paper streamers and a rich fruit cake in preparation for Christmas and set out from Calcutta on December 18th.

4
Led North by the Sacred Thread

When Lieutenant-Colonel Forrest's party left Calcutta on December 2, 1807, to journey to Delhi, he wrote:

> None accompanied us for mere state. Our party consisted of seven persons. We had three howdah-elephants, that is, animals trained for riding, hunting, and shooting, well broke, and with able mahauts, or leaders. Four others carried the camp equipage, which consisted of two large marquees, each a sufficient load for an elephant, being about eighteen or twenty hundredweight. There were two smaller tents, besides others for the servants and guard of Sepoys; a light gig and horse, several saddle-horses, four palanquins, a cart, and hackery, or common cart of the country, with two bullocks to each. About two hundred servants and followers, and a guard of Sepoys, or native infantry, of forty men and a native officer, attended us. (*A Picturesque Tour along the River Ganges and Jumna*.)

I took a knapsack, a small shoulder bag and, wanting to travel as lightly as possible, had now left even my shaving equipment, preferring to go to barbers who used cut-throat razors. I walked alone away from the noises and congestion of Calcutta, happy to be walking again, though it would be several days before I would reach the end of the urban sprawl. Only then would I be able to breathe clean air and hear squawking parakeets flying among palm trees.

After four hours of walking I reached the international headquarters of the Ramakrishna Mission. Well-to-do families were strolling on the lawns around a pink building, said to represent a Hindu temple, Moslem mosque and Christian church. I asked to stay in the *ashram* but this was 'Not possible,' and only with difficulty could I extract from the monk in the office the name of another *ashram* half a mile away. Though unable to speak Bengali and with no one speaking English to be found at this latter *ashram*, there I was led upstairs into a hall where two boys, dressed in orange, were laying out two rows of tin plates beside narrow carpets of bamboo matting. I sat cross-legged on the mat and, being a visitor and thus without my own metal plate, a disposable plate of four leaves pinned together with thorns was set in front of me. One of the boys dumped out a mound of rice on each plate from a metal bucket, followed by potato and turnip *subzee* (spiced, cooked vegetables) and water in a clay cup. A grey-haired man in orange garb sitting opposite me was guarding three plates and complained at the miserable portions he had been given. His neighbour, who looked like an Old Testament prophet, found this humorous and the two of us laughed together, our mirth transcending the language barrier. The cantankerous holy man was given an extra portion after everyone else had been served.

I took a bath in the Hooghly after the meal, the first I had taken in the heavily polluted river since starting out. I entered the cold, brown water slowly down the marble steps. How quickly the dust and weariness of the miles of walking were washed away! I was now quite adept at washing and changing clothes in public and within twenty minutes I was asleep on a bamboo mat on the floor of the dining hall.

After our afternoon snooze, I was taken to meet the head of the *ashram* by a man who could speak some English. The *baba* was a short, plump man, perhaps in his forties, who held audience sitting cross-legged on a carpet in front of a mattress in his small room. He was dressed in red and wore an enormous red turban. The translator explained where I was going and where I had come from and the six people in the room were amazed that a foreigner would come to walk beside their sacred river. There was also laughter that the richly-endowed Ramakrishna Mission should refuse hospitality and pass me over to the Lal Baba (meaning red father) which served poor people. We listened reverently to the *baba* speaking softly while an attendant dressed him in a red cardigan ready for evening prayers. He seemed to smile even when his face was relaxed and he received the homage of two men, who touched their heads at his feet, with smiles and a gentle patting of their heads.

Praying and reciting sacred Sanskrit texts, such as the *Bhagavad-Gita*, continued day and night in the *ashram*, either with all the 80 residents or just two *sannyasins* (monks) keeping the cosmos in order and attending to the gods, a task believed to be just as necessary as the work of farmers in the fields. Two *sannyasins* sat reciting together the dialogue in the *Bhagavad-Gita* between the god Krishna and the warrior Arjuna, who asked Krishna to number all his heavenly powers and forms. Krishna said he would give only the chief of these:

I am the Atman that dwells in the heart of every mortal creature: I am beginning, the life-span, and the end of all.

Among purifiers, I am the wind; I am Rama among the warriors: the shark among fish: Ganga among the rivers.

In the alphabet, I am A: among compounds, the copulative: I am Time without end: I am the Sustainer: my face is everywhere.

I am death that snatches all; I also am the source of all that shall be born; I am glory, prosperity, beautiful speech, memory, intelligence, steadfastness and forgiveness.

But what need have you, Arjuna, to know this huge variety? Know only that I exist, and that one atom of myself sustains the universe.

There were no buildings or people when Lal Baba arrived beside the Hooghly in 1932 and cleared the forest to build his grass hut. He often sat in silence in the evenings gazing at the holy river and, though he died in 1967, his life-size statue still sits in a gaudy cloak in a grass hut looking out across the river. Many pilgrims come to see the place where he was cremated, which is marked by garlands of fresh yellow and orange marigolds.

Seven of Lal Baba's disciples remain in the *ashram* which is now a three-storey building of concrete and bricks. There are small rooms for the *sannyasins* built round a large courtyard, handpumps for fresh water and stables for the milch cows. One of the seven disciples sent his own disciple to make tea for the three of us. The boy was 12 years old, dressed in red cotton pants and head cloth and had bright eyes and infectious laughter. At suppertime, he served his *guru* and then came to eat with me at the other side of the hall. Another of the original disciples, a jovial, portly man with rosy red cheeks, came from his room to give me three *chapatis*, and another came with a little potato and cauliflower *subzee* to supplement the official menu of chunky rice and *dal* for supper.

After sunset, while there was still light, we sat looking out across the river, which even 102 miles from the sea was tidal. Suddenly, the calm of the river water was broken by a splash and ripples. We watched and waited and moments later a brown dolphin surfaced ten yards from shore and dived again. It came up once more and then was gone. It was the first Gangetic dolphin I had ever seen and the sight was magnificent.

These brown mammals live exclusively in the fresh water of the Ganga and Brahmaputra rivers and are well adapted to the murky water. Their sonar is so sensitive that they can distinguish between dead or live fish which they catch and eat, and their hearing is also very sensitive, but they are almost blind and able to distinguish only light and dark. The four- to six-foot-long dolphins swim on their sides with one eye peering towards the light and drag one flipper, usually the right, along the muddy river bottom. This helps them stay oriented in the river's currents and enables them to swim in water as shallow as eight inches. It is believed that these dolphins sleep only very briefly and that they never stop swimming in order to stem the swift currents, especially when the river is in spate. In 1976 there was an estimated total population of 4–5,000 Gangetic dolphins, called *susa* in Hindi after the sound made when they surface for air. The fishermen along the river seem to regard them as bringing good fortune and, I believe, do not net or try to kill them.

Bedtime came as soon as it was dark and I slept on bamboo matting on the floor of the dining hall under my mosquito net. Early next morning I met the *baba* coming from his morning prayers and bath in the river just after sunrise, and offered a donation of ten rupees. He smiled and held up his hand to refuse the money.

'It is our gift for your journey', I think he said, and he led me to his room to have tea. While we waited for the tea to be made he unwrapped the enormous red turban coiled on his head. It was only now that I realised that the turban was twisted around his own hair which, when he unravelled the coil, stretched nine feet across the floor.

Thick mist cloaked the half-mile wide river every morning until the sun was high and strong in the pale blue sky. This was the best time of day to be walking, while the chilly air carried the clatter of tin buckets being filled at the taps on street corners and the rumble and fumes of traffic had not yet begun. I was heading north on the Grand Trunk Road with a buoyant heart, stepping aside for the tinkling bells of men cycling to the early shift at jute or cotton mills beside the river and the bicycles laden with cauliflowers being taken to market. I passed men with little shopping-bags scrutinising dead fish displayed on cloths or live ones swimming in plastic bowls at a roadside market and I stopped for sweet, milky tea at stalls outside factory gates.

By lunchtime I reached the town of Serampore, founded as a trading post by Denmark in 1755. The settlement did not prosper but the Danes gave asylum in 1800 to six Baptist missionaries whose college and influence continue today. The men had sailed up the river in defiance of a ban on missionary activity strictly enforced by the East India Company who were interested exclusively in trade.

Three of the six Baptists, William Carey, Joshua Marshman and William Ward, who produced translations of the Bible in many Indian languages, published the first vernacular newspaper in India and operated the Mission Press, printing in Indian languages. They also established Serampore College in a palatial building with a portico of seven huge columns overlooking the river. It was the first theological college in Asia, though today only 54 out of more than 2000 students study theology and active missionary work is discouraged.

The Serampore Missionaries were the spearhead of missionary work in northern India in the 19th century. Their Christian activity was a direct challenge to the moral and intellectual energies of Hinduism and Islam. They provided education to the rising urban middle-class Indians, and provoked a response from both Hindus and Moslems demonstrating the compassion and ethics of their own faiths

'Most missionaries presented the gospel in its western dress and they were therefore apostles of the west as well as of the pure spirit of Christ. By their manners and conduct, by their very existence, they were influences in favour of the western outlook', according to Indian historian Percival Spear's *Oxford History of Modern India*.

Eight miles up the road from Serampore I crossed a narrow stone bridge flanked by two pillars, each carrying the inscription: 'RF, Chandernagore, Liberté Egalité Fraternité'. I was entering the former French colony of Chandernagore.

The French arrived in Bengal in 1673, 22 years after the English and 136 years after the Portuguese. Ships sailed up the Hooghly twice each year with money to pay for return cargoes which had been collected and stored in the warehouses during the previous months. The station prospered until March 15th, 1757, when Robert Clive used the pretext of war in Europe to attack England's commercial rival in India by besieging the town with 900 European and 1500 Indian troops. The town was captured ten days later after a bombardment from ships on the Hooghly and the victory left the English in complete control of the river.

Chandernagore was returned to the French six years later when the Treaty of Paris was signed in Europe. It was recaptured by the English in 1794, returned in 1815 and handed back to the newly-independent India, along with Pondicherry, in 1951. I entered the town hoping to meet an ageing *matrone*, or at least to perceive some links with the recent European past. There were none. All street names, all shop signs were in Bengali. There was no trace of the Paris Hotel and all that remained of the grand houses were crumbling, ornate gateways plastered with cow-dung cakes, leading into empty gardens where pink and orange bougainvillaea had gone wild. The only indications of the French presence were the Administrateur's house (now a library and a dusty museum of Gallic relics) and the College Dupleix, now a Higher English School.

One other manifestation of the European occupancy has remained—the Sacred Heart Church built by Italian missionaries in 1726. Its thick, pale orange walls still glow in the sunshine. I arrived at the church while workmen were fixing Christmas lights to the roof and enjoyed a marvellous, if unofficial, view of the town and river. Then I strolled along the promenade beside the river, shaded by mature banyan trees, until I rejoined the grass bank where water buffaloes were grazing and women were pounding laundry on flat rocks, or knitting in groups outside their brown adobe homes.

I was walking happily in sandals, *lungi* and *kurta* and completely at peace with the world, when I passed two men filling buckets at a handpump. As they watched me pass along the footpath, I was amused to hear one say to the other 'No, he's not English. He's from Kashmir.'

It was a fiction that changing my appearance could really help my comprehension of the country and people. But wearing the local clothes was a symbolic act which many people were to warmly appreciate in the months that followed.

I passed through the former Dutch town of Chinsura a few miles on from Chandernagore. It had been the strength of the Dutch East India Company in the Far East that lured the English to trade in India, and English success in India that pushed out the Dutch when they exchanged the island of Sumatra for Chinsura in 1825.

At teatime I reached another Roman Catholic church, at Bandel, and after explaining about my journey, asked if I could stay in the church retreat house until Christmas which was five days away. I was told this was not possible without advance reservation, eventually I was shown to a dusty room with bed, table and chair. The air was thick with mosquitoes but there was a wide view of the river from the window. The cleaner who swept out the room and the man selling pamphlets at the church porch were welcoming and talked to me. Although I knew that I was imposing on the church and being accommodated on sufferance I wanted to spend Christmas in a church so much that I did not mind being thought rude.

Bandel is the oldest church in north India, having been founded in 1599 by Augustine friars beside the 'bandel', or port, of the Portuguese at Hooghly. The fortunes of the church reflected the adventures and misadventures of the Portuguese who had begun trading in Bengal 62 years earlier. By 1620, Hooghly had become the major town on the river, superseding nearby Satgaon which was silting up. The Portuguese controlled the river and Hooghly was a famous and cosmopolitan town with a reported 10,000 Christians. Portuguese merchants dressed like Indian princes, living in luxury, and they traded in slaves, spices, china, jewels and salt while enjoying the patronage of the Mughul emperor in Agra who was happy with revenue from the thriving commerce. The church flourished and the statue of Our Lady of Happy Voyage attracted great devotion from Christian sailors and from Hindus who called her 'Guru Ma', Mother Guru, regarding her as another goddess with her own cult following.

Bandel's success and control of traffic on the river was seen as a threat in 1627 by the Emperor Shah Jahan, who was also sore at the Portuguese for not supporting his earlier civil war against his father. Shah Jahan's forces besieged Bandel and Hooghly in 1632 and sacked the town and church after three months. This was the same year that the emperor started construction of the Taj Mahal in memory of his late wife Mumtaz. Rather than allow the statue of Our Lady from the church to fall to the Moslems, who would have destroyed it in accordance with their iconoclastic religious principles, the statue was sent across the river with a strong swimmer. Unfortunately he was killed by an arrow and the statue was apparently lost.

Four thousand prisoners from the settlement marched to Agra, where many were eventually released, ransomed or died. The next year, the priests and leaders were fetched out of prison to be executed in public by four elephants. However, when Father Joao da Cruz was thrown at the feet of an angry elephant, 'the elephant, abandoning his natural fierceness, knelt at the feet of the said father, paid him his obeisance and defended him with his proboscis (trunk),' according to one Catholic account. Whatever the circumstances of this 'miracle', the prisoners were released and sent back to Bandel with gifts from Shah Jahan to rebuild the church.

According to the Bengal Catholic Herald of May 1842, a second miracle occurred when the statue of Our Lady was found at daybreak on the river bank. The statue now stands at the top of the church belltower, reached by steps well-worn by pilgrims who have continued their adoration and petitions for intercessions to Our Lady for over 350 years. I was warned that thousands of people would be arriving in Bandel on Christmas morning and most of them would be Hindus.

However, the greatest Bandel miracle is that the church has never been flooded or washed away, though it stands beside the river.

'We believe it is a holy place,' I was told in the Baba Cabin, one of two local teahouses. The river has receded during the past 100 years and left a lawn the size of two soccer fields. Grazing cows keep the grass short and their dung is collected in baskets by women from the village.

Now, overlooking the calm, flowing Ganga, I was suddenly aware of the existence of a Divine, incomprehensible being. Those who believe in the bounty of Mother Ganga will take this revelation as her blessing; other people will say the thought came from days of quietude beside the water. It doesn't matter. I sat, supremely content, beside the river, watching a kingfisher diving into the water then emerging and flying to a clump of hard earth.

This incident prompted me to buy a small notebook in which I wrote out prayers and hymns to begin and end each day. The five days before Christmas passed quietly and pleasantly in reading and chatting with a group of men in the Baba Cabin, where I was taking my meals. One of them, Ranadhar Biswas, invited me to go to the Bengali service on Christmas Day at the Protestant Church and to Christmas lunch with This family.

I have always enjoyed the anticipation of Christmas and waited, therefore, until Christmas Eve before putting up the five paper streamers which I had brought from Calcutta. I went to Midnight Mass in the plain, thick-walled church. The service was conducted in Bengali and English and the building was full. People greeted each other after the Mass and though I stood to one side, not wanting to intrude, a small queue of men and women formed to greet me and shake my hand or push forward uncertain children to wish me Merry Christmas and receive the same from me. I believed that I was being mistaken for a priest. The congregation gathered in the refectory of the monastery attached to the church to drink tea from disposable clay cups, eat the ration of two biscuits and watch a display of fireworks shooting up over the river. For the first time in the week people came forward to ask who I was and where I was going. Far from being unfriendly and allowing me to stay on sufferance, it transpired that the prior and monks had not wished to disturb my retreat and I felt very cheap to have thought myself snubbed.

Ranadhar, his mother and sister took me on Christmas Day to the Protestant church in Chinsura, and although I did not understand a single word of the Bengali service, I enjoyed humming the tune of 'Hark the Herald Angels Sing'. There is no traditional menu for Christmas dinner but we ate a big meal of sweet, sweet basmati rice, thick *dal*, chicken curry and a delicious home-made tomato chutney. I took along the rich fruit cake I had bought and carried from Calcutta.

At least 50,000 people were thronging the street of Bandel by mid-afternoon to pass through the church to see the Nativity crib. Many, if not most, of the pilgrims were Hindus and I found something appealing in people of one faith embracing symbols and personalities venerated by another. A line of bobbing black heads coiled slowly through the church, past paintings of the miracles of Christ. People scattered coins in front of one of the side altars and looked at the crib, with its backdrop of stars in a blue sky, and finally emerged into the congested street of Bandel where, appropriately, two carpenters were working in a workshop.

The area beside the river in front of the church was now crowded with families and lines of hawkers selling peanuts, balloons, toy windmills, images of Jesus, Mary, Shiva and Ganesh, posters of Indian cricketers, with air rifles and target balloons to shoot, spicy or sweet snacks to eat and a hundred other amusements or nibbles. It was impossible to distinguish pilgrims from the day-trippers thankful to be away from Calcutta or Howrah, just as it was impossible to analyse the essential significance of Ganga herself. Not all pilgrims creep forward on their hands and knees, nor fast, nor gaze with solemn piety; the joy and love shared among families and friends on such festive days may be just as much a blessing as singing carols. I was learning not to try to separate daily life from religion.

It began drizzling late in the afternoon and the crowds dispersed quickly when heavy rain started towards nightfall. I was spending my last night in Bandel with a family in their well-equipped, brick-built bungalow and I sat at the dining table with husband, wife and son while we watched a film on their black and white television. Professor Deb and his family wanted me to stay longer and when in the morning it was still raining hard, I was delighted to accept. This made me all the more eager early the following morning to be moving again, after one week in Bandel.

By ten o'clock, having splashed through puddles on the asphalt road, I reached the end of the urban sprawl that had stretched 33 miles north from Calcutta. I stopped for a glass of tea and biscuits, answered questions from 20 men who gathered at the tea-stall, then crossed a small suspension bridge onto a dirt cart track. For the first time in weeks I saw a red-crested woodpecker with golden back, flying in a grove of bamboo and uttering its 'he-he-he-he' squeak. Perhaps it was laughing at me, already knowing how stupid I was being in walking briskly, despite my hurting feet, and after a week's inactivity, intent on reaching Kalna by nightfall.

I did reach the town, having walked 20 miles, and being unable to find hotel, *ashram* or warehouse in which to sleep, went to the Catholic boys' hostel. After supper of rice, stewed fish, and cauliflower and potato *subzee* at a nearby *dhaba* that was popular with truck drivers and mechanics, I hobbled back to the hostel for a cold shower and inspection of my feet. A deep crack cut across the ball of one foot. A large blister covered the ball of the other foot. I had walked too far again and was obviously too stupid to remember the self-inflicted damages which had marred the start of the walk.

Next day I walked four miles before admitting that I could go no further. I was 12 miles south of a pilgrim town where I was sure to find accommodation so I took an UP steam train up to Nabadwip (pronounced Na-baa-deep) and by rickshaw, ferry boat and slow, slow walking I reached the mighty *ashram* of the International Society for Krishna Consciousness, whose orange-robed and shaven-headed devotees chanting 'Hare Krishna, Hare Krishna' have long been a common sight on the streets of London, Paris and New York. Having once had a close encounter with the Moonies (a frightening experience), I entered the ISKCON ashram with trepidation and waited half an hour sitting on a mattress on the floor of the office before being interviewed and admitted. Charges were R25 for the room and R25 for three meals. Smoking and tea drinking were prohibited. Procedures were streamlined and rigid and I was shown to a gleaming single room on the second floor of a long hostel block containing 80 guest rooms and communal bathrooms.

I flopped on the bed and slept until early evening when I was visited by one of the devotees. He was a tall American, originally from a Catholic family in Brooklyn, New York, who entered in orange robes with his small bag of *japa* beads (similar to a rosary) dangling from one hand.

'I saw you coming in and I hear you're a walker, so I figured I'd ask you some questions 'cos I've been thinking of doing some hiking,' he said, sitting on the bed. 'See, I'm doing all these *japa* beads, walking up and down here every day and I could be out there walking in the Himalayas. Maybe go up to the source of the Ganga. Now, how about that? Wow!

'I've been in this place seven years. Seven years in India—Wow! I gotta get out. A man could go bananas here. You know, he really could. Well, I came to India to please my *guru*. He said to come here. I'm not really one with the people, y'know. I came here to please my *guru* and I guess I've done that.'

It was hard for me to hide my curiosity about how Kanva Das, for that was his new name, and the dozen other foreigners had come to be at the *ashram* at Mayapur amid quiet countryside over the river from Nabadwip.

'See, I was in Hawaii. I was not doing too good, I tell you. Well, I was rejected F4 by the military for the Vietnam war—that's fucking useless—I was doing drugs and all kinds of shit. I'd been working as a clerk on the New York Stock Exchange. I was spending my big salary on clothes and going for hours from Brooklyn to Wall Street on the subway. And I just looked round and I said, "Jesus Christ! Is this all there is? For the rest of my life?"

'Well, I'd heard Hawaii could be pretty good with all that sunshine, so I was working there picking pineapples or working as a "boy" on fishing boats. I kinda liked that, y'know.'

Living off the land, swimming, sunbathing and sleeping in caves, he finally went to the ISKCON temple on the island for free food. He said he'd joined ISKCON and worked on their farms in the United States for ten years before coming to India.

'We don't work here. Everything's provided if you just keep the simple rules—no intoxicants, no illicit sex and so on, and learn the devotional songs and beads.'

From being rejected by the US military, Kanva Das was now Head Gardener employing 40 labourers, though he did not speak too much Bengali, and providing vegetables to feed several hundred people each day. But now he wanted to get out.

Visitors' meals were served on the second floor verandah of the temple and administration block and about 100 people sat on the floor in two long lines behind strips of banana leaves on which rice, *dal*, spinach stew, cauliflower and potato *subzee* and a sweet were served from buckets on wheels. Eating and sleeping occupied my first two days in the *ashram* after both feet swelled up, throbbing painfully. My right foot had two long cracks and my left a big blister under the ball of the foot. Both feet were going to take a long time to heal and meanwhile I could only put pads on them both and limp slowly across the garden to go for meals. I decided to hasten the healing process by cutting open the big blister which revealed a half-inch diameter spot of raw flesh. The damage was far worse than I had suspected, and much more painful, but it was all my own fault, and there was nothing to do but wash both feet with antiseptic, walk as little as possible and pray the injuries would not get infected.

The *ashram* at Mayapur is one of many ISKCON *ashrams*, farms, hotels, villas and recording studios around the world. The organisation is big business and is reported by *Newsweek* to have spent US$1 million on full-colour promotional supplements distributed in Australia's major daily newspapers. Much of its wealth is donated by members when they join. These gifts, together with the members' free labour and the entrepreneurial spirit which permeates all its activities, such as its boast of serving 5 million free meals as if a charitable McDonald's, has made ISKCON a prosperous enterprise. In the West, this has passed almost unnoticed. In India, the oasis of affluence that is seen as a foreigners' playpen has attracted increasing envy. Guards armed with bamboo sticks patrolled the locked compound at night and three months after my visit a gang of robbers armed with bombs and guns broke into the temple and stole an idol and silver throne worth R75,000. Two of the robbers were shot dead by ISKCON guards and two devotees were injured. Since then, the guards' bamboo sticks have been replaced with rifles.

All this seemed to be far removed from devotion to Krishna, a god of love sometimes compared to Jesus Christ, and the message of ISKCON's founder Swami Prabhupada, who died in 1977. A massive mausoleum, with a dome reaching 160 feet above the ground, was under construction at Mayapur at a cost of R2 crore to house the flower garland worn by the swami when he died (his body has been preserved elsewhere). Land has also been bought around the *ashram* on which to build a city 'the size of the Vatican', according to ISKCON's leader, the *gurudeva* William Erlichman of Buffalo, New York.

'It's going to be a spiritual Disneyland,' Kanva Das told me one evening. It was shortly before supper time and I suggested that we should go to eat. Kanva Das looked at me and said proudly, 'That's okay. I don't eat with you guys. I can't eat food touched by just anyone. I'm a Brahmin. I gotta cook my own food.'

When my feet were starting to feel better, after several days, Kanva Das took me out to see a field spread with a mulch where 50,000 ears of sweet corn had been planted for the thousands of foreign devotees expected for a big festival in three months' time.

'They're just wild for it,' he said. 'And I make a good buck on that— twenty-five hundred dollars. Course, it all belongs to Krishna. We do everything for Krishna. But if I want to do my experiments on the farm or go visiting state-side, then I gotta have the cash.'

Worship in the *ashram* began at 4.30 a.m. with four hours of ecstatic dancing and chanting in the temple, similar to the Sufi devotion of Islam. Worship of Krishna, an incarnation of the god Vishnu, had been developed in Bengal by the fifteenth century Hindu saint Chaitanya who is said to have lived in a mud cottage on the site where the ISKCON establishment has been built. I wondered what had happened to Western Christianity to cause thousands of people to see God through this branch of an alien religion? Now, paradoxically, the West was receiving missionaries from India.

The old year ended and 1984 began while I was recuperating at the *ashram*. My feet were slowly healing while, day after day, I lay in bed reading the *Bhagavad-Gita* or sat in the rose garden enjoying the winter sunshine and the peace of the *ashram*. By January 3rd, after a week's inactivity, I felt ready to walk again. I paid my bill and left the *ashram* to walk the 12 miles before Nabadwip that I had travelled by train. That night I slept on the outskirts of Nabadwip on a string bed in a cold, draughty *dhaba*, shivering much of the night and eventually wrapping myself in the heat-reflecting emergency 'space blanket' I was carrying, though I felt like a roasting chicken wrapped in this sheet of tin-foil.

I was invited for tea to a neighbouring house at sunrise the next morning. An armchair was fetched from the house and placed on the chilly verandah and my host presented his wife and daughters and explained my pilgrimage to them. One of the daughters immediately dropped to her knees in front of me and kissed my feet.

'No! No!,' I exclaimed, putting out my hands to raise her up. This was completely the wrong response because the young woman thought I was rejecting her and refusing her my blessing, and I swiftly regretted my instinctive repulsion of a veneration I did not deserve.

My left foot was still sore and this was sufficient excuse to stay on the asphalt road when the river meandered off to the right. During the morning I decided there was little purpose in my wearing a wristwatch. I was waking before sunrise, eating when hungry and sleeping after sunset. My watch was therefore put away at the bottom of my knapsack and in the next few days I began to observe the changes in colours of light, shadows, and the noises of each time of day more distinctly. In putting away my watch I was also putting away a symbol of modern affluence in India. No one thinks it odd if a watch doesn't work or shows an incorrect time; wrist-watches are talismans of progress.

I stopped for tea and four *samosas* at midday and bought a bread bun to chew on the road. The road was straight and empty, running above fields planted with rice seedlings. I ate most of the bread bun and without stopping threw the crust to a stray dog. A hundred yards down the road, I turned round to see the dog chasing towards me. I opened out both hands to show that there was no more food and continued walking. The dog followed at my heels. A mile further, I stopped to answer a sudden call of nature and the dog lay down on the road and waited. When I started again, the dog followed. I ignored the animal and gave it no encouragement, as my mind filled with the difficulties and complications that having a dog as companion would bring in a country like India.

After four miles, a doctor invited me to his makeshift surgery for tea and the dog went to sleep outside. By now I really was becoming anxious that the dog had become my companion, thus barring me from hotels, homes and *ashrams*, though I was simultaneously gratified that the dog wanted to come along. I left the doctor after half an hour and had walked three hundred yards before the dog woke up and came running after me to walk at my heels panting for breath. The mutt would run ahead and sit in the road until I caught up with him, or chase after another dog with a bone, but always he came back to my side with tail wagging. I did not want any companion but secretly resolved that if he was still with me after 24 hours without my paying him any attention, he would be welcome and we would face the uncertain future together.

We walked together for the rest of the afternoon, passing barking dogs, and near sunset reached a village where one man was irrigating a rice field by the age-old method of hanging an open-ended canoe on a counter-weighted boom. I stopped beside the water ditch to watch him push the canoe down with his foot to submerge it. The canoe lifted as the counter-weight fell, and the water spilled out into a channel in the rice field on the higher level. Meanwhile, the dog went off on his own, giving me the chance to get away. I set off briskly along the open road and a quarter of a mile further on, when three men called to me, I went down into their field. I was then astonished when I saw the dog standing out on the road looking in my direction, and I cursed my selfishness. Even months later I remained convinced that the dog would have willingly completed the journey with me, but I was relieved to have left it behind. In India, it is easy to see the Divine in every aspect of living. Days later when I mentioned the dog to a young student, he replied easily, 'it is from such animals that we learn love.'

I slept that night on straw in a small room in a dilapidated *ashram* where hymns of love and devotion to Krishna were being sung non-stop day and night by pairs of men sitting in the temple. They had been praising Krishna in this way for 35 years and intended to continue for a thousand.

'Of course, we shall not be here. But generations will carry on the work,' explained the elder in charge, a retired civil servant.

I handed him a donation when I left at dawn after a day's rest. Mist lay over the dark river and black rowing boats were bringing over big baskets of tomatoes. I waited at the water's edge watching as groups of three men raised each basket onto one man's head and that man then went off towards the market at a running shuffle. At length, the sun rose through the mist, spreading a warming glow as we crossed the river. The opposite bank was revealed less than a quarter of a mile away and I set out along a footpath towards the site of the battle of Plassey.

Day labourers were already chopping the stands of sugar cane with sickles and I passed youths on the path carrying home bundles of cane leaves for fodder. Others were carrying the cane on their heads to heaps at the side of the fields where they would be crushed through mangles driven either by small petrol engines or by pairs of bullocks goaded by boys with sticks. Then the juice would be boiled in pans, like giant woks, over fires fed with the crushed and dried cane by women and children, and a smell would drift across the fields, similar to that of tinned tomato soup. The syrup would thicken to molasses and eventually crystallise into hard balls called *gour* which would be sold in the local market as sugar, or used in sweet making.

'Ah! Ah! Ha!' called the men who ploughed with pairs of bullocks, preparing the sandy fields for the year's second crop of rice or wheat. I had counted only six tractors in the 205 miles from the Bay of Bengal, one of them actually working the land and the others towing trailers of bricks or people.

It was here in the flat countryside at the start of the monsoon rains in 1757 that Robert Clive and the forces of the East India Company met those of the Nawab of Bengal in battle. Fighting began at eight o'clock with the Nawab's guns outranging the English and causing Clive to withdraw his men. At noon, the sky darkened and monsoon rains fell for nearly an hour, drenching the fields and dampening the powder of the Nawab's artillery. The Nawab's cavalry charged expecting the English artillery to be similarly disabled but their charge was repelled by the English guns, whose powder had been protected under tarpaulins. However, Clive's forces were still boxed in. But the Nawab was having his own problems. His army had refused to fight until they received arrears of pay and the Nawab was terrified both of fighting and of losing. One of his most capable officers was mortally wounded by lunchtime, and another had already signed a secret treaty to support Clive.

When the Nawab's troops began withdrawing to their entrenchments at three o'clock, the English Major Kilpatrick pursued them and sent word to Clive, who was changing out of wet trousers at the time. Clive was furious at this insubordinate act but having once advanced could not withdraw. Meanwhile, courage had at last failed the 20-year-old Nawab and he fled on a camel with 2000 horsemen. Word of his escape quickly spread and his forces surrendered. Two hundred of the Nawab's men and 50 of Clive's had been killed in the day's exchange. A memorial stands today on the site of the battle, surrounded by rice fields and scattered trees.

Had it not been victorious at Plassey, the East India Company would have been pushed out of Bengal. Victory brought great wealth and limited power. Real power and a permanent presence in North India were another seven years in coming, after the battle of Buxar.

After six days I entered Murshidabad alone and found a decaying and decrepit city. The population has fallen by two thirds since 1982, and the buildings have also declined or fallen down due to lack of repairs and lack of money. People seemed to be living in the ruins of yesteryear. The great palace of Murshidabad was the best example of this decay. Built by the English in 1837 as a £167,000 gift to the Nawab, it was a replica of an Italian palazzo. Its first-floor banqueting hall was almost 200 feet long and over 54 feet wide, illuminated with a chandelier burning 110 candles. This hall opened into a ballroom of the same size and there was also a circular *durbar* room, with throne of ivory and gilded flowers. I wondered if ghosts with thick beards and heavy turbans might gather here, when the tourists had gone, to hear once again the petitioners and plaintiffs appealing to the Nawab. Echoes of the servants' chatter and soft footfalls on the stone stairs had long since faded. The paint was now peeling, the plaster cracked and crudely repaired, furniture had been removed and cobwebs covered the cabinets of sea shells and stuffed game birds which stood in the corners of the rooms as in an English country house. Tourists had scratched graffiti on the walls, next to notices telling people not to spit. There was nothing Indian about this building or its contents. The landscape paintings were of England, family portraits were painted in European style and hung alongside pictures of the British royal family.

But the Nawab seems to have had little taste for this imported culture, and the 1881 edition of Murray's guide to Bengal noted, 'It is strange that with so noble a residence the Nawab should have preferred to live in a range of low, small buildings to the east, while his mother resides in a barge.'

Why the mother lived in a barge was not disclosed, but there has long been a close association between the Moslem majority of the city and the river. A Moslem raft festival is held on the river every year in late August and combines Moslem practice with much of Hinduism. For example, there is music, normally forbidden on Islamic religious occasions. The prow of the raft looks like a crocodile, the animal which according to Hindu tradition carries Ganga, and the Moslem festival is held in accordance with the Hindu calendar.

Celebration of the Bera festival on the Ganga demonstrate the respect that Bengali Moslems have for the river, though it is also a convenient stretch of water. It was in the guise of a man of Bengal that a village poet once asked of the Ganga:

Who is that woman
whose presence is a blessing,
whose embrace redeems us,
whose kiss can bring us immortality?

I returned to the room where I was lodging for the night in Murshidabad to wash my feet with antiseptic and to put on antiseptic cream and bandages over a deep crack and areas of tender flesh. Every time the strapping of my sandals broke and was repaired by a street cobbler the position of my feet in them changed, causing new blisters. My legs were also suffering from sudden cramps and I would wake during the night in momentary agony. I was certainly learning to respect my body, but felt somewhat down-hearted now that the euphoria of actually beginning the walk had faded after seven weeks. I was looking forward to reaching open spaces and silent miles along the Ganga in Bihar, but this was still weeks ahead, and I was still being hindered by crowds and constant questioning in Bengal.

I was furious to discover that there was an extra R5 charge, above the R10 room charge, for the quilt which was standard equipment everywhere else during the winter months. It was a grimy, dismal room, without padlock, without water, with a dirty bed sheet and a mosquito net with long tears. This contrasted so much with the hotel room I had enjoyed several nights previously for R10 that it angered me to feel I was being cheated. As often happened in India, I went out of this fleapit hotel feeling very indignant yet was immediately mollified when I found friends and good food in the congested market. I carried with me in my knapsack two cassette tapes of my favourite music and that evening the owner of a *dhaba* and his customers invited me to play a cassette on their tape recorder. I'm sure that this was the first classical music ever to be heard blaring in the dim, dirty streets of Murshidabad. The tape was a selection of my favourite melancholic music, and the pace was much too slow for the customers of the *dhaba*. One man, wrapped in a green shawl, crouched on a bench while his transistor radio played Bengali songs in his ear.

However, conversation was respectfully whispered while I floated away with the music and the effects of the *beedis* I was smoking. Just as the last 'Amen, Amen,' of Handel's *Messiah* was being sung, the electricity cut out and we were in total darkness.

'Load-shedding,' called a disembodied voice.

'It is the curse of every day,' explained another.

Hurricane lamps were quickly brought and we continued eating supper.

Three days later, I reached the Jangipur Barrage and was within sight of the main course of the Ganga. Here was the apex of the Ganga delta, where the two arms of the river joined, and the river was as wide as a sea. But first, I had to be ferried by rowing boat across the 150-yard wide canal which flows from the Farakka Barrage on the main river into the Hooghly branch below the Jangipur Barrage. It is this canal that keeps the port of Calcutta alive by flushing out some of the silt choking the river bed.

The current in the canal was swift and the boatmen were obliged to punt some distance upstream before rowing away from the canal bank. The sky was overcast and it began to drizzle, which was beneficial for the second crops of rice and wheat that had just been planted.

I reached the main Ganga half an hour later, and had now walked 268 miles from the ocean. I stood at the edge of the 40-foot escarpment and looked down at the grey ribbon of water that flowed from left to right across miles and miles and miles of empty sands and mudflats. Somewhere here runs the border between India and Bangladesh. It looked as if the tide had gone out.

5

The Inland Sea

'To talk of a call from God is not popular now. People like to speak of their work. To me, it has been a call.' Miss Gudrun Saether took another sip of her strong coffee and sliced another piece of processed cheese to put on top of a bread roll.

'I was not happy when the call came, yah! I was a nurse in the operating theatre. It was a good job, I had a beautiful flat. My life was comfortable. But—huh!—God comes to shake us from this. Yah! One day I knew Jesus was calling. He wanted me for his holy work. I was not happy at this. I kept those things in my heart for a time. I prayed in the church. It was God's call, so I must answer. It was hard to tell my mother and my father that I would leave Norway and be a missionary in India. My mother, she said to me, "Gudrun, it has taken you so long to come to this? I have always known." I have been here thirty years. You see, God is wonderful. I am not lonely here. I have the main mission in Bihar to go to, but I do not wish. I have my work and my reading and letters; oh, so many letters.'

The breakfast of instant coffee, cheese, bread rolls and marmalade provided a welcome change from spiced beans. Afterwards, we went across the road to the mission hospital and passed a large signboard with 'Norwegian Mission' written in green lettering. I had arrived the previous afternoon in front of this sign, soaked after two hours' walking in heavy rains, and so astonished to come across a mission beside an isolated village amid banana trees and date palms that I walked up the garden path and knocked on the door of the small, white bungalow.

Miss Saether, the solitary missionary, invited me for tea on the covered-in verandah, and we sat on comfortable cushions in wicker armchairs, overlooking the waterlogged beds of red flowers in the garden. She smiled at me and asked how I had come to her village.

'Yah!' She exclaimed when I told her, and sipped her cup of tea while the warm rain clattered on the verandah roof. She seemed not to notice the water dripping from my hair nor the trickle, running down the inside of my clothes, dampening her cushions. She asked for an assurance that I was 'genuine' and that I planned no evil deed.

'A woman on her own, so I must ask you,' she explained.

She made me comfortable on a spare bed in the office she used for literacy lessons, to which was attached a bathroom; this was a hole in the concrete floor and a bucket of cold water under a tap.

'My servant—one must have a servant if you want to do other work in India—he is away. I'm sorry I can give you no food.'

Half an hour later, I was walking briskly down the waterlogged road towards a town four miles away to get a hot meal, wearing a borrowed gaberdine raincoat over my *lungi* and *kurta*. The mission station was about two miles from the Ganga and I had retreated from the muddy, slippery path along the river bank after slipping onto my backside in a field of young wheat. Most of the shops in the town were closed because few people ventured out in the rain, but I found a place serving the inevitable rice, *dal* and *subzee*. I returned to the mission station at dusk just twenty minutes before torrential rain started again. The teenage son of the mission nightwatchman was already encamped on the verandah doing his school homework by the light of a hurricane lamp.

I was thoroughly tired, having walked twelve miles from Jangipur on slippery paths and eight miles further on wet roads, and it was only now, resting on the edge of the bed, that I realised I had walked those extra miles unnecessarily. I found four tins of fish and a packet of cheese that I had bought for just such emergencies at the bottom of my backpack.

In the morning the sky was gloriously blue and clear when Miss Saether and I strolled across the road to the mission hospital after breakfast. The long, white huts and the dark faces standing on the porch of the small dispensary reminded me at once of photographs of Doctor Albert Schweitzer's hospital at Lambourane in West Africa. There were 101 patients in the Norwegian hospital, which was run by one nurse, two auxiliary nurses and a doctor who visited once a week. A white clapboard chapel stood in the middle of the compound and there was also a dispensary stocked with about two dozen different drugs to treat 20,000 people suffering everything from hookworm to severed toes after accidents with sickles at harvest time.

'Is there no government dispensary?' I asked Miss Saether.

'Yah! Yah!'

'Why do people come here for treatment when you charge two rupees and the government dispensary is free?'

'A woman from the village said to me, "If we go to the hospital, we die",' she replied.

I was to hear this criticism of government health services again and again along the Ganga, and in particular in Bihar, the most rotten state in the country, whose border I was soon to cross.

In addition to the dispensary and hospital, the mission organised regular eye camps sponsored by the Lutheran World Service. About 9 million people are blinded by cataracts in India. At the last eye camp, a few months earlier, 2262 people had arrived blind and, after surgery, returned home with their sight restored. It must have seemed like God's greatest miracle.

'It is a wonderful thing when men and women can see again. My servant—oh, he reads and reads all the time now. Yah! He cannot believe he can read again. It is God's work,' explained Miss Saether with a big smile across her pale, wrinkled face.

Then I was on the move again, keeping to the asphalt lane until the mud on the footpaths dried in the strong sunshine. I stopped several times for tea and always someone would ask where I was going and where I had come from. It was easy to tell whether they understood when I answered them in Hindi. Their eyes would open wide, their jaws fall open and I would hear them whisper, 'Oh father. You are walking?'

'Yes.'

'Alone? One man? Only one?'

To each of these I would murmur the short and expressive Hindi word, 'huh!' (yes) while nodding my head from side to side.

'It is strange. It is wonderful. Will you take tea?'

'Yes, I will take tea.' And twenty people would quickly gather while one or two men asked questions in English, Bengali or Hindi and translated for the audience.

In one record-breaking morning, I drank tea, smoked *beedis* and answered the same questions 16 times within four hours. I tried to see a spark of the Divine in each person, especially when I was tired and grumpy, and not merely yet another stranger who asked the same tedious questions. It no longer sounded preposterous to give the glacier at Gau Mukh as my destination though it was still more than 1200 miles away. Almost everyone knew where the source of the Ganga was, but no one I met had seen the Himalayas.

Two days after leaving Miss Saether, I saw the barrage that holds back the Ganga and causes the wide river bed to look as if the tide had gone out, leaving miles and miles of grey sands. The Farakka Barrage remained a blur across the horizon for hours, gradually emerging from the shimmering haze as I walked along the edge of the bank that dropped 40 feet into the river. I was walking beside fields of *dal* bushes and sat for a while overlooking the empty river. This was a moment to savour: the first time in six weeks that I was able to be alone.

.I reached the Farakka Barrage at teatime. It is here, behind 109 massive, metal gates stretching two miles (I estimated) across the Ganga, that the mighty river is diverted into the canal that is prolonging the life of the port of Calcutta.

Twelve miles downstream of the Farakka Barrage, in Bangladesh, the dam's impact has been devastating, according to the Government of the People's Republic of Bangladesh. The water level has fallen five feet, allowing salt water to penetrate 83 miles inland from the Bay of Bengal. Irrigation has been damaged and rice production in 400,000 acres has fallen by 20 per cent.

The Indian Government claims that diverting water helps Bangladesh by reducing flooding during the monsoon. Bangladesh says diversion during the monsoon is irrelevant because then there is too much water for everyone. It is during March, April and May in the hot season, when the river is at its lowest, that the effect of diverting water is so devastating. According to Indian Government statistics, more than half the water in the Ganga during the hot season is diverted by the Farakka Barrage, leaving Bangladesh with a puny serpent of water flowing across the sandy desert between river banks that are miles apart.

I rested at a tea-stall beside the guarded barrage and decided to make a side trip away from the river by the evening steam train over the barrage and slowly north to the town of Malda, 25 miles from the Ganga. I found a hotel that would take me, after three attempts, and booked a single, clean, quiet room painted entirely in lime-green gloss for R12. The food, produced from a dark, smoky room in the hotel, was fresh and tasty and after rice, *dal* and *subzee*, I went off to the market to buy tangerines before enjoying an early night's sleep.

After one day's rest, during which I abortively tried to make a telephone call to England via Calcutta, I went out of Malda sitting comfortably on a cycle rickshaw. My shawl was wrapped round me against the breeze while the rickshaw-*wallah*, who was my own age, pedalled hard along the flat road. We were going to Gaur beneath an avenue of big mango trees, a round trip of 10 miles at a cost of R15 which had already been agreed. It is more than four hundred years since bullock carts and camel trains loaded with spices, brassware, rice and other grains last travelled this route to Gaur, for three hundred years the capital of Bengal.

When Ludovico di Varthema came to Gaur from Venice at the start of the sixteenth century, he reported on the size of this city's commerce, but omitted to mention the multitude of street entertainers, bands of singers, snake charmers, or men with bears and monkeys. Fifty ships were loaded with cotton and silk stuffs every year, he reported. Like Venice, canals connected Gaur's port with the remainder of the city. Arab merchants from Baghdad and Basra had settled in Gaur and they had no doubt overawed visitors to the Golden Mosque, built with 44 handsome domes in 1526 by the Mughul ruler of Bengal.

The port traded with far-away China, and Portuguese merchants, visiting Gaur shortly before 1540, described its streets as straight and broad and crowded with traffic and people. The city, they said, had a population of 1,200,000 families though they did not say how many members individual families might contain. The city measured seven and a half miles from north to south and was between one and two miles broad. It was well fortified with high, thick ramparts, deep entry gates and, in places, double or triple defensive ditches. Gaur was situated at the head of the Ganga delta where the river divided into the Bhagirathi (being renamed the Hooghly lower down) and the Padma (flowing into present-day Bangladesh).

Gaur was created because of the Ganga; and what the Ganga gave, she also took away. We know the date of the death of Gaur because it was sudden and it was caused by the river. In 1575 the people of Gaur were enjoying renewed prosperity after their city had been sacked 18 years previously. The rivers rose and broadened for three months as usual during the monsoon but, as the monsoon flood waters receded, the main channel of the Ganga shifted several miles to the south. Gaur was marooned by sandbanks and with no water. In the festering conditions of Bengal, in the heat and humidity, the stagnant riverbed soon became a breeding ground of mosquitoes and malaria. Dreaded pestilence broke out in the city late in 1575. The result was predictable. W. W. Hunter wrote, in *Annals of Rural Bengal*, in 1897:

> Thousands died daily . . . The living, wearied with burying the dead, threw their bodies into the river. This created a stench which only increased the disease. The governor was carried off by the plague. The city was at once depopulated and from that day to this it has been abandoned. At the time of its destruction it had existed two thousand years. It was the most magnificent city in India, of immense extent, and filled with noble buildings. It was the capital of a hundred kings, the seat of wealth and luxury. In one year, it was humbled to the dust, and now it is the abode only of tigers and monkeys.

The rickshaw-*wallah* offered to take me on the lane around the remaining ruins of Gaur for an extra R10 and we visited the northern gate of the old citadel, which now led into a mango orchard. We visited ruined mosques and climbed a brick tower. But I was distracted from the intricate work of the tiles and the beauty of the domes by a sudden association of the ruins with Shelley's 'Ozymandias':

'Look on my works, ye mighty, and despair!'
Nothing beside remains. Round the decay
Of that colossal wreck, boundless and bare.
The lone and level sands stretch far away.

The Ganga never returned to Gaur and its ruined walls have only recently been opened to visitors by the Archaeological Survey of India. Today, the Ganga flows 25 miles to the south and the river is so wide above the Farakka Barrage that it looks like an inland sea. Even at nine o'clock in the morning, before the haze thickens in the sky, there was only a blurred green line on the horizon across the expanse of water. I walked briskly in this chilly, morning air, happy to be beside this river again after two days away, though it was necessary after a few miles to watch where I was walking. The footpath by the river might well be called The Toilet Route.

Late in the morning on January 21st, I sighted the brown Rajmahal Hills emerging from the white haze on my left. These volcanic hills were the first relief in an otherwise completely flat landscape devoid even of stones in the past 300 miles from the Bay of Bengal. An asphalt road led north-west between quartz and kaolin quarries where purple, white and golden rocks were being broken up. Men were smashing boulders into fist-sized chunks with hammers, women were carrying baskets of the rocks on their heads to mechanical crushers and more men were loading the gravel into trucks with shovels. The work was hard and dusty, for a pittance—but it was work and people must eat and feed their children and offer something to the deity at the local temple.

The quarries, the all-important fields and people's little homes were squeezed onto a shelf of green vegetation between the Ganga and the Rajmahal Hills, which had now closed in on my left. There were few handpumps here and those I did see in the small villages were broken, or rusting from disuse. People took water from open, brick-lined wells, dropping their metal buckets down 10 or 15 feet on ropes with a clatter and a splash. The round, cow-dung cakes I had seen in the delta were now replaced by sausage-like ingots. These ingots of the precious material were stacked on the verges of the road and in front of people's homes to dry in the afternoon warmth. Cooking fuel was every family's priority, but the loss of fertiliser for the rice fields has been serious. Bio-gas digesters, converting manure simultaneously into gas for cooking and nitrogen-rich fertiliser, are rare. I was to see six digesters during the entire walk but only two of these were working.

I reached Maharajpur railway station at 1 p.m. with aching feet and a blister the size of a large coin under the ball of my left foot. This time, I was smart enough to know not to walk any further and after half an hour's wait took the steam train up the line to Sahibganj. I had seen many trains go by while I was walking over dusty paths and had been showered by particles of ash from the engines' funnels (the ash is said to be good for rice cultivation). Any secret desire that I might have had to be aboard a train instead of plodding along on foot vanished when I boarded that UP train from Maharajpur to Sahibganj. Every carriage was packed with people, packages and sacks. More people forced their way inside at each of four railway stations while others tried to leave the train by squeezing themselves out like toothpaste from a tube. I was glad not to be going far.

After half an hour I emerged into daylight and fresh air at Sahibganj and went immediately to a local barber for a shave before walking the mile to St Xavier's School. Like many Catholic schools in India, this had a reputation for excellence and attracted the children from well-to-do families who could afford the fees and meet the academic requirements.

Six jovial Jesuit fathers from Malta and Sicily ran the school, and were training Indian Jesuits to take over from them. They were a hearty band, undaunted by being so far in distance and culture from their islands, enjoying minestrone, green salads and leavened bread at their dinner table. I had been given an introduction to one of the fathers and received a warm welcome when I arrived in time for tea, bread, butter and jam. I was put up in a comfortable bed in the original schoolhouse overlooking the Ganga. The bungalow, with its pretty flower garden, had formerly been the home of an Anglo-Indian family who emigrated to Canada after Independence.

'Why are you making this walk?' asked one of the thousand St Xavier schoolboys, dressed, like the five friends standing beside him, in blue shorts and white shirt, with his black hair cut short and neatly combed.

I answered the question while the boys looked me slowly up and down.

'Why are you wearing *this* dress?' asked one boy.

They were terribly enthusiastic, though I think it was all quite outside their comprehension.

'After this, will you continue as a hippie?'

I laughed and excused myself to walk back to the railway station at Maharajpur and thus make up the section I had covered by train the previous afternoon. The baked earth that lies between the river and the volcanic Rajmahal Hills has acted as a buffer protecting the town of

Sahibganj from being washed away by the monsoon floods. Groves of mango trees covered this hard earth and cattle grazed on the short, sparse grass. I approached so quietly up the shaded slope of a wooded ravine that two girls continued singing while collecting fallen leaves into wicker baskets to take home for fuel. I was 30 yards away when they saw me and they stopped singing and shyly turned away, though only after gazing at me for a long time.

Two miles further into the mango grove, I was called from the footpath by an old man with a club foot who was tending a small herd of goats nibbling grasses. This was only my second day in the Hindi-speaking area and though the man spoke slowly I could only surmise what he was saying. He began miming his questions in order to clarify them, keeping his balance by clutching his bamboo staff in one rough hand and waving the other hand up and down in the air, while his small body, dressed in a scruffy tweed jacket of dark design and patched khaki trousers, bent and twisted from side to side. I eventually guessed his question: 'Do you have cows in your country?'

'Yes.'

He smiled through the only two teeth in his mouth and wiped his greying moustache. 'What country are you from? Do you cultivate the earth? Do you harvest with a sickle?' This was easier, and question followed question until, at length, he seemed satisfied and waved goodbye, swinging his staff in front of him and walking away with a heavy limp to round up the goats which in the meantime had wandered off.

Further along, I reached a steep-sided hillock rising like a monolith above the land and climbed 95 broken steps to the white, Moslem mausoleum at the top. There was hardly space to park a bullock cart, but the view over the Ganga was astounding. The river flowed like a broad, silver ribbon gleaming in the afternoon sun around a large, flat island about four miles away. Four villages and yellow and green fields were visible in the bleaching haze across the riverbed. There seemed to be no end to the expanse of the floodplain miles beyond the island. The opposite shore of the river was invisible through the haze, yet all this plain and the low-lying island would be flooded by Ganga-ji during the monsoon. I had already heard people referring to the river as Ganga-ji, the suffix denoting respect, and after eight weeks living beside her it no longer seemed impertinent for me to do the same.

I looked down from my pinnacle and was surprised and intrigued to see two paddle steamers lying high and dry on a beach below. It did not take long to reach the marooned PS Marjorie and PS Ganga nor to creep up the gangplank aboard PS Marjorie, hoping not to rouse the two watchmen who slept noisily on the forward deck. I tiptoed over broad, wooden decks and peered into the First Class Saloon, now bereft of its accoutrements. Third Class was in the hold, with bare plates and crude shelves serving as benches and bunks. All the steamer's fittings, such as her lifeboats, had gone, and I was saddened to see the vessel, once so grand, now abandoned. Alas, there are no longer any steamboats on the Ganga.

Inevitably, the two watchmen awoke and I escaped, quickly, pursued across the sands by Hindi abuse. The river has shifted north in recent years and Sakrigali Ghat has been stranded a quarter of a mile up the beach. Goods trains could no longer be loaded and unloaded from river steamers at this ghat, beside the rows of red brick terrace houses that were still noisy with families, dogs and cows. The ghat, or steps for bathers down to the river, was buried in sand and the silent marshalling yard was now a graveyard for rusting, broken wagons with 'booked for stabling' scrawled on their doors. The railway tracks led up a slope to the main line and I eventually reached Maharajpur punctually for the evening UP train back to Sahibganj in time for evening prayers at St Xavier's.

After a supper of meat loaf and boiled potatoes, I sat down to read *India Today*, the country's news magazine. One story was more disturbing then usual. Nine children, a youth and a man from a village along the Ganga where I would soon be walking had been kidnapped and all but three massacred. 'The dead are said to have been the victims of a long-drawn-out inter-caste war between the Yadav and Dhanuk castes in the village . . . a war that has its roots in the struggle for land, less and less of which is available as the river eats into it every year,' said the report.

'The lawlessness of the area is all too well known. Criminals have in recent years made it a practice to dump their victims in the 350 km stretch of the "holy Ganga" between Mokamhtal and Bhagalpur. They have also perfected techniques to prevent bodies floating to the surface—they either chop them into little bits or slit their stomachs,' it continued. I was just ten days' walking distance from this area of Bihar, but I could not turn back now and must just hope for the best.

Next morning, the sun was high and hot by the time I had said my farewells, received a blessing from one of the fathers and answered further questions from a delegation of schoolboys. I walked briskly along the road at the base of the Rajmahal Hills. The hills soon faded into the white haze on the horizon and I was left on the vast Gangetic Plain with 1000 miles still to walk before I reached the foothills of the Himalayas. Though utterly flat, the land was not boring, being crowded with villages of adobe houses with thatched or red tile roofs, with lines of green trees and with orange or brown fields where women were bent double weeding the new crop of young wheat. I was often confused in India by the wheat and barley in the fields because the wheat had bearded ears like barley.

This was the second crop of the year and its success was dependent on irrigation. After the famine of 1967 great efforts were made to increase and improve irrigation, but by 1977 only one-third of Bihar's crop land was irrigated, compared to over three-quarters in the Punjab. The latter is India's most advanced agricultural state and Bihar is probably the most backward. Yields of the major crops (rice and wheat) have remained low in Bihar compared to other states, despite the Green Revolution: 87 bushels of wheat are produced per irrigated acre (66 bushels per unirrigated acre) compared to 260 bushels of wheat (115 unirrigated) per acre in the Punjab. Yet in the sixteenth century Bihar had exported grain to other parts of northern India. The development of irrigation has depended on the goodwill of politicians, the maintenance of law and order and the willingness of farmers to work together without fear of fighting. All these conditions have been lacking in Bihar and are the main reasons for the state's continued stagnation. Production of food-grains, such as wheat and rice, has been very unstable in Bihar, increasing 21 per cent between 1974 and 1978, then falling 30 per cent in 1982. Meanwhile the population has increased 24 per cent in the ten years from 1971, up 13.6 million to 69.9 million. Production in the Punjab has almost doubled in the same period while its population has also increased 24 per cent.

Almost three-quarters of Bihar's water comes from canals and ponds, with the remainder being drawn from underground wells. Water is drawn from shallow, open wells by two methods which have been used for centuries—buckets on big wheels which are turned creakingly slowly by bullocks, or single buckets which are raised by men pulling on counter-weights on long poles. The modern method uses electric or petrol motors to drive pumps attached to deep wells each made of a single metal pipe inserted into the ground. These wells are called tubewells and one pump can irrigate 44 acres. Electric pumpsets for tubewells are the cheapest but less than half the villages of Bihar have even nominal electric power, which often means one light bulb in the house of the local baron. Officially, there are over 182,000 electric pumpsets but the power supply is so erratic that in 1981 parts of the state were getting power for irrigation for only one hour per day. Small wonder therefore that the farmers of Bihar who can afford the requisite R5000 or who can borrow the money buy petrol-driven engines.

I followed the asphalt road beside the Rajmahal Hills parallel to and a few miles inland from the river. I walked in a deep reverie and on one occasion caught sight of a brown and green snake coiled by the roadside just before I trod on it. Occasional billboards advertised irrigation pumpsets or family planning. One advertisement in English seemed a poor joke in a land 200 miles from the sea and where 26 per cent of the people cannot read or write even any Indian language. It declared, in English, 'For adventure and fulfilment in life . . . Join the Indian Navy.'

The changes from Bengal to Bihar had been gradual but now the landscape looked completely different. The soil was sandy and unable to hold water. There were no ponds in the villages. There were no ducks nor flowers nor banana trees nor date nor coconut palms. The open land was light or dark brown in colour under a cloudless blue sky and there were so few trees that it was possible to count them.

Seven miles on from Sahibganj a man came running from his field one afternoon to invite me to sit with him. At first I declined, as this was the fifth invitation within a few miles, but then I followed him down the bank and across to where an eight-foot spray of water gushed from the mouth of a tubewell to flow across the field through a shallow ditch. My host scooped up a bowl of the clear water and offered it to me. It tasted warm and flecks of sand and mica settled to the bottom of the bowl as I drank.

'Please stay five days in my house,' he said in English after a few minutes' questions.

As always, I was eager to keep moving and was ever conscious of the endless miles ahead across the Gangetic Plain. The deadly heat of the dry season was now only three months away and I wanted to have walked as far as possible before conditions became physically unbearable. But how was I to learn about the land and the river if I always declined local invitations? When my host invited me a second time to stay in his house, I accepted for an overnight halt.

From his wristwatch, his command of English, his clean, white *dhoti* (the dress of Gandhi) and his self-assurance, it was obvious that this was no ordinary villager.

Shri (Mr) Prakasha Nand Singh, my host, courteously fetched out some potato *subzee* and thick *parathas* (similar to *chapatis* with a high oil content) and after the meal we settled down on a blanket to while away the sunny afternoon. The petrol engine behind us worked with a slow, steady cough and water sprayed from the mouth of the tubewell like the torrent from a fireman's hose. The water gushed into a shallow settling pond then flowed smoothly into the field of young sugar cane where a solitary man was working with a hoe.

I was carrying several books in my knapsack, having anticipated a lean supply of English language books in Bihar, and was reading a biography of Jawarharlal Nehru, India's first prime minister and the late Mrs Gandhi's father. My host picked out a book by Mahatma Gandhi on nonviolence and read while his labourer travailed in the field.

The petrol engine choked, spluttered and died once during the afternoon, and when it stopped a second time near sunset the labourer was called from the field to carry home the petrol can, tools and hoe while we strolled home wrapped in shawls against the chill of early evening.

The male members of the family turned out to welcome me to their single-storey brick house with its wide, covered verandah and brick-paved yard where water buffalo cows were effortlessly munching sugar cane. Shri Nand Singh had eight sons, three of whom were married, and all of them living in the one house. None of the women saw me arrive but every question and answer was reported back to them as they brewed tea in the kitchen. We talked in a mixture of Hindi and English, laughed and smoked *beedis*, looking on while a man carried baskets of chopped hay to the 20 cows tethered at feeding troughs in the yard. He was short and muscular, perhaps in his twenties, and blinded in one eye by a cataract. The animals also needed water and a boy spent over an hour drawing up water in a bucket from the open well in the yard.

I was reluctant to ask my host's caste because it seemed such a personal and irrelevant question, like asking an Englishman his class. But there was no such reticence in India and many people had already asked *me* the question. To know someone's caste was to pigeon-hole them exactly, not only into their religious division but, with thousands of sub-castes, also into their occupation and place of origin, and thus their social status. So I summoned up courage and asked.

He named some sub-caste but I was embarrassed to ask further and its significance escaped me.

'Milkman,' he said.

When it was dark I was called into a room lit by the yellow light of a hurricane lamp to eat hot *puris* (much, much lighter, but similar to *parathas* and deep fried), fried potato, fresh tomato slices and spring onions and spiced cauliflower which was the vegetable in season. Six men of the family stood behind as I ate, ready to serve whatever extra was required. The food was delicious but my hosts were always too generous. I had established two techniques to minimise the discomfort. The first was to say that I was full and could eat no more after the first helping of food. But more food would always be brought and with luck my protests might be taken seriously by the third helping. The second method necessitated finishing all dishes at the same time; with the last piece of *chapati* wiping clean the bowls of *dal* and *subzee*, because if half a *chapati* remained then another bowl of *dal* would be served and the generosity could go on and on. The meal was finished with a bowl of warmed water-buffalo milk sweetened with a melting meringue. This milk is as rich as the cream of a Jersey cow and enjoys a favoured status in India. Strangely, Hindus hold the white domestic cow, not the black water buffalo, as being sacred.

'Do you have water buffaloes in your country?' people sometimes asked me.

'No.'

'You do not have buffalo milk?'

'No, only cow's milk.'

'But, you are a rich country,' they would say, unable to comprehend why the rich man did not keep water buffaloes.

It was time to sleep after finishing the rich milk and rinsing my hands and mouth. I don't know when the family ate, perhaps while I had dozed earlier in the evening. One man was already asleep on the verandah under a thick blanket, apparently unworried by mosquitoes on such a chilly night.

This same man began his prayers at 4.30 a.m. the next morning, singing in a monotonous, gritty voice. I turned, over, blocked my ears and slept until shortly before sunrise. When I woke, my host led me out with a big brass jug into the field to defecate. I had been unable to explain that I merely wanted to urinate, something permissible without trekking into wheat fields along a narrow path slippery and muddy with morning dew. So I crouched down with bare bottom among green plants and watched the gorgeous sunrise over the flat land and the delightful orange light illuminating the distant Rajmahal Hills.

6

Where Angels Fear to Tread

After eight weeks I was finding the footfall of walking something of a hypnotic drug to which I had become addicted, and I was beginning to resent the frequent interruptions from curious wellwishers at the roadside. But I continued west along the road to Bhagalpur, having rationalised that I should not follow the river pedantically around a meander because it would necessitate imposing on a village for accommodation. In fact, I was apprehensive about walking into an area shown as blank on my map, but was still determined to keep going, despite all the warnings and advice to take the train through the troubled areas of the state. This was not youthful brashness: I knew that most battles and massacres were being fought between serfs and landowners backed by the police and would not affect an outsider.

Bihar's reputation for violence, superstition, misery and political corruption is so extreme that I had found it difficult to believe accounts such as I had read in *India Today* before I travelled through the state for myself. The opportunity to gain access to remote, forgotten areas, such as parts of rural Bihar, was another reason for walking beside the Ganga. But I was not prepared for the squalor and human degradation which gave rise to the violence.

'Rural Bihar—the very name conjures an image of a land full of gun-toting youths and caste feuds. A land where murder is not news anymore, where whole villages are demolished or set on fire if an individual refuses to pay for a fund. A land where poor peasants dread sending their womenfolk to the fields for fear of sexual assault,' reported a writer in *The Hindustan Times*.

Bihar is a state lagging far behind the achievements and conditions of other parts of the country, where standards of living for most people are slowly improving. It is not unknown for witches to be pursued and victims ducked underwater—if innocent, they drown, and if guilty they survive to be burnt or beaten to death. The anger of the gods is real and strong measures must be taken to protect the majority from people possessed.

The simmering violence of rural Bihar is between people 'with' and people 'without'—land, food and employment. Battles are fought on caste lines, in line with the traditional social structure, but the fights are caused by economic inequalities.

The Ganga itself has been one of the causes of the tension leading to this violence, as each year the river shifts, washing away valuable land and making destitute the families who lived there. Nearly half the 700 million people in India grow their food on their own land and nearly three-quarters of these holdings are less than five acres, yet the largest 3.1 per cent of the holdings occupy 26.2 per cent of the land. To lose land is so fatal that people are willing to murder to retain title to any land or steal it from weaker people. The conditions of the peasants have improved since Buddha's time and in the decades since Gandhi's death, but progress is frighteningly slow.

Despite much noise about change, neither state nor central government has promoted land reform, which would break up large farms into family smallholdings, because the big landlords and landowners employing labourers are the powerbase of the Congress (I) Party. The need to grow more food for the extra workers in the cities has been equally important. India's population has doubled since Independence and food production has more than kept pace. Many people still cannot afford the food but India's record is remarkable. The introduction of high-yielding seeds, tubewell irrigation, fertilisers, pesticides, additional and improved machinery and credit to finance the Green Revolution has been carried out in India by the better-off farmers. They are the leaders of the traditional society and the main supporters of Congress (I) in the countryside. It is these people who have been most receptive to new ideas and who have been able to afford to take risks with unknown seeds, unfamiliar methods and newfangled machinery.

The power and grip of the landlords over their villages and peasants have been further increased by moneylending. The landlords are often able to borrow money from banks at low rates of interest and relend the money to illiterate labourers at interest rates varying between 25 and 400 per cent. The moneylenders may forgo interest payments in return for free labour on their fields until the debt has been paid. They may forbid borrowers to take any other work or may make them work so many hours that they have no time to take paid employment. Thus, without cash, the debt can never be paid off and the moneylender-landlord gets free labour for his fields indefinitely. The borrower and his family become his slaves. It is not rare to find a son or grandson still paying off a debt of R50 or R100 incurred 20 years earlier by their father or grandfather, perhaps to buy food or to replace a sick cow or bullock.

In theory the peasants of Bihar have the vote like all adult Indians. However, the parliamentary system imported from England has been grafted onto a traditional feudal power structure. The landlords decide who will work at planting and harvest times, how much they will be paid, what rate of interest will be paid on debts, what split of share-cropped land they will take, who will benefit from government development projects and who will receive cheap bank loans. Controlling the parliamentary vote is a small matter. The notion that landlords do not have these rights is novel but the spread of education, talk of democracy on radio and the large rise in the numbers of families without land is bringing resistance.

The battles in the countryside are being fought between two main organisations, the Mazdoor Kisan Sangram Samiti (MKSS), representing factory workers and cultivators, and the Bhumisena, the landlords' army. Both organisations police their own areas, punish wrongdoers and raise money.

'The only difference is that MKSS kills the most cruel of landlords on provocation, and the Bhumisena kills even innocent people because they are poor and, therefore, suspect,' said one Bihari police inspector quoted in *Probe Magazine*.

I was optimistic that Hindus would venerate a lone man walking unarmed beside Mother Ganga, whatever their politics and hatreds. I walked in peace and saw no reason why I should not be received in peace.

The red-orange sun was setting far away across the Ganga on the fourth evening after I had left the Singh family. I was in the town of Sultanganj and asked a boatman to take me two hundred yards out to a small island rising 70 feet above the flat waters of the river, on which a temple had been built. The boatman wanted R10 for a trip that normally cost about 50 paise, and we settled for R3. By now the sun had set and it would soon be dark. I had no place to sleep but felt no disquiet. Something would turn up. We landed with a bump against the stone steps on the Fakir's Rock and I left my sandals half-way up the steps leading to the white temple. I entered the dark interior of Shiva's temple by ducking through a low doorway to find three *lingams* set in the stone floor inside. I knelt beside a priest in front of them and he mumbled prayers and poured a teaspoon of holy water into the palm of my right hand for me to drink. I left 50 paise which was apparently acceptable.

The boatman was keen to return to the shore so I asked to speak to the *baba* of the temple. He was sitting on a terrace overlooking the river and the fading pink sky. He was already wrapped in a blanket and a red balaclava to keep warm. Dressed in this garb and with his grey-stubbled chin, he looked like a haggard survivor of Scott's last expedition to the Antarctic. I explained in a few words of Hindi about my pilgrimage and asked if I could spend the night on the rock. The *baba* sent away the boatman but did not seem to have answered my question. I could always swim back, I supposed. Another holy man sat with us with a basket between his knees and began preparing a pipe of *ganja* (marijuana), which is smoked at all times of the day by the religious, the oppressed and the indolent in India.

We smoked two pipes to keep ourselves warm and when the night was dark and the stars shone in the black sky it was time for evening worship. Two men beat drums, another shook a big, brass bell, two others beat cymbals with sticks and the *pujari* carried incense and a candleholder inside the temple to perform the *puja*. The noise of the worship must have been easily audible across the river in the town. Sitting cross-legged among the musicians on the windswept terrace, lit by candles and two electric lights, I felt as though I was sitting in a tower with two sets of bells striking midnight simultaneously for half an hour.

The electric lights cut out, as did the power in the town, just as the *chapatis, dal* and *subzee* were being served on leaf plates. After our meal and ablutions over the parapet, I was led down the big, stone steps to sleep the night on the floor of a room at the front gate. This was to be my coldest night. One blanket, kindly fetched for me, and my own blanket and cotton sleeping bag were inadequate for the long night. There was nowhere to hang up my mosquito net and the blood-suckers were the first to attack, buzzing round my face and biting through the blankets in a dozen places. The concrete floor was hard, which was bearable, but it acted like a heat sink, draining my body of warmth. As each buttock and side of my body numbed with cold, I would roll over to allow the other side to chill and curl up tighter in a ball. I would pull up the blankets and thus expose myself to more mosquito bites. The door of the room stayed open all night, for a reason unknown to me, and a junior member of the temple slept snugly in a heap of blankets at the back of the room. Winds got up during the night and it began to rain hard. My sandals were still outside and I worried lest the river rose and washed them away.

It was a long, uncomfortable night. I lay awake with the buzzing of mosquitoes and the howl of the wind in the dark and longed for morning to come. Eventually I could stand it no longer and resorted to my 'space blanket' again, though it was supposed to be only used once. I had resisted all gadgetry for the walk but was glad of the slim packet which opened with a great deal of crackling into a large insulating blanket. I wrapped the silver blanket around me and felt renewed warmth. I was cheered by knowing that I was now impervious to the mosquitoes and fell mockingly asleep.

I opened my eyes hours later to a clear sky and warm sunshine, but shrank from plunging into the pale, green river with the priests, though I needed to wash before another day's march. I found my sandals on the steps and was happy enough to sit in the sunshine while waiting for the boatman to retrieve me. He came soon enough, saying he'd already been out for me once while I had been asleep. We rowed round the island before returning to the shore to enable one of the priests to anoint two carvings of unrecognisable deities in the pink porphyry boulders with Ganga water and vermilion paste. Each of the boulders, which were heaped up to form the island, was bigger than an elephant and the morning light picked out the large crystals like a thousand sequins on a red cloth.

That day I passed a line of over 300 barefoot pilgrims walking to a three-day festival. Although I did not recognise the name of their destination I was told that the round trip was 400 miles. Each man or woman carried a bamboo pole over one shoulder, from which hung two wicker baskets carrying incense, *ganja*, vermilion powder, scriptures and other supplies. The women walked in groups and were vastly outnumbered by the men trotting, limping or walking on the asphalt road.

My own feet were bearing up well. I'd finally learnt to respect their vulnerability, but now both feet had toughened, the skin hardened and muscles strengthened. I did not feel too tired therefore, when I reached Monghyr after sunset having walked 21 miles, and sat down at a tea-stall in the bazaar while a cobbler sitting at the side of the street repaired a broken strap on my sandal. Monghyr was the largest bazaar I had entered since walking out of Calcutta over a month earlier and after days of gentle walking and of being almost alone I found the crowds and clamour of the city startling. It was a surprise to see shops stuffed with fruits, silks, bicycles, jewellery, rice, dry foods and many other commodities stacked on shelves in the open-fronted shops, and the wide streets congested with bicycles, rickshaws and men in white clothes carrying small shopping bags.

'You are from the Bihar School of Yoga?' asked a man while we sipped our tea together. I had not previously heard of this school but decided to find out whether I might stay there for a few days. It was easy to locate the *ashram* because when, suddenly, all the lights in the shops and streets went out it seemed to be the only building in the city affluent enough to have its own generator. The bright lights shone out from the top of a hill overlooking a narrow spot on the Ganga, above the pinprick lights of candles and hurricane lamps in the marketplace. However, when I reached the correct entrance gate, I was apparently too late to be admitted. An old man in orange clothes unlocked the padlock of the main gate and examined my passport before sending me off to the school's old quarters until morning.

'Our charge for one week's stay is one thousand rupees,' said the young Indian man blandly at the desk in the office next morning.

I gasped and nearly fell off my chair. In Bihar, R1000 was the average man's income for a year. My surprise was evident.

'This is for food, lodging and yoga teaching.'

'I would like only to stay, please,' I said.

'If you want to stay only, then give a donation. As much as you can.'

I bunked in a room with a 24-year-old Frenchman who was a devotee of Swami Satyananda, the founder of the school. 'I have no religion. I follow Swamiji. That is enough,' he told an Indian lady who asked his religion. I was more of a coward and said I was a Christian. Over half the inmates of the *ashram* were foreigners from Australia, England, France and Germany and half of these were women. Almost all wore the orange clothes that marked them as *sannyasins*, or monks, and wore their hair either cropped or shaved.

An Australian man in his twenties sat down on the step beside me at teatime with a mug of sweet, black tea in his hands.

'I've had no job for two years, I've done work here and there, yet I've more money now than then,' he explained, as evidence of the fruits of renouncing one's ego. This was a necessary part of accepting one's karma, he said. It was a process he was uncovering for himself with delight and eagerness.

'As you sow, so shall you reap,' he told me, explaining the law of karma which applies to every action, every event, every thought. The kind man receives kindness and the thief comes to a bad end, eventually; perhaps after many lifetimes.

'Course, the first thing you do when you accept karma is to become honest—because you know there's no escape from your actions,' he said, and chuckled at the futility of all the Indian businessmen who routinely adulterate every food in the marketplace.

Swami Satyananda's *ashrams* are scattered worldwide; India seven, USA four, Greece three, Scandinavia five, Australia 17; and one each in Singapore, France, Italy and Spain. The *swami* was away touring in Australia, but remained much in the minds of his followers learning ego surrender and realising the illusion of 'I'. Ego and ambition, which have fuelled so much achievement in the West, are barriers to spiritual progress, according to the Swami's teachings. Only God is eternal and therefore relevant. This God is not a deity but a Divine Spirit existing in all creation. Distinctions of the material world between dog and tree, American and Soviet are therefore irrelevant. Cooling down and calming down are the prerequisites to spiritual progress.

> Thinking about sense-objects
> Will attach you to sense-objects;
> Grow attached, and you become addicted;
> Thwart your addiction, it turns to anger;
> Be angry, and you confuse your mind;
> Confuse your mind, you forget the lesson of experience:
> Forget experience, you lose discrimination,
> Lose discrimination, and you miss life's only purpose,

according to the *Bhagavad-Gita*.

The purpose of life is to know that God contains all creation and to become released from the concerns of the material world. This is not easy. Even Mahatma Gandhi thought he had failed to attain an unattached state of mind:

> Not shaken by adversity,
> Not hankering after happiness:
> Free from fear, free from anger,
> Free from the things of desire:
> I call him a seer, and illumined.
> The bonds of his flesh are broken.
> He is lucky, and does not rejoice:
> He is unlucky, and does not weep.
> I call him illumined,

said Krishna in the *Gita*. According to Swami Satyananda, this elevated state of mind can be reached through yoga, which includes meditation, work, devotion and physical exercises. By these avenues, the aspirant wrestles with the ego and the intellect until these are controlled.

Sitting in the manicured garden of the *ashram*, I interpreted all this as a philosophy of material sloth, but I could feel myself calming down in the quiet, ordered atmosphere, in a luxury undreamt of by 95 per cent of India's population.

A quarter of a mile down the road from the *ashram* there was another community. Here were poor people who lived in conditions not fit for pigs. About 60 people occupied a dozen tents built of rags and discarded plastic bags over bamboo poles. Each family's home measured about seven feet by five feet. A thin hand reached out from the opening of one tent when I proffered my worn-out 'space blanket'. I wondered what these people would make of the enthusiastic Westerners reciting the Law of Karma which placed them at the top of the hill and these people at the bottom. It is just as the English Victorian hymn, 'All Things Bright And Beautiful' says,

> The rich man in his castle
> The poor man at his gate,
> God made them high or lowly,
> And order'd their estate.

Perversely, I knew the struggling families in the make-shift tents would accept that their plight was indeed their karma.

Whatever my doubts and personal conflicts, I did leave the *ashram* after three days' rest feeling relaxed and more generous of spirit towards the incessant questioners. The date was February 2nd and though the hot season was at least six weeks away, the sun was already noticeably stronger. I walked contentedly repeating the day's list of new Hindi words to be learned. Even my feet seemed in good humour, barely noticing the miles along an embankment at the edge of the permanent river bank. The actual flow of water was probably several miles away, beyond green fields and white sands, where a band of haze crossed the horizon like a broad stroke of white paint. I was back on the main road that ran parallel to the embankment a few hours later and stopped in a village to drink tea, answer questions and eat a dish of *chena* (similar to chickpeas). Down the road, an old man stepped out from the ditch and stood in my path revealing his three yellowed teeth with a smile.

'Do you know God?' he asked.

'Yes,' I answered.

'Where are you going?'

'To Gau Mukh. To Gangotri.'

'Is it so?' he asked with disbelief. 'Where is God?'

'He is in you, he is in me.'

'Then he lives not on the outside.'

'Yes. Inside and outside,' I said.

'Yes,' said this seer, slowly speaking the English words and smiling. 'God is everywhere.'

'Yes,' I replied.

'If God is everywhere, what is the use of travelling from Ganga Sagar to Gangotri?'

I smiled. 'It is a pilgrimage.'

'How can you see God?'

'With an inner eye.'

'How can you see with an inner eye?' he asked.

I tried to answer in Hindi. 'To see a tree with an eye, you must have good eyes. To see with an inner eye, you must have a good inner eye.'

'How?'

'Through pilgrimage and yoga,' I said, taxing my knowledge of Hindi to its limit.

'Yes. You will have to search out a *guru*. Lord Krishna was Arjuna's *guru*. You will have to search out a *guru*.'

I nodded.

'Thank you,' he said and walked away, leaving me with my eyebrows still raised.

My first attempt to rejoin the embankment away from the road was stopped by two men blocking the way through their village. They were adamant but not unfriendly. Unfortunately I couldn't understand what they were telling me. I was, nevertheless, now entering the area where the eight boys had been kidnapped and murdered four weeks previously.

I made a second attempt to rejoin the embankment by following a cart track that wound through a hamlet. I made it through this time and was already on the footpath beyond the houses when a group of children called me back and I stood in front of a middle-aged man while he spoke. I didn't understand a word but when he had finished I asked, '*Dacoit?*'

The man smiled. 'Many, many,' he said.

But I still did not want to leave the river and detour miles inland.

'*Dacoits*. Go by road,' said the man in Hindi, running his hand across his throat to demonstrate how dacoits deal with their victims. Reluctantly remembering the wisdom of the Three Kings departing to their own country by another route after being warned of danger in a dream, I opted for safety and took his advice. The guardian looked relieved when I bowed gently to him and retraced my way through the hamlet. It was disappointing to be on the road yet again, but at least I was walking towards the bright splendour of a late afternoon sun.

The detour would add 10 miles to the journey, taking me on two sides of a triangle while the river flowed directly from the west. I felt myself to be walking around the perimeter fence of a forbidden area. I walked through this area of menace still relaxed from the influence of the *ashram*, passing like a fool where angels might fear to tread. The landscape seemed to shrink all of a sudden, and was broken up into a chequered pattern of squares and oblongs by small earth ridges, as if by a legion of moles. No rectangle was larger than a garden plot and each was someone's field. Everything was yellow and lifeless. Stubble from November's rice harvest was still standing, wherever women had not dug up the roots to take home as fuel for cooking. This land was not irrigated and therefore had no second crop, effectively more than halving people's annual income. Not even weeds grew amongst the dry stubble. Yet I crossed a bridge over a dried-up river a few hours later and the irrigation and green colour of wheat, vegetables and tobacco, an important cash crop, were to be seen in some of the fields.

My diet changed little from day to day, except for the vegetable in season from week to week. One week, every meal was cabbage, the next, cauliflower. That week it was a tomato week and I enjoyed a most delicious plate of heavy, chewy *puris* and several plates of sweet, spicy tomato *subzee* made with chillies. It was the best food I'd eaten in weeks but people looked at me strangely. Perhaps they knew what happens when one eats too many spicy tomatoes at once.

I arrived in darkness to lights and shouts and a troupe of horse-drawn *tongas* outside the small railway station of Mokameh Ghat, and stopped for a meal at one of the half-dozen *dhabas*. It was here, in 1898, on a dark night like this, that the young Jim Corbett arrived by train to take on the contract for transhipping goods from railway wagons to ferries across the Ganga. Mokameh Ghat was the coupling between the broad-gauge railway on the south bank of the Ganga and the metre-gauge branch railway on the north side two miles away across a narrow stretch of the river.

Corbett was told that the prospect of clearing the massive backlog and congestion at the Ghat was hopeless, but he hired his own labour force at piece rates, cleared the backlog, and was to hold the contract for 21 years even while he was away in France and Waziristan during the First World War.

He was a robust man, one of 15 children, who enjoyed shooting both for the table and for sport. He used to travel on a trolley with friends nine miles down the railway track at night to shoot geese when, as he described it, 'the full moon was rising over the palm-trees that fringed the river, and the cold brittle air throbbed and reverberated with the honking of geese and the swish of their wings as they passed overhead in flights of from ten to a hundred.'

The river was then the wintering ground for many barheaded and greylag geese, but these have now almost totally vanished. 'The geese, literally tens of thousands of them, spent the day on the islands in the Ganges and in the evening left the islands to feed on the weeds in ponds, or on ripening wheat and grain crops beyond.'

I was now 58 miles from Patna, which with luck would take me two days to reach, three at most. Reaching the capital became my goal and the walking became a deliberate route march. Mile after mile, passing field after field of red chillies, only stopping briefly to gobble down

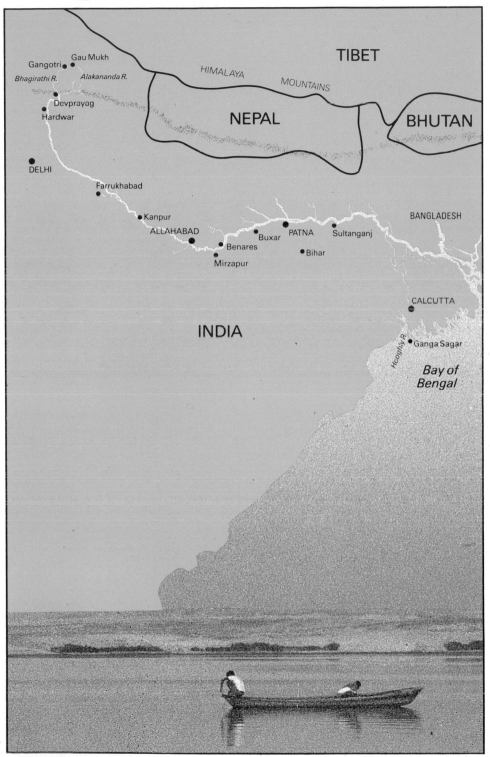

In the cool before sunrise, fishermen from the village of Arjunpur in Uttar Pradesh check their night fishing lines.

Boating on the Hooghly north of Calcutta on a Sunday afternoon.

Early morning bathers 120 miles up the Hooghly from the Bay of Bengal, where the river is still tidal.

Strong, sweet, milky tea poured from a pan by a tea-*wallah* in Uttar Pradesh. The wristwatch may not work but it is a sign of being modern.

In Bihar, a craftsman models the figure of Saraswati, goddess of learning, in clay daubed over a skeleton of straw in preparation for the goddess' festival in February.

The Shiva temple in the middle of the Ganga at Sultanganj.

Outside a village in Uttar Pradesh, a man irrigates rice seedlings prior to transplanting.

Krishna as a boy cowherd, detail of an etched mirror in a temple in Buxar.

Across the Ganga from Arjunpur, an ingenious arrangement of bamboo levers allows one man to raise and lower a net into the shallows to catch sardine-like fish.

Walking beside the Ganga near Benares, as yet without the umbrella that kept the sun off during the hot season.

Looking like slices of salami to a weary hiker, the terraces above Devprayag are bare before planting of the rice crop at the start of the rainy season.

In the foothills of the Himalayas even the houses stand on terraced rows. Families live upstairs, with their cattle, sheep and goats in the room below.

Devprayag – where the Bhagirathi and the Alakananda merge to be called the Ganga.

The young river gurgles and surges through the confines of the hills above Tehri.

The brown Gangotri glacier, birthplace of the Ganga, at 13,450 feet above sea level.

meals at roadside stands and then walking again. Hardly time to answer the endless questions and no time at all to sit for a smoke and a chat. How difficult it was to override my preoccupation of striving to achieve each day's destination and to take pleasure in the journey itself.

I did stop once, when called by eight men sorting tomatoes in big baskets. 'Which is your home? Where are you going? Is it so?' They offered me tomatoes for the long journey. I accepted two, but could not get away with less than several pounds. Another man was also accepting tomatoes: a pedlar from Nepal, walking the lanes of north India selling asafoetida to housewives for cooking. This resinous gum comes from the root of the *Narthex asafoetida* plant, which is related to the great fennel, and is known as *hing* in northern India.

We set off again together, conversing as best we could in Hindi, and laughing a lot. He was a short man whose tanned face had so many creases that he looked much older than his 30 years. He wore baggy grey pants, patched in many places, a well-worn shirt and worn-out tweed jacket. I peered, when unobserved, into the leather satchel around his neck in which he kept the *hing* and small balancing pans for weighing. Ropes over both shoulders secured a woollen blanket over his back. I was embarrassed that he carried so little in contrast to my own load of bric-à-brac. We were called into a brick house by a housewife who wished to inspect the *hing*, which was the colour and texture of used chewing gum. Its smell is unpleasant and it has been called 'Devil's Dung', but it brings out the flavours of other spices in cooking. The housewife claimed that it was too dry but bought a piece the size of a marble for 25 paise. She wanted to pay for it in tomatoes but this was flatly refused so she paid with coins and in turn demanded a free sample. The pedlar gave her a little extra and muttered at her penny-pinching as we walked away.

We joined his companions half a mile along the road; another man with satchel and weighing pans and a man and a boy carrying large wicker baskets on their backs full of cooking pots, blankets, vegetables and firewood. They welcomed me to their party and we walked together for some miles. But our strides were different and I was keen to get along though the day was ending and I had no idea where I might sleep.

'I request you to rest at my house.'

The man's voice broke through my day-dreaming. Not more questions and another tea, I groaned to myself.

'I request you to rest at my house.'

I did not want to stop, knowing too well how long it would take for tea to be served.

'Come, come.'

'Sleep,' I said.

'Come, come.' He took me across the grass verge and up the front steps onto the verandah of a big house of brick and light-brown stucco.

'Yes, yes. Please sit here,' said my host, Shri Surendra Singh, smoothing down a blanket on a low table. Tea was soon fetched and a cigarette offered.

'I smoke *beedi*,' I said and took out a bundle from my pocket and offered them round. This was a popular gesture, for cigarettes are a status symbol in the countryside and something I wanted, therefore, to avoid. The men, boys and young girls of the family gathered on the verandah to hear my story, and this was relayed sentence by sentence to the women in the kitchen by the children dashing back and forth.

'Do you have your father's permission to be here?' someone asked, which always struck me as an odd question. We proceeded in Hindi and in smatterings of English through the routine questions and answers. Without a better knowledge of Hindi, I was gradually becoming remote from my surroundings, like a tourist passing across a land without contacting its people. Worse than this I was still enmeshed in my own thoughts, holding myself back, not becoming immersed in the Ganga or the people whom I had come so far to meet. Perhaps I had been naïve to believe I could live in someone else's surroundings and begin to see life from their point of view. I had come to this country knowing I was ignorant; but the blunder had been in thinking that I could learn.

After tea, it was necessary to go out to the latrine in the field before daylight faded. I was handed a brass pot of water and led to the appropriate place while the red and orange embers of sunlight died in the western sky. I was then compelled to take my bath back at the house. The end of the day was not the ideal time to take a cold shower, but I was sweaty and dusty and wanted to be clean, and I stood on the grass verge beside the road in front of the house and stripped to my *lungi*, suffering an ascetic mortification as I poured the cold water over myself. After weeks of being perpetually observed by the curious I was now inured to bathing with an audience.

As the first stars appeared in the blue-black sky, a teenager fetched out a long bamboo pole, and after several patient attempts linked up two illegal wires to the electricity supply of the village. Almost one quarter of the electricity generated in Bihar in 1981 was either pilfered by illegal wire-taps or lost in transmission.

We sat on the verandah of the house in the light of a hurricane lamp. The stolen electricity was to light the small white-washed temple next door. In the gloom of nightfall I was left alone with the lamp to read the evening prayers I had written out in my exercise book. I sat cross-legged on the low table, with a blanket wrapped over my shoulders and my hands held in my lap.

When we had completed our various prayers my host asked, 'Bread or rice?'

'Your food is my food,' I replied in Hindi.

A tray of tomato *subzee, chapatis* and various pickles was brought to me. As usual the family ate separately after I had finished my meal.

Then it was bedtime and I was taken into the large room at the front of the house. A wooden table and three *charpoy* beds were the only furniture. I was handed a blanket and lay down with my own blankets on the wooden bed. It was like sleeping on a huge coffee table. Five members of the family huddled on the floor beside the bed, round a fire of crackling, orange flames and thick smoke in the dark room. All the wooden window shutters were closed, and the room soon warmed up and the smoke fumigated against mosquitoes.

I lay with my eyes closed and fell asleep, happily anticipating my arrival in Patna late the next day. But I could not foresee the hospitality awaiting me at St Xavier's School when I arrived at teatime having completed more than 500 miles since Calcutta.

'If you come early and with a bit of luck, there's hot water for half an hour at six o'clock,' explained Father Kunnankal, my sponsor at the school. The luxury of hot water! It spoilt me for weeks afterwards and I enjoyed every glorious drop.

7

Round and Round the River Bends

Joyous groups of Patna's young men carried down each goddess from the top of the broad steps towards the Ganga. For three days, these models of Saraswati, the goddess of literature, art and music, had stood adorned inside magnificent pavilions of bamboo, cloth and paper, and had been the objects of the petitions and prayers of millions of Hindus. In some villages, two or three of these pavilions had been erected, and hundreds had blocked streets and narrow alleys in cities such as Patna. Each had a record player or a tape cassette player blaring out Hindi disco music or hit songs from Bombay's movie industry. Volume was preferred to quality. The festival of Saraswati, in common with festivals throughout the year, was as much a social as a religious occasion. Youth clubs competed to raise the most money, build the gaudiest or biggest pavilion, play the loudest music and order the largest model from local model-makers. The older generation inspected the work of their offspring and attended to the *puja*.

Saraswati's festival ended after three days. The last rites had to be performed and the goddess given a good send-off, just as Kali had months earlier in Calcutta. In the most elaborate and expensive processions in Patna, noisy brass bands and high-spirited boys throwing purple, red or green powders over themselves and spectators escorted Saraswati to the amphitheatre of steps that led to the Ganga. Saraswati might also arrive in a rickshaw or in the back of a chauffeur-driven car.

During one hour, I saw more than 30 statues of Saraswati being carried down the long flight of steps to the water's edge. It was almost sunset with the orange disc sinking behind silhouettes of rooftops in a pale blue sky. The bright, peach light shone in the faces of the crowds and glistened across the flat river water. The sun's rays were like theatre lights highlighting the beauty of the heroine who, on this occasion, was made of straw and baked mud with china-white face, rouged lips and long, black hair. The largest statue I saw was over eight feet tall and the smallest was carried in the hand. In all of them, Saraswati sat side-saddle on a swan with a lute in one hand and holding a book in the other. The grace of these statues was stunning; never a roughly hewn shoulder nor a hand with clumsy fingers. It was easy to imagine that Saraswati herself might stand up suddenly from her seat on the swan and set aside her lute.

Flower garlands were removed from her neck at the water's edge and she was lifted carefully aboard big, black rowing boats for her final journey. Hindus have a strong belief in cycles; of death and new life, of influence and weakness among the gods, of the giving and taking of land by Ganga. To cling on to any model, and to want to possess it would be futile. However beautiful and however costly the figures of Saraswati, her own cycle must be completed. The statues had been created from mud by craftsmen and the deity invited to dwell in each of them for the festival. The divine presence was now gone and the models must be destroyed and the mud returned to the river. The last prayers were spoken and each boat in the flotilla, a hundred yards from the shore, manoeuvred so that Saraswati faced the east. Then, with a final heave, the statues were thrown overboard and immediately sank in the water of the holy Ganga. Bare straw skeletons would be washed ashore within days and poor people would take these home to dry out and use as fuel for cooking their meals.

Five days after the official end of Saraswati *puja* I met six elephants in the market street of Patna. Brass bells clanged against their hot, grey flanks as they strolled past the shops in a procession led by a marching band in stiff tunics of blue and red. A second band in yellow and gold braid paraded behind the elephants and four camels walked with characteristic pride behind them. Each band was playing a different tune and the street was filled with this joyful cacophony. Goddess Saraswati, ten feet tall riding on a swan, came at the end of the procession looking out from the back of a truck. She appeared as lovely as ever, gazing serenely over the jostling crowds while the animals and the bands pressed forwards through the congestion towards the waiting river boat.

It was the middle of a warm afternoon, that time of day when people are somnolent after their midday meal. I was on my way in a petrol-driven rickshaw to look at the new road bridge over the Ganga. It extends for miles like a concrete pier across the brown water to an embankment far away on the north shore and is said to be the longest road bridge in Asia. The last ferry steamer on the Ganga stopped soon after the bridge opened and a handful of wooden boats carrying sand, propelled by sails and oars, are now the only vessels on the water. Yet Patna had once been a major port and for over a century an important call for the steamers plying between Calcutta and Allahabad.

The city had been built beside the Ganga at its confluence with the Son river 2400 years ago by a king who wanted to move his capital to a more militarily strategic site. Buddhist legend states that Buddha himself prophesied that Pataliputra, as it was then called, would become a prosperous centre of trade and the chief port of Aryan north India.

The ambitious King Ajatasatru had gained the throne by murdering his father, and by the end of his reign his kingdom stretched 300 miles along the Ganga and its hinterland from Kashi (or Benares) to the eastern outposts of Aryan civilisation in Bengal.

The kingdom was later weakened by rivalries for the throne and some time between 324 and 313 BC, the city and kingdom was defeated by Chandragupta Maurya. Pataliputra then became the capital of a single kingdom controlling the Ganga basin and north India. Buddha's prophecy had come true. Trade in exotic commodities with the Roman Empire flourished, as did art and agriculture, and an organised bureaucracy grew up to regulate many aspects of rural and urban life. Chankya, the king's chief minister, was an able, scheming man, sometimes compared to Machiavelli, who wrote a book on state-craft called *Arthashastra* (or 'The Science of Polity'). His book sets out in detail the intention, if not the practice, of kingship and government, and maintains that prosperity is dependent on effort.

According to Jainist tradition, King Chandragupta Maurya abdicated his throne to become a Jain monk and is said to have fasted to death.

His grandson, Ashoka, came to the throne in about 269 BC and was to rule for 40 years. He is believed to have been the greatest and noblest of India's rulers and among the great kings of the world. He erected stone pillars throughout his kingdom with inscriptions detailing in local languages his achievements and policies. It is Ashoka's *chakra* wheel representing the cycle of life—not Mahatma Gandhi's spinning wheel—that now decorates India's national flag.

Ashoka became a Buddhist in the eighth year of his reign, thereafter renouncing aggressive warfare and stressing good government throughout his empire, which covered the whole country except for three kingdoms in the southern tip. He encouraged religious tolerance, banned animal sacrifices (at least in the capital), planted fruit trees along roads to provide shade and food, dug wells and established travellers' resthouses. Medicinal herbs for humans and animals were grown and distributed to health centres. 'Officers of Righteousness' checked the work of local officials throughout the empire, and Ashoka promoted a personal code of ethics for each citizen, called *dharma*.

Interest rates of 60, 120 and 240 per cent for merchants, overland caravan traders through the forests covering much of the Gangetic Plain and seafaring merchants respectively, reflected both the profits and risks of trade in ancient times. Merchants travelled overland in convoys of 500 for protection against bandits on forest roads. River boats had to be protected from pirates, who continued to menace the Ganga into the early nineteenth century.

Diplomats and missionaries were sent west to Syria, Egypt and Macedonia and east to Sri Lanka (Ceylon), Burma, Thailand and the Orient. Buddhism became a world religion and Indian colonies sprang up as far away as Bali in Indonesia. At home Buddha's teaching and Ashoka's practice appealed to a people weary of the rituals and exclusiveness of the priest caste.

Ashoka died in 232 BC and the Mauryan empire quickly disintegrated. It was 500 years before Pataliputra again became a capital; capital of the Gupta empire which extended across northern India in a Golden Age of science, technology and art during which Hinduism replaced Buddhism as the popular religion. Contemporary astronomers recognised that the world was round and rotated on its axis, and mathematicians adopted both the so-called Arabic numerals and the symbol for zero.

However, repeated invasions in the sixth and seventh centuries AD, from Central Asia, Iran and Afghanistan sapped the energies of kingdoms already weakened by squabbles, internal jealousies and an excessive rigidity in the caste system. Foreign travel was discouraged to the extent of being effectively banned. Centuries later, Mahatma Gandhi defied this ban and lost caste by sailing to England to study law. The process of withdrawal from the wider world and isolation from fresh ideas took several centuries but ultimately suffocated India's cultural inspiration.

'Losing the art of creating beauty, her children lost even the capacity to recognise it,' wrote Nehru. 'There was decline all along the line—intellectual, philosophical, political, in technique and methods of warfare . . . and there was a growth of local sentiments and feudal, small-group feeling at the expense of the larger conception of India as a whole.'

No sense of Indianness developed under the Mughuls although, by the end of the seventeenth century, they controlled almost the whole country. However, internal trade continued throughout medieval and Mughul times. Widespread distribution of salt was essential in the hot climate, and wheat and rice from Bengal and Bihar were required up country to feed the great cities of Agra and Delhi, with the rivers being the arteries of trade.

The East India Company opened a trading post in Patna in 1658, several years after the Dutch, but it was to be another 99 years before Robert Clive's forces arrived in Patna fresh from victory at Plassey and Buxar. Ships of 300–500 tons sailed the Ganga and its tributaries carrying cloth, metals such as imported copper and lead, and food-grains. Distribution of the latter was not good, especially away from the rivers, and most people lived off the land in villages that were largely self-sufficient. Scarcity and famine were never far away. In many areas, peasants were wholly dependent on the monsoon to grow one crop. Too little rain or too much rain at the wrong time of year brought disaster.

Famine broke out across northern India two years after the arrival of the East India Company in Patna. It broke out again in 1671 after the monsoon failed and in Patna alone 90,000 people starved to death. Drought combined with the devastation of war to produce a gruesome famine across Bengal and Bihar, in which ten million people are estimated to have perished.

Despite this calamity, the East India Company collected its usual land tax. 'Notwithstanding the loss of at least one-third of the inhabitants of the province, and the consequent decrease of the cultivation, the nett collections of the year 1771 exceeded even those of 1768,' Warren Hastings told the Court of Directors of the Company in London in 1772, the year he became Governor of Bengal.

The monsoon failed again in Bihar 11 years later and food was scarce and expensive. Memories of 1770 were still fresh, so Warren Hastings commissioned a series of granaries to be built to hold reserves. Only one store was built, shaped like the top half of a 96-foot-high boiled egg, and this has become the main tourist attraction of modern Patna. 'For the perpetual relief of famine' reads the inscription in English and Persian, the language of the Mughul court. Brick steps on the east and west sides curve steeply up the outside of the Golghar (round house) and, from the top, visitors can enjoy an uninterrupted view over Patna and the Ganga. The river flows from the north-west across miles of flat sands and tall grasses, half-hidden in the white haze. It turns sharply eastward in front of the city, past the cremation ghat and electric crematorium, past the hovels of the urban poor and the minarets of the city's mosques.

The Golghar was never filled with grain because of its flawed design. It stands now as a reminder to well-meaning visitors, especially foreign experts on Third World development, of how good intentions can be ill-conceived. The intention when the Golghar was built in 1786 was to purchase up to 137,000 tons of rice during bumper years. Porters would carry sacks of grain up one flight of steps, pour the rice through an opening in the top of the brick structure and descend by the second staircase. Grain could then be retrieved through four doors at the base. However, several snags spoiled this superb plan: the steps were too steep for porters to climb when carrying 200-pound rice sacks, and it was argued after the Golghar had been built that the rice would spoil if stored loose in such quantity. It was also thought that having such a reserve might encourage peasants to work less hard. Lastly, it has been claimed that the doors at the base of the structure were built to open *inwards*, making entry impossible. The doors now open outwards and sacks of rice are stored in the hot, humid gloom for the Food Corporation of India which buys and distributes grain throughout the country.

The main road out of Patna passes in front of the Golghar, and after over a week of hot showers at St Xavier's and a respite from questions and crowds, I was once again walking westwards beside the Ganga. One-third of my journey (500 miles) was now accomplished, to my relief. It was already the third week in February and in four more weeks the hot season would begin. People had already warned me about the perils of April, May and June with their heat and hot winds and dust, and outbreaks of dysentery and cholera. I was determined to cover as many miles as possible before the hot season began but wanted to avoid being force-marched. Nor could I allow myself to think of dangers which the future might bring. To do so would have been to invent my own nightmares. I must walk on, I told myself, staying beside Mother Ganga, handling difficulties when they arose with a mixture of prudence, endurance and faith.

Out beyond the congestion and brick houses of Patna, the narrow footpath led north-west for miles along the edge of fields of maize and peas beside a 20-foot drop into the swift, brown water. The river was steadily undercutting this bluff and the path deviated among the tall plants wherever the bank had already collapsed. This was one of the Ganga's innumerable meanders, eroding land on the outside of each bend and extending mudflats and sandy beaches on the inside. Hunched figures crouched in the double-cropped fields with sickles, cutting pea vines from among the rows of young, green wheat, but there was no village to be seen and I could not tell where the people had come from. I was questioned three times and warned of dangers ahead. The message was always the same.

'*Dacoit! Dacoit!*' they would say, brandishing their sickles.

I discounted these fears because I had already been cautioned again and again about thieving people in the next village, only to be received in each one with hospitality and warned about thieving people in the next.

Towards evening, when the cool breeze stirred up the white sands on the other side of the one-and-a-half-mile wide river, a man came running from the field and I waited for him on the footpath. He shook his head when he heard where I was going. 'No, no, no,' and pointed back to Patna. 'Train,' he said firmly.

With some impatience, I told him I had just come from the city and would not return, though I was becoming concerned at these continual reports of *dacoits*. It was obvious that I was not going to listen to reason, so he held up his sickle in my face and demonstrated how robbers would assuredly cut my throat and seize my bag. It was not yet time to quit the fields and go home across the river, so I was told to sit down and was left with a handful of fresh pea vines to nibble.

A line of men, boys and women came out of the green field over an hour later with great bales of pea vines on their heads, and we went down to where several rowing boats waited. There was hardly room for the dozen passengers after we'd stacked up the green bales but everyone clambered aboard, women dressed in orange or red saris with gold rings through their nostrils sitting together in the bow, bales smelling like newly-cut grass amidships, and the men in the stern.

The evening brought relaxation and laughter and the questioning of a stranger. There was a murmur of pleasure and approval when I said I was going to Gangotri. An old man took out a tin of chewing tobacco and rubbed the fibres in his thick, coarse hands, mixed in a pinch of white powder and offered it round. Our boat seemed set apart on a lake of sparkling diamonds as the light caught the swell of the river. It was a slow crossing. The current was not slack and the two oarsmen were tired. At length we reached the landing below a village on the north bank. No one would take payment from me and everyone wished me well on my pilgrimage, though I'm sure they thought I was mad.

I followed a path through an orchard of *dal* bushes to a narrow asphalt road, and half a mile later, in the increasing gloom of nightfall, reached what people called a 'line-hotel', an English military expression adopted by Hindi. A single electric light bulb dangled on a wire over blackened kettles and pans on a large earthen hearth. The hearth was built like a kitchen counter and shaded from sun and rain by a thatch roof supported on four corner poles. The tea-*wallah* made hot tea and I settled down on a wooden bench, wrapped against the cold in my shawl, to the day's Hindi lesson. The electricity went off after half an hour and then we sat in the weak, yellow light of a hurricane lamp smoking *beedis* and drinking tea. Load-shedding whenever there was a shortage of electricity generated was a recurrent curse of Indian life that was endured with the stoicism that tolerates inaction in post offices, banks, government offices and development projects.

The evening meal of five fresh, hot *chapatis*, fried potato, raw onion, *dal* and a dish of spinach was delicious. I had lost some weight and was now conscious of the need to keep up my calorific intake. After the meal, drinking tea, chatting and smoking *beedis* with the tea-*wallah* and his friends in the semi-darkness, I retired to a straw bed on the floor of a shed that was open on one side. The night was chilly, despite two blankets and the insulation of the straw. I woke several times to rewrap myself and to check that my knapsack and shoulder bag were still safely beside me. I was aware, as if in a dream, of trucks passing in the middle of the night on the main road north from Patna's road bridge and of a succession of customers stopping at the line-hotel.

The cost of the evening meal, teas, straw bed and morning tea at sunrise was R4-30. No one could argue with that. I had already stopped asking prices before eating meals and snacks, which laid me open to daylight robbery, but I was prepared to pay whatever within reason was asked. Occasionally I had then to pay double the going rate but mostly tea, meals, fruit and *beedis* were sold to me at regular prices. Sometimes tea was given to me by generous people bursting with questions.

These were days when I had to pinch myself to be sure I was not dreaming. I was now addicted to the regular footfall of my sandals as I walked on, for eight or ten hours each day, and to the rising and declining sun. The shores of the Ganga were three miles apart here but the flow of water had shrunk to a few hundred yards, as it was now five months since the monsoon. The water divided into channels and lakes around cultivated islands and banks of sand and grasses, rejoining and splitting, merging and dividing like the braiding in the tail of a mythological horse.

I headed south along a cart track away from the asphalt road after lunch on my third day west of Patna. Fields of wheat, peas and yellow mustard thinned until the soil gave way to sand with well-spaced rows of melon plants, and beyond that white sands extended to the horizon beneath the cloudless, deep-blue sky. Navigating by the sun, I headed approximately south-west across several miles of a curious landscape of undulating sand covered by a veneer of baked mud. The mud had cracked in patches of crazy paving, and in the bottom of hollows, like bunkers on a golf course, the mud had dried out so slowly that the veneer had curled like dry parchment or pastry rolls awaiting cream. I did not know exactly where I was; but it was fun being away from paths and the asphalt roads. The warm afternoon breeze was filled with the songs of birds fluttering overhead, and it was a great relief to be the only human being on this expanse of hard mud and blowing sands.

In this frame of mind, I did not wish to go near the rowing boat I caught sight of in the distance, ferrying people across the Ghaghara river near its confluence with the Ganga. I turned northwards into the wind and followed the Ghaghara towards the railway bridge marked on my map, passing two pairs of red-brown ducks on a sandbar. It was joyless knowledge to realise that by clever internalised arguments I was ingeniously avoiding the remote reaches of the Ganga. I was convincing myself of the good sense of keeping near roads, villages and towns and was managing to miss much of what I had come to see and experience. The whole purpose of my being beside the river was to follow a varied itinerary, through cultivated fields and wastelands out on the floodplains.

I came ashore from the mudflats and sands and walked several miles on a road to the tea-stalls and a school, clustered at the foot of the embankment beside the railway bridge. I took my bath at the hand-pump of the school and ate food cooked specially for me by one of the tea-*wallahs*. I was allowed to sleep on two desks pushed together in a classroom where the nightwatchman and a teacher were also sleeping. The bed was hard but I always fell asleep quickly after each day's 15-mile walk. I was also eager to rest my feet for as long as possible. After more than 500 miles, my feet were toughened and accustomed to the daily pounding and the rigours of the trail. All my blisters had healed during the rest in Patna but now hard skin around both heels was cracking. Although this was not painful it might easily become infected. Every night, therefore, I inspected both feet and applied antiseptic cream and clean dressings to give them an overnight cleansing.

My breakfast of two boiled eggs, bread rolls and glasses of tea at a tea-stall was an extravagant meal in the eyes of the three men crouched near the flames of the hearth, wrapped in shawls with only their faces and hands exposed, but this might be the only tea-stall I passed all day and I wanted a good meal.

I crossed the railway bridge by stepping from sleeper to sleeper and listening for approaching trains. Fortunately, the sight of water flowing 40 feet beneath my feet was blocked by metal plates but the wind was strong and cold and it made my ears ache. I walked with quick paces, passing a man pushing his bicycle along the railway track, and got across the bridge before any train arrived.

The Ghaghara is the largest tributary of the Ganga. An estimated total of 20,766 million gallons of water and topsoil from Nepal flows down it each year. The *Times of India* has reported that a United Nations aerial photograph reveals an island of 19,000 square miles growing from the seabed in the Bay of Bengal at the mouth of the Ganga. An apocryphal rumour says that the government of Nepal has claimed sovereignty over the island, declaring that the island is Nepal's topsoil!

Destruction of forests and the consequent erosion of soil is a serious problem throughout the Indian sub-continent. Just 7.5 per cent of the total land area of Bihar is covered by forests, compared to 14.3 per cent of the whole Ganga drainage basin. India's forestry policy calls for 33 per cent coverage. Deforestry and increasing silt in the Ganga and India's other major rivers is causing more and more flooding each monsoon. Damage to homes, crops, roads and other public utilities reached a record R2459 crore in 1982 (£1640 million).

Three of the Ganga's largest tributaries join it within 30 miles of Patna, though the river is so wide here that it is impossible to discern the confluences. The Son comes from the south and the Ghaghara and the Gandak from the Himalayas. These rivers submerge the desiccated floodplains during the monsoon with a swift torrent that is miles across and thick with silt. The surging water destroys homes and roads, and leaves behind new layers of fertile soil. Three rivers provide more than one-third of the total flow of the Ganga yet they are quiet, unassuming rivers for nine months of the year.

I was determined not to walk miles and miles inland from the Ganga, though neither was I keen to plod into the middle of nowhere without food. Having started three months earlier with stove, pressure cooker and food when I did not need them, I was now in need of these and able to buy only glucose biscuits from village shops. I followed a deserted lane for three hours without knowing where I was going, and at length, when the sun was high and strong, I reached the end of the road. It stopped suddenly just outside a village where three women were chattering and doing their laundry on flat rocks. I set off along a path through green wheat and yellow mustard, zig-zagging towards the earth embankment crossing the horizon like a high wall about a mile ahead. The Ganga was behind this dyke, I was sure. I scrambled up the bank, breathless with excitement at being reunited with the river.

But when I looked over the top, there was no river, no water, no sand dunes. I was staring at miles of green wheat and yellow mustard. The Ganga must be miles away, I thought, disappointed. There was nothing to do but turn west and follow the serpentine embankment to see where it might lead. I tramped for hours in the sunshine with shawl folded over one shoulder and my mind wandering. Solitary babul trees, with crooked, black stems and green canopies, stood amid the surrounding expanse of young wheat, yellow mustard flowers and clusters of red, white and violet pea vines. The field seemed unending and was so pleasant to walk through I almost wished that it was. But hidden by the crops, the land had been splintered into tiny pieces by the irregular grid of low boundary ridges. The arable land which appeared a single expanse of green was actually a quilt of ten thousand patches, some as small as people's homes, and most little more than twice that size, on which the majority of people in the country had to grow their food and crops to sell.

One family might own several scattered pieces. Each of these will be divided between brothers on the death of their father. Four brothers in a family owning four parcels will receive one-quarter of each separate field and the four fields will be split into sixteen. In this way each male member is assured an equal share of the land on which he and his family must depend in a land-hungry country. It is no surprise that the country's courts are clogged with disputes over land ownership or that the arable land has been fragmented over generations into inefficient plots. Ploughing in little fields takes more time because of the frequent turning at the end of each short row. Then the bullocks must be led, with the plough carried on the farmer's shoulder, to another field perhaps a mile away to repeat the operation.

Communal schemes such as irrigation become almost too complex to administer amongst the myriad of little landholdings. The development of agriculture through increased irrigation, electricity for machines, fertilisers, pesticides and high-yield seeds bought with cheap bank loans becomes difficult and the Green Revolution delayed. Efforts to regroup scattered fields into consolidated holdings have had varied success. The feudal conditions and mentality of Bihar's landlords and tenants is one of the main barriers to change. The powerful few resist change because they fear losing their traditional power and economic advantages. The impoverished majority fear that change will make their conditions even worse. Change involves risk and trust. Periodic hunger, disease, ignorance, debt and bondage to landlords and moneylenders, superstition and fear have reduced millions of people to a crippling bondage. It is a miracle that the human spirit has not been overcome. Joy, gaiety and love have persisted.

I walked all day along the embankment and finally reached an asphalt road and a tea-stall under a tent of bamboo and thatch. I sat here in the shade sipping tea, downhearted that I had never once sighted the Ganga. Further along the asphalt road I came to a village, but not desiring another night sleeping on top of school desks or sleeping in straw I caught a local bus 17 miles into the town of Ballia 75 miles west of Patna. (I returned by bus two days later and walked the 17 miles back to Ballia, thus keeping my pilgrimage and sponsored walk intact.) A sharp bend brought the Ganga beside the road and I realised, on the bus ride into Ballia, that I had never in fact been far from the river. My isolation, my sense of wandering along an irrelevant route and of being distanced from the Ganga were now proven to be imaginary. I saw at once that the river was changed. The water was clearer and paler, upstream of the silt flowing in through the three major tributaries.

I reached the broad streets of Ballia feeling very tired and eager to sleep and asked a man for the name of a hotel. Even large towns like Ballia have few hotels and I expected to arrive outside some grotty flophouse with peeling paint and bedbugs. Instead, the cycle rickshaw stopped outside the Sarang Hotel. I was flabbergasted. There was a doorman in clean, red jacket; there was a red carpet leading into a spacious lobby with leather armchairs and clean walls. My own appearance was grubby and unkempt and I was grateful that the eager receptionist allowed me to stay in a spotlessly clean double room, with clean bed sheets, fan and air conditioning, attached bathroom with a tap that worked and gleaming toilet bowl, all for R25 per night.

A small, elderly man with grey stubbled chin handed me the room service menu and took my order for tea and toast. I sat back on the bed with a great sigh and began laughing with relief. Feast or famine, poverty or riches, palace or a place in the straw; God bless India! I thought.

Enlivened by a shower and changed into clean clothes, I went down to eat in the large, clean dining room which had sets of basins for washing hands and mouths before and after eating. I enjoyed a feast of tomatoes stuffed with vegetables in a ginger sauce, peas cooked with cheese, fried *dal* and several different breads, of which there was a choice of twelve on the menu. It was a delightful change to find that items on the menu were actually available, since many establishments, particularly government-run tourist bungalows, had big menus but each request would be met with 'not possible' until visitors were reduced to the standard rice, *dal* and *subzee*. There was too much food to eat but I ate it all just the same, thankful for the opportunity.

Later, I sat in bed in my room with a tray of coffee, reading Jawarharlal Nehru's *Discovery of India* by the blaze of an electric light. Not even the music of a wedding in the street tempted me from this cosiness and from learning about Nehru's own wrestling with the culture of his motherland.

> It was not [India's] wide spaces that eluded me, or even her diversity, but some depth of soul which I could not fathom, though I had occasional and tantalizing glimpses of it. She was like some ancient palimpsest on which layer upon layer of thought and reverie had been inscribed, and yet no succeeding layer had completely hidden or erased what had been written previously.

My enthusiasm for the luxury of the Sarang Hotel was tempered only slightly the next day when I began to feel ill after drinking a cup of mid-morning coffee. I was still in bed, enjoying the quiet and luxury of breakfast in bed and reading Nehru's book all morning. I got up for lunch but had no appetite despite a rumbling stomach, and slept through the afternoon and night with an aching belly but no vomiting. It was not for another day that my appetite returned. The diarrhoea continued for days.

I left Ballia determined to stay close to the Ganga wherever that would lead. A path led out across fields and rough pastures, down the river bank into the sand and reeds of the dry floodplain. I kept away from men and women cutting reeds to avoid their questions and warnings about robbers. Three times I met groups of people carrying bundles of reeds on their heads, rustling with the motion of their strides, and we passed with a brief greeting, 'Jai Ram' (Victory to God).

Tall, thick reeds, rustling in the morning breeze, soon encircled me. I walked slowly for miles, sometimes unsure of the path and unable to see the direction of the sun. I was never lost but for three or four hours did not know exactly where I was. Several clearings broke the monotony of the jungle and on one occasion a jackal paused 100 feet ahead on the path and looked back at me for half a minute before trotting away. My eyes watched the baked earth for snakes while my mind enjoyed the peaceful solitude. For me, being alone has always been an opportunity, not a penance to be endured.

The sun was high in the sky when at last I emerged onto a vast, empty beach beside one channel of the Ganga. The main river was a mile away across the sands on my left. The wasteland of white sands and brown reeds receded as the river's course straightened and the high banks narrowed. I walked along the 30-foot cliff looking down at a line of seven-inch turtles sun-bathing on rocks, and I gazed at the blue water of Mother Ganga, in which to lose one's thoughts.

A recent concrete road bridge with eleven graceful spans crosses the Ganga at the town of Buxar, but otherwise I doubt that the countryside has changed since the 23rd of October, 1764, when the 50,000 soldiers and cavalry and 194 guns of the Mughul emperor in Delhi, the ruler of Oudh, and Mir Kasim, ex-nawab of Bengal, crossed the Ganga onto the south bank to fight the 7,200 troops and 28 guns of the East India Company. The Company's forces were led by Major Hector Munro, who had already suppressed a mutiny among his troops by putting its 24 ringleaders in front of the mouths of his cannons and blowing them to pieces.

The allies were routed, and 2,000 of their soldiers died in the panic when a pontoon bridge over the Ganga was destroyed by the ruler of Oudh to bar pursuit. The emperor in Delhi then switched sides. The

ruler of Oudh was reinstated by the Company and thereafter 'protected' by four English garrisons in his territory.

> It was this battle, the culmination of an obstinate campaign, which
> determined the British mastery of Bengal. Hitherto they had been rivals and
> manipulators of existing authority; their power was fortuitous and hedged
> with doubt; the issue was still open. It was now unchallenged . . . Plassey
> marked the beginning of the British expansion in Bengal; Baksar determined
> the success of the enterprise (Percival Spear, *The Oxford History of Modern
> India 1740–1947*).

I stayed the night in the rooms of three students in their early
twenties studying Aryuvedic medicine after one of the young men had
stopped me in Buxar's main street and offered accommodation.
'Is Buxar famous for its medical college?' I asked.
'We are not the best students. It is very difficult to study in Bombay.
So my father donated five thousand rupees to the college here and so I
was admitted, you see,' was the frank answer.
Before leaving Buxar the next morning, February 29th, I was taken
to the main temple where Vishnu was the presiding deity. A new room
had recently been opened in the courtyard around the main temple
building. Large mirrors etched in red, gold and silver with scenes from
religious myths covered the walls and ceiling of the room. It was the
most beautiful display I was to see in India. The fun-loving Krishna, the
monkey-god Hanuman, Saraswati and Ganga were all depicted in
traditional scenes known to every pilgrim and shown on posters,
calendars and books in shops and homes. Pilgrims come here for
darshan—religious sightseeing. To see a deity or holy man, such as
Gandhi, brings its own blessing. The small room was crowded with
two dozen chattering women dressed for their outing in saris of
resplendent reds, blues, yellows and greens. Each wore clusters of glass
bangles on her wrists and a streak of red paste, showing she was
married, in the parting of her black hair, which was tied in long pigtails
down her back.
After Buxar, I followed a path on the edge of a 25-foot drop into the
river, enjoying the breeze that was whipping up whitecaps on the water
and hampering the efforts of boys in an orchard to collect fallen mango
leaves for fuel. That night I slept in another schoolroom, and after a
breakfast of two boiled eggs, bread and tea at 6 a.m. I waited to be
shaved in a barber's cabin painted pink. Upstream, the river curved
northwards in a wide bend and dolphins broke the surface of the water,
several times so close to the bank that I could hear them gasping for air
before diving again. Red-wattled lapwings, with long yellow legs, red
eye make-up and loud calls of 'Did-he-do-it? Did-he-do-it?' paced up

and down looking for food at the water's edge. Ducks with bright red-orange plumage, inevitably called Brahminy ducks, watched warily from the mudflats further out. The high banks crumbled into gentle slopes as the course of the river straightened and the grey water moved away to my right across sand dunes and dazzling white beaches.

I walked all morning on the floodplain between the water and the bank, crossing the hard, cracked mudflats or the sand formed in ripples and coated with silver flecks of mica. There were no homes or trees, nor any other colours in the bright sunshine except white, off-white, grey-white, pale beige and the blue-white of the wide sky. It was stark and barren like a desert. Small, fluttering birds seemed to hang in the air above my head and sometimes yellow butterflies flickered over the sands. Small gardens of wild flowers grew from the hard mud in the shallow hollows or stood alone in clumps on the beaches, with tails of wind-blown sand. The power of the sun was increasing each day, and the left side of my face was beginning to peel and my left foot was more tanned than my right. I carried no water though I knew this could not continue much longer. I always seemed to be thirsty. The temperature in the sun felt over 90°F, much below the 116°F in the shade expected within ten weeks. I stopped at noon to munch a dry bread bun which, like much of the food, had been adulterated with what tasted like plaster.

The river turned to the left, and during the afternoon I found hundreds of ducks and lapwings and other waders in flocks in the shallows and on the sandbars. For over an hour I sat watching terns flying back and forth over short stretches of the river then plunging suddenly into the water wherever fish were spotted. But I never saw one fly off with a fish in its beak.

I was now in the state of Uttar Pradesh and in four days' time, 70 miles, would be reaching the only city along the river whose gaze is always towards the water. It is officially named Varanasi; is known to Hindus as Kashi, the city of light; and is called Benares in the countryside. I followed the meanders of the river on footpaths at the edges of fields or along the beaches and became very keen to reach the city. I felt well, cheery and not lacking energy, but had frequent bouts of loose stools. My digestion had been upset ever since that cup of coffee in bed in Ballia and I stopped often to defecate. I wondered if excessively spicy food was the cause, or drinking a lot of water after being dehydrated after hours in the sun. I knew the latter was irresponsible abuse of my body. Whatever the cause, I hesitated to assault my intestines with any drug from my little medical kit and thus risk making myself more vunerable to further infections. I hoped the problem would pass and meanwhile I had to defecate in the open beside the river, though I hated this filthy and unhygienic practice which is the established routine in the countryside.

'Where are you going?' called a man's voice in English while I was walking past the fence surrounding a baked-mud home in a field.

I was surprised to hear English and replied in Hindi, 'To Kashi.'

A young man emerged and greeted me. His mother came out and, with her hands on her hips, looked me up and down. 'Ah yes. Yes! It is him! It is him!' she exclaimed in Hindi, and I was ushered into the small yard to sit on the ground beside bundles of animal fodder in front of their home. Water was fetched for me to drink and to wash my hands. Cold *chapatis* and a dish of cold, spiced peas were brought.

'He is making a *padyatra* (foot-march) beside Ganga-ji,' said the mother. 'He is coming from Ganga Sagar. He is going to Benares. He is going to Hardwar and Gangotri. All by the shore of Ganga-ji,' she explained in Hindi to a visiting neighbour.

I had not yet said a single word.

'He is making *padyatra* and now he has come to my home!' This dear woman was beside herself with delight and for a moment I understood something of what *darshan* means to Hindus. It was evidently being applied to me. I had never grasped just how special the Ganga is to Hindus until this moment. I could only guess that the mother had seen me in the mirrored room at the temple in Buxar three days before and that, unknown to me, the party of women had asked who I was and where I was going. Of all the women who had been to Buxar, she counted herself to be indeed blessed that Ganga had sent this foreign pilgrim to accept the hospitality of her house.

A small girl came to hear the story and to look at me, and I gave her a toffee from my pocket. The family pressed me to stay one or two days but I wanted to keep moving. We exchanged addresses and I left their home with full belly and both hands full of freshly picked pea pods. The son escorted me along the footpath beside the Ganga for a quarter of a mile and then I was alone. I regretted my haste in wanting to keep moving, because I believed this family thought I felt that their hospitality was too simple to accept.

The immense size of the river has ensured its perennial flow, unlike thousands of streams and lesser rivers which dry out in the hot season. The Ganga is an important habitat for hundreds of varieties of mammals and birds, many of the latter spending winter on the Ganga and flying north to central Asia and the Soviet Union in March and April, either up over the Himalayas or up the Indus and Brahmaputra valleys. However, the absence of the flocks numbering thousands reported fifty years ago was very noticeable.

My interest in the waders and waterfowl was gradually increasing. I was pausing more and more to listen to unusual bird calls or to wait for dolphins to surface and dive again. At the same time, the strain of speaking only a little Hindi combined with the endless repetition of questions was becoming almost unendurable after three months. I enjoyed the solitude of the daytime so much that I was gradually withdrawing inside myself, a definite handicap in such a thickly populated area, which added to my tension. The increasing need to defend my privacy and personal space made me reluctant even to bathe in the Ganga wherever there were people or to stop for tea and face the questions. It was not a dislike of India but contentment with my solitude. With this mentality, people wanting to talk to me became unwelcome interlopers. It was an unhappy turnaround from the eagerness to meet people with which the journey had started. In my withdrawn frame of mind I often detoured round villages rather than face more questions, despite the automatic offer of water from people.

I wandered hour upon hour along the path beside the Ganga, north then south round meanders on the river, often with my mind straying. There was so much of this country that I could not understand or for which I had no sympathy. It was not the poverty of millions of people that appalled me but this squalor in the midst of so many resources and so much potential that baffled me.

'India is not a poor country. She is abundantly supplied with everything that makes a country rich, and yet her people are very poor.' This seems as true today as when Nehru wrote those words while in jail in 1944, despite the progress that has been made in the face of a population which has doubled. Fertile soils cover an area larger than France. There are big reserves of coal, iron, and 50 other minerals, abundant water in rivers and underground, and a great many people. At present, they achieve little of their human potential in a country so often divided against itself. My own bewilderment and frustration were nothing compared to the frustrations of many educated and cultured Indians, and I began to understand the apparent indifference and impatience often displayed by them towards illiterate, superstitious peasants.

Late afternoon was heralded by squawking, rose-ringed parakeets flying round clumps of bamboo trees. I must have been crazy to think of reaching Saidpur in one day, a distance of 26 miles from the previous night's schoolroom. But I wanted to reach Benares as quickly as possible. The spire of a temple in Saidpur never seemed to get any closer as the sun finally set and grey gloom settled over the green wheat fields and the clatter and cries from scattered hamlets became more distinct. I was miles from Saidpur and my feet were aching. I walked on the beach, for the softer ground, but went back to the track after being attacked by two dogs. Darkness came and I carried two clods of baked earth in my hand in case of attack.

I walked on. There was nothing else to do. But this was no night to admire the stars. I stopped outside the front yard of one home to ask directions and was inevitably showered with questions by two teen-agers. I was reluctant to waste time chatting, I thought, but answered their questions as patiently as I could. They invited me to eat and to stay the night and they fetched their schoolbooks to hear me read English.

Their mother emerged after half an hour. 'What are you doing? Bringing a foreigner into our home?' the angry woman demanded of her son.

'Go, go!' she said, turning to me.

'Where is the path?' I asked as I hurriedly left the property, but no one replied. I was now in difficulties. The night was black and my small flashlight was not powerful enough to show where the path lay. Dogs were likely to attack me and it would be easy in the dark to miss the bridge across the river to Saidpur. I was worn out and did not know what to do so I crept forwards, step by step, with clods of earth grasped in both hands ready to throw at dogs. I called out plaintively in Hindi, 'Friend! Friend!'

I had walked no more than a hundred yards, though it felt much, much further, my progress exceedingly slow, when a voice answered my calls. I stepped forward, shining the flashlight in my face so that whoever was answering could see my face, and I found myself approaching, through buffaloes and cattle tethered at feeding troughs, a small, brick house.

'Where are you going?'

'Saidpur.'

'The bridge is here.' A man stepped forward to show me the way.

'I am going for night halt,' I said, not completely unaware of the response this might produce.

'Night halt? You may sleep in my house.'

Relieved and grateful, I crouched down on the brick verandah by the heat and orange glow of a fire that illuminated the smiling faces and bald heads of three men warming their hands. Food was fetched and I ate as little as was polite and drank much water. Then I passed round my *beedis* and we crouched round the fire while I answered the inevitable questions. At length they saw that I was exhausted and hospitably unrolled bedding over straw spread out on the verandah adjacent to the fire and wished me goodnight.

I woke hours later, when the fire was dead and everyone was asleep, with an urgent need to defecate. There was no water with which to wash myself to carry out into the field, but I could not delay and walked out quietly to a nearby field of castor oil plants to do my business in the dead of night. I cleaned myself with dry earth and halfway back to the verandah I met my host coming out to the field with a tin of water in his hand.

'Bad stomach?' he asked.

'Yes,' I replied, and we tiptoed back to our places.

Milk was already squirting into buckets when I woke just before sunrise to see the cows eating at troughs in front of the verandah. Four men and women were scraping up the manure produced during the night. This would be dried and stacked in piles shaped like the nose cones of space rockets in preparation for the monsoon rains. Other boys and men were warming themselves round a fire, and for the first time I could see their faces clearly and they could see mine. A dozen pairs of brown eyes were watching me with both curiosity and friendship. It was not possible to leave without smoking many *beedis*, answering innumerable questions already answered the night before, and eating four balls of *gour* washed down with several glasses of water. They wished me well but my words of Hindi were inadequate to convey my gratitude.

A chill wind was blowing across the sands as I trudged forward, wrapped in my shawl, with aching ears, and I saw the pontoon bridge which I had missed in the dark. From Saidpur the river swung south towards Benares and I followed part of the way behind a camel on a path shaded by mango trees at the edge of wheat fields.

Two men joined me on the track, thus ending my Hindi lesson, and forcing me into conversation. I was in a bad mood and wanted only to be left alone. The taller and stouter of the two men, dressed in blue *lungi* and plain cream shirt, was intensely curious about my belongings and wanted to know what I was carrying.

'Do you have camera?'

'Yes.'

'I will see.'

'No,' I replied with annoyance, not wanting his awkward hands handling my precious camera. He insisted and, not wanting to give greater offence, I took it from my shoulder bag and handed it to him. He was ignorant of its purpose and fumbled with it in his big hands.

'It's not a doll, it's a machine,' I said in Hindi, and infuriated by yet another example of asinine curiosity, I put the camera away and we walked together to the next village where I bought tea and glucose biscuits for our breakfast. I refused to take photographs but was filled with a moment's dread when a police officer wearing clean, pressed trousers, green sweater and sporting a leather gun holster walked up to me. It was impossible to refuse his request to hold the camera and, having looked through the viewfinder, he handed the camera to the tall man in the blue *lungi*. The events of the next few minutes happened quickly. As soon as the camera was in his hands, the man ran off down the lane with it. I gave chase, crossing a vegetable patch, behind a washing line, up an alley, round a house and back down the path but I was carrying my knapsack and was unable to catch up with him. I could feel the knot securing my *lungi* coming undone.

A crowd gathered in the main street. 'He ran and ran,' explained a small boy who had seen me chasing the man, adding with glee, 'and then his *lungi* came down!' There was laughter and I smiled through my anger.

'I am a guest in your village,' I said in Hindi. 'I am making a pilgrimage beside Mother Ganga and going to Benares. I am one man.' I refused the hospitality of tea and water and the tension increased. Someone must have known where the thief had gone, and I was depending on people's goodwill to get the camera returned, though I knew that my own conduct had provoked the theft. A message was sent to the local police station, but the camera was returned to me after half an hour while we were waiting for the constable to arrive on his bicycle.

There was still a great deal of tension and I was escorted down the village street by some forty men and children. We stopped outside a tea-stall where someone volunteered: 'Camera comes. Now you will take tea.'

'Yes,' I agreed, nodding. The tension broke and our laughter swept away embarrassment and anger.

8

Benares: City of Light, City of Dark

For seven days I stayed in the compound of the tourist bungalow in Benares, and did not venture out further than to a Chinese restaurant seven yards from the front door except to collect 15 letters awaiting me at the main post office. I lay low knowing I was too weary to be in a receptive mood for exploring India's holiest city. I needed a short time apart, away from the crowds and the questions. I enjoyed fried eggs, coffee and buttered toast every breakfast; tea and glucose biscuits sitting in the garden washed with the glow of afternoon sunshine; reading and writing. Above all else, I enjoyed the tranquillity of a week's respite from the mental bruising outside. My dark mood eventually began to lift a little and then I walked two miles through congested and noisy streets to look for a place to stay near the Ganga.

'We do not take foreigners,' said a young man sitting on a bench in the cramped entrance to a little hotel. 'This is South Indian Hotel.'

I hate racial discrimination but there was no point in arguing and I sat down for tea with the man and his friend. Both were flabbergasted when I told them of my journey, and one of them explained apologetically, 'When foreigners came here, so many troubles with drugs and police.'

It was already dark outside, so he arranged for a guide to escort me through back alleys to the house of a family who rented rooms to foreigners. I stayed for two weeks in a little room in this house while I grappled with my distaste for Indian squalor, languour and violence and my paradoxical admiration and love for the country. I often sat alone in the evenings on the broad, stone steps leading down to the the Ganga, watching the calm flow and gradually feeling calmer myself. I began to share the mood of the poet Jagannatha, who wrote a love poem to Ganga called *Ganga Lahari*, 'The Waves of the Ganga', in the 17th century:

> I come to you as a child to his mother.
> I come as an orphan to you, moist with love.

I come without refuge to you, giver of sacred rest.
I come a fallen man to you, uplifter of all.
I come undone by disease to you, the perfect physician.
I come, my heart dry with thirst, to you, ocean of sweet wine.
Do with me whatever you will.

None of the six million pilgrims who come each year to Benares would miss bathing in the Ganga. This place, the city with the river, is the easiest crossing place or ford to heaven to escape rebirth in this world and to reach liberation. These *tirthas*, where heaven and earth touch, exist all over the country but are especially powerful at Benares, Hardwar and Ujjain where the potency of prayers, chants, sacrifices and penances for spiritual gain and worldly success is increased. Benares stands on the left bank (looking north on the map) at one of few places where the river flows in a four-mile crescent northwards. This is believed to be especially beneficial by the pilgrims who have been coming to the city since the beginning of recorded history. Some of their actions and devotions are the same today as almost three thousand years ago, when the city was founded.

'When Athens was growing in strength, before Rome had become known, or Greece had contended with Persia, or Cyprus had added lustre to the Persian monarchy, or Nebuchadnezzar had captured Jerusalem, and the inhabitants of Judaea had been carried into captivity, she had already risen to greatness, if not glory,' wrote Rev. M. A. Sherring, a Christian missionary to Benares in the nineteenth century. The city has had many names throughout the centuries: the most ancient, Kashi, is said to refer to a kingdom of which the city was capital about 1000 BC. Kashi also means, 'one that enlightens', and this is the City of Light which devout Hindus respectfully call Kashi-ji. Its present name, Varanasi, recalls another ancient name. Popularly, this refers to the Varuna and the Asi rivers flowing to the north and south of the city which are said to be the 'averter' (*varuna*) and the 'sword' (*asi*) that protect the city from evil. The British had called the city Benares, a corruption of the Moslem name 'Banaras', from 'Baranasi', meaning 'Varanasi' in the Pali language, and after independence it was officially renamed Varanasi.

Long ago, before there were buildings or streets, the area was forested and there were temples where teachers gathered with their students. This was Anandavana, the Forest of Bliss, the last of whose trees were cut down only at the beginning of this century.

The city is pre-eminently the home of Shiva, the creator. 'Although Shiva dwells everywhere and in everyone, he is said to dwell with special intensity here, where the membrane between this world and the transcendent reality is so thin as to be virtually transparent,' explained

Diana Eck in *Banaras: City of Light*. It is to this *tirtha* that the pilgrims come on their journeys of holy sight-seeing, to wash away their
sins, to imbibe spiritual purity and to receive the blessing of the holy
places.

There are an estimated 100,000 Shiva *lingams* in the city and
innumerable temples. Few pilgrims would miss the main Shiva temple.
Like most buildings in the city, this is not old, having been built in 1750
on the site of previous temples, and has been dubbed 'the golden
temple' after a maharaja paid for the spires to be gilded in 1839. It is
properly called the Vishvanath Temple (Vishvanath being another
name for Shiva), and the temple, of red stone, is now crammed between
other buildings and reached through narrow lanes.

Untouchables were only allowed to enter the precincts of this temple
after the 1955 Untouchability (Offences) Act forbade the banning of
Untouchables from temples, shops, restaurants and village wells.
Mahatma Gandhi called these people, at the bottom of the social heap,
'Harijans', meaning Children of God, and campaigned vigorously
against the religious and social taboo that still stigmatises one in five
people in the country.

'Untouchability is not a sanction of religion . . . There is neither
nobility or bravery in treating the great and uncomplaining scavengers
of the nation as worse than dogs to be despised and spat upon,' said
Gandhi.

Strict Brahmins in the golden temple decided that the presence of
Harijans was polluting, so a New Vishvanath Temple was built to
which Harijans are allowed entry, but forbidden to touch the *lingam*,
making *puja* impossible and thus effectively barring them from using
the temple. The new temple stands with many others above the 81
ghats lining the bank of the Ganga. It is on these steps that people begin
their pilgrimages with physical and ritual purification in the river. Such
is the power and grace of Mother Ganga that no one, not even a
Harijan, is too sinful to be embraced.

Some are old and feeble, weary with long journeys of life, emaciated by
maladies, saddened from losses and troubles; and the morning air blows
sharp, the river wave runs chilly. Yet there they stand, breast-deep in the
cold river, with dripping cotton garments clinging to their thin or aged
limbs, visibly shuddering under the shock of the water, and their lips blue
and quivering, while they eagerly mutter their invocations. None of them
hesitates; into the Gunga (*sic*) they plunge on arrival, ill or well, robust or
sickly; and ladle the holy liquid up with small, dark, trembling hands,
repeating the sacred names, and softly mentioning the sins they would
expiate and the beloved souls they would plead for! (Edwin Arnold in *India
Revisited* in 1886).

Such scenes have continued unchanged for centuries. An outsider should neither comment nor make assumptions. It should be enough only to observe, I thought, when I went down at first light to sit all day at the most popular *ghat*.

A young mother, her patience with her two children gone, beats her fists on her small son's back making him cry even louder. Her strong fingers pinch his cheeks with such ferocity that suddenly he sits in silence with mouth agog and spittle drooling, watched curiously by his naked baby sister.

'No,' says the grandmother, putting her wrinkled arm between son and mother. Quickly mother calms down, packs up the clothes and drags her family away.

Muscular youths in jock-straps stretch their limbs and gyrate their necks while dozens of pot-bellied businessmen from Delhi and Bombay float on their backs in the river, their heads shaved clean of every hair for this, the start of their tour of the holy city. Other men, standing apart from the women, are towelling themselves dry or are already changed and sitting cross-legged under big, bamboo umbrellas on the wooden platforms of the *pandas*. The *pandas* have guarded the bathers' belongings and are now reciting appropriate Sanskrit verses before marking each forehead with three parallel sandalwood paste lines in the sign of Shiva, and accepting as much or as little payment as is offered.

'Hello, hello. Cold drink? Campa cola? Thumbs Up? Yes, yes,' call the stallholders, who stand beside their red boxes of ice and cold bottles while American, English, German and Japanese tourists saunter past. It is true that we tourists are interlopers here, arriving as soon after sunrise as we can get ourselves out of bed, woken by the tour bus's horn. We come with fresh films in our cameras, our lenses cleaned, our telephotos poised for bare female breasts and dead bodies floating in the river. We come to see the 'real' India, the one we think we have not seen at the railway station or on the streets.

At midday, the barber puts away his cut-throat razors, scissors, brushes and soap into a small, tin suitcase and snaps shut the faded black umbrella which has kept off the sharp sun all morning. For five hours he has squatted on sackcloth laid out meticulously in front of the wooden block on which his customers have sat to be shaved.

How invitingly the cool, green river glistens in the hot afternoon. How empty and quiet is the *ghat* in this lull when everyone sane is sleeping. There is hardly a flutter in the clothes hung up to provide shade and scarcely a bird in the sky.

The sun gradually sinks behind the city. Shadows extend across the *ghats* and the river, and a breeze cools the air and stirs the white sands of the beach beyond the water. When the first stars appear in the sky the *ghat* becomes crowded again with families taking evening strolls and men selling balloons, toys on sticks, crispy *popadoms*, clay cups of tea served from kettles wired to buckets of glowing coals, and *chena* piled on leaf-plates from mounds on brass trays garnished with flowers. Their chatter mingles in the dusk with the sound of sitars played by a group of skinny hippies, wearing loose pantaloons, braided waistcoats and necklaces, and with evening Sanskrit chants emanating from loudspeakers outside temples.

Later, when the river is calm, without a ripple, and men sit in hushed groups on the steps, an Indian skimmer flies back and forth by the light of the full moon over the black water, its lower beak scooping through the water and its top beak ready to snap shut on any fish caught.

The inhabitants of Benares have not all approved of the adoration of the river nor the multiplicity of temples and shrines in the city. Both Hindus and Moslems have rebelled against this clutter of objects and dogmas separating the people from God. A man called Kabir in the 15th century was one such iconoclast. He was a low-caste weaver whose poetry is still celebrated in northern India, even in Benares whose sanctity he disparaged:

> There is nothing but water at the holy bathing places;
> and I know that they are useless, for I have bathed in them.
> The images are all lifeless, they cannot speak;
> I know, for I have cried aloud to them.
> The Puranas and the Koran are mere words;
> lifting up the curtain, I have seen.

One of Kabir's disciples was Guru Nanak, who later founded Sikhism as a reconciliation between Hindus and Moslems. An apocryphal story tells what happened one day when Guru Nanak was taking his morning bath in the Ganga. When everyone else cupped their hands and offered the river water in prayer to the rising sun, Guru Nanak turned towards his own village.

'What are you doing?' the Brahmins asked.

'Well,' said Guru Nanak, 'if the water can reach the sun so far away it can surely irrigate my garden at home.'

Hours of observation with as much inner silence as I could muster were showing me that the formalities of worship and dogma were irrelevant, and that the purpose of worship was primarily to uplift the worshipper, not the deity being worshipped. That millions of people in India believe that the water of the Ganga is the actual goddess, is no different from millions of Roman Catholics believing that the bread broken during Mass is the actual body of Jesus Christ.

Looking at the Ganga, day after day, I saw a powerful symbol of life's continuum, its rapids and shallows, fast flows and meanders, and I decided it would be inauspicious not to bathe in the Ganga at Benares despite the sewage and corpses and Hindu disdain of ignorant foreigners who play-act.

I was woken by the first Moslem call to prayer wailing over rooftops, through empty streets and alleys strung with telephone wires like abandoned cat's cradles. Six women were already selling petals and flower garlands and a few rickshaw-*wallahs* were cleaning their bicycles near the top of the popular Dasawamadh Ghat. I waited for the sun to rise above the band of haze along the horizon on the far shore, then joined a dozen men already in a group at the water's edge. I left *kurta*, sandals, towel, money and clean pyjamas on the wooden platform of a *panda*, pulled up my *lungi* around my waist, exposing thin, white legs and knobbly knees, and stepped down the slimy steps into pale, green water. It felt tepid, perhaps because the early morning air was still chilly. A dazzling streak of sunlight broke across the river and men standing beside me or further out began their prayers, calling on Ganga to be present. They scooped up water with cupped hands and poured it out between their fingers towards the sun in prayers to the gods and their own ancestors.

I cleaned away the surface of the river in front of me and with eyes closed and nose held, ducked under the water. I had no prayers to offer so I lathered myself in soap and smiled at the cameras of tourists sightseeing from boats. I was now quite proud that I could publicly bathe, dry myself with a towel and change into dry pyjamas and *kurta* with ease and modesty. When I was changed, the *panda* handed me comb and mirror and then I sat cross-legged on his platform, shaded from the morning sunshine, while he mumbled a prayer in Sanskrit and painted my forehead with sandalwood paste. The *panda* was amused by it all, though his expression turned to shocked delight when I said I'd reached the city from Calcutta on foot. He asked for five rupees in payment and accepted one without much hesitation.

Behind us at the top of Dasawamadh Ghat pilgrims were clanging the brass bells of the Shitala temple, alerting her to their presence. Shitala is the goddess of smallpox and other diseases and is particularly worshipped during the hot months of April, May and June when innumerable illnesses strike. Even in the rainy season, when the Ganga rises 40 feet submerging the steps to her temple, people go out by boat or swim to the temple to make *puja* and have *darshan* of three-eyed Shitala who rides a donkey. They pray both to forestall infection and for Shitala to bless sick family members by leaving, and thus curing them. Because the goddess herself inhabits the infected, those who die of smallpox are not cremated because this would injure the goddess.

Day after day the brass bells sound, the flowers and offerings are made and prayers recited just as they have been for centuries, but I could not suppress the suspicion that it was these rituals and religion that perpetuate the miseries from which Hindus pray to be released. Shitala and the other gods have had thousands of years to abate the diseases which still ravage humankind. Epidemics of smallpox, typhoid, cholera, tuberculosis and diphtheria, for example, have been abated in the West through improved public hygiene, not through piety! My mood of revolt against temple worship was quite inappropriate to Benares. I was weary and not even trying to understand what I knew I disliked. In a city full of temples, there was not much else to do but take myself off to see a Soviet aeroplane disaster movie and to hope that my depression would pass. The film (or the projector) broke three times, but there was, of course, no denying that the Aeroflot planes and pilots were heroes, unlike the man sitting two rows in front of me spitting into the aisle.

After the film I still felt dislocated from my surroundings, and for the second time in four months I borrowed a tape recorder one evening and retired to my little room. I closed the door and wooden window shutters, lit a candle and turned out the light. I lay on the bed listening to the music of Beethoven, Brahms and Grieg. I closed my eyes and imagined I was at home in Canada, watching the beavers that live in the riverbank opposite my home. That night I yearned to hold and to be held by another human being.

My feelings of loneliness and disillusionment were slow to pass, and weighed down every day of my three-week stay in the city. But I was considerably cheered when, one Sunday morning, I journeyed four miles north of Benares in a 6-seater auto-rickshaw to the gardens and ruins of Sarnath where Buddha preached his first sermon in 588 BC.

'There are two extremes, oh monks, which the man who has given up the world ought not to follow—the habitual practice, on the one hand, of self-indulgence which is unworthy, vain and fit only for the worldly-minded—and the habitual practice, on the other hand, of self-mortification, which is painful, useless and unprofitable,' Buddha apparently told five monks in this first sermon. 'To satisfy the necessities of life is not evil. To keep the body in good health is a duty, for otherwise we shall not be able to trim the lamp of wisdom, and keep our mind strong and clear. Water surrounds the lotus-flower, but does not wet its petals.' Buddha preached an eightfold path of Noble Truths to guide every person: right views, right aspirations, right speech, right behaviour, right livelihood, right effort, right thoughts and right contemplation.

His message spread over India, Sri Lanka and the Far East. Numerous Buddhist monasteries were built at Sarnath and occupied by over 1500 monks, and the emperor Ashoka erected a tall thick pillar called a *stupa* (commemorative mound). But by AD 600 the faith was fighting a popular and rejuvenated Hinduism, and the tree at Bodh Gaya under which Buddha had been enlightened was chopped down by a Hindu king and the shrine converted for Hindu worship. Buddha himself became deified by his followers and was the centre of elaborate rituals, which became increasingly similar to those of Hinduism. Buddhism gradually lost its popular following, and the monasteries and universities were all that remained when Moslem invaders destroyed these institutions and sacked Hindu Benares in the twelfth century. Hinduism recovered. Buddhism did not.

The ruins of Sarnath lay buried until British archaeologists excavated the site in 1836 and it has since become an important place for Buddhist pilgrims. I watched one such pilgrim muttering prayers as he paced round and round the *stupa* with his rosary in the hot sunshine. Sarnath was peaceful and clean with birds chattering in the bushes or standing out on the green lawns with beaks open wide. Splashes of reddish-purple, yellow and pink bougainvillaea enhanced the atmosphere of calm beauty which was in such contrast to the dust, noise and congestion of the city. Groups of teenage boys or girls sat in groups, shaded under trees on the lawns, listening to recitals of sitar music or poetry while families came to stroll and gaze at the deer and crocodiles in a small zoo.

I made one other outing from Benares, 50 miles north by bus to visit a kindergarten in Jaunpur sponsored by Save the Children Fund. The local Jaycees (a service organisation similar to the Rotary Club) established and supervised the project near the rubbish dump on the edge of the city. The little school had been built in the midst of the people it served—rickshaw-*wallahs*, beggars, basket weavers and leaf-plate makers. Shri Virendra Kumar Pradhan, chairman of the *Balwadi* Committee and a local carpet manufacturer, took me out to see the school on his scooter at lunchtime. On the day I visited, 84 children attended but there are usually nearly 100, aged between two and fourteen years. Attendance can be erratic because the children are often needed to work, for example at collecting leaves to be pinned together into disposable leaf-plates. Classes are held in Hindi. All the children learn mathematics and English and the older ones are taught general knowledge, art, Sanskrit and Moral Science (hygiene, manners etc.). They also receive regular medical check-ups.

Parents had originally been reluctant to send their children to school even though they get a free hot meal at noon. Hearing that a foreign agency was involved, they feared their children might be kidnapped and sent abroad but their confidence was now growing. When I visited it, the project was entering its last year of sponsorship and the Jaycees were expected to find another sponsor or become self-financing. They were meeting this challenge confidently and energetically.

The festival of Holi was celebrated half-way through my stay in Benares, beginning on the night of March's full moon with the lighting of bonfires in the streets to consume the witch Holika. Holika had tried to burn up a great devotee of Vishnu's, called Prahlada, but he was saved by the strength of his faith in Vishnu. I was warned to stay indoors the following morning for fear of being doused with the paints and powders thrown by enthusiastic youths. Within a few hours they manage to cover themselves and everyone else in colour until the city's alleys and streets look as though they have been invaded by green or red people with white teeth.

According to custom, this messy frolic ends at midday when people take baths and, if they have them, change into new or clean, white clothes and wish one another 'Happy Holi', patting each other with a little red powder, exchanging gifts of sweets and drinking a pleasant tasting concoction of milk and hashish called *bhang*.

'How do you feel? Oh dear, oh dear. It frightens me so much when I give these things to a foreigner,' said a kindly man whom I had met in a shop one day and whose Holi hospitality I was now enjoying.

'I feel fine,' I said.

'Dear, oh dear.'

There was one *ghat* in Benares where foreigners were not especially welcome. This was a subdued place where the serious business of cremation was conducted. About 35,000 bodies are cremated each year and I sat watching the Untouchable attendants prodding five funeral pyres with bamboo sticks to ensure fast, even burning.

Benares is the best place in the world to die, and thousands of people come to the city for that purpose. To die here is to be certain of release from the cycle of karma and endless rebirths in this world. To die in Benares is so beneficial that even those who have enjoyed all pleasures of the flesh will be liberated without penances or sacrifices.

In Kashi, as elsewhere, the living must perform rituals for the dead and the body must be properly disposed of. The corpses are carried on bamboo stretchers in a chanting procession and are each dipped in the Ganga before being laid on the funeral pyre and covered with wood and clarified butter. I watched six men arrange a body wrapped in white cloth (white cloth denotes a male and red cloth a female) and bring forward a boy to walk round the pyre anti-clockwise five times and then light the pyre with a bundle of burning reeds. Smoke and flames quickly engulfed the logs. The boy would later break open the skull in order to release the soul, and this also prevents the skull from exploding when the brains heat up.

There were no tears, for that would bring bad luck to the departed. Fifty mourners were crouched in silence watching five pyres. One man sat alone, looking at the flames from time to time but otherwise gazing at the grey river. He looked to be thirty years old, though it was hard to tell as his head had been shaved bald to signify mourning, and his body was wrapped in a single piece of coarse, white cloth.

Women, if they came at all, stood behind railings at the top of the *ghat*. Water buffaloes watched from the river and a dozen mangy dogs waited to fight over pickings with vultures and crows.

Wealthy people cremate their dead with sandalwood which burns hotly and emits a sweet smell. Merchants at the *ghat* supply gradings of sandalwood from logs to sawdust at prices to suit every pocket. Cremation is an expensive business, costing between R500 and R5000 compared to the average annual income of R995 in Bihar and R1313 in Uttar Pradesh. Inevitably, some people cannot afford the 700 pounds of firewood necessary to incinerate a body so when their wood is all burned, what remains of the corpse is cast in the Ganga for the dogs, vultures, crows and fish.

Despite the sizzling and the blue smoke, the burning *ghat* was not a gruesome sight. 'For Hindus, death is not the opposite of life; it is, rather, the opposite of birth. The great transition which death occasions is not from life to death, but from life to life,' wrote Diana Eck in *Banaras: City of Light*.

Each pyre burned for about three hours and when the flames were well settled amid grey ashes, I saw an old man with fleshless arms and shrunken eyes being led to a fire by younger relatives. They turned him round so that he stood with his back to the fire, and held an earthen pot of Ganga water to his shoulder so that he could ceremonially douse the flames by dropping the pot over his back so that it smashed in the fire with a hiss. Then he stepped forward with his walking cane without looking back. Later the mound of ashes would be dumped into the river and the site prepared for another body.

The city authorities have been trying for ten years to install an electric crematorium, such as operates in Patna, but there has been strong opposition from the family that controls and profits from the main burning *ghat*.

The river is also polluted in Benares by the twenty million gallons of untreated sewage which flows daily into the river from outlets between the *ghats* where people bathe. Ten years ago the World Bank built five pumping stations in the city to move sewage downstream of the city before it was discharged into the river, with the idea of eventually building a treatment plant. None of the pumps has ever worked, though all the money has been spent, according to Professor Veer Bhadra Mishra whose mission it is to fight pollution in the Ganga. Professor Mishra was a professor in the Hydraulic Engineering Department of the Benares Hindi University, a priest at one of the riverside temples and head of the Clean Ganga Movement.

In the hot months only 615 thousand million gallons flow past the city compared to over 24,637 thousand million gallons during the four months of the monsoon. More and more of the river water is being taken for irrigation during the hot season and the concentration of pollution is therefore steadily rising. The Ganga is unfit for bathing or drinking even after sterilisation during May, according to Government of India statistics. There is more than three times the maximum allowable biochemical oxygen demand and 24 times the maximum total fecal coliform count. The water in the Ganga at Benares is suitable only for wildlife, industrial cooling, irrigation and controlled waste disposal, according to a report published in 1984 by the Central Board for the Prevention and Control of Water Pollution.

Professor Mishra and the Clean Ganga Movement have been fighting not only the ineptitude and apathy of engineers, bureaucrats and politicians but also the religious dogma that maintains that Mother Ganga cannot be polluted because she is so pure.

'How do you combat this?' I asked.

'People say to me that Ganga is our mother. So I ask them, "Do you wish your own mother to be treated with this disrespect, spitting and sewage and such things?" You see, they have no answer,' explained Professor Mishra.

There is little industrial pollution at Benares because the major industry is silk weaving and brocade making which is carried out in small workshops or people's homes. Daily sales of silk saris are estimated at more than R10 million, as millions of pilgrims combine religious observance with bargain hunting in the abundant silk shops, each stuffed with rainbows of colours and innumerable designs. The men who run these shops control the silk industry, as no silk yarn is produced in Benares, and these middlemen supply yarns and patterns to the weavers who bid to make each length of cloth which is then woven by themselves, their wives and children. Naturally the profits of the transactions go to the middlemen, while the weavers work in a labyrinth of backstreet workshops where conditions are appalling. Overcrowding and dirt are exacerbated in the ferocious heat of the summer because fans cannot be used as the silk threads would tangle.

The same fabric patterns were repeated again and again in the shops as if nothing new was being created. Many designs were identical to those displayed in the museum at the palace of the Maharajah of Benares, and although the colours were stunning and the precision of the handicraft exquisite, I wondered where Indian creativity had gone. The absence of anything innovative was unimportant if confined to silk saris and brocades, but I recognised that it spread to almost every aspect of Indian life. I observed that there was nothing original in design of any nature. It was not only the packaging of Colgate, Cadbury's or Nescafé, but even wholly Indian merchandise would have looked at home in any supermarket in the West. Even the designs of posters and the statues of Hindu deities seen in every village, shop and home were imitative stereotypes, which indicated a total absence of any creative impulse.

It was time to get out of the city and return to the countryside, heading towards the fresh clean air of the Himalayas 850 miles away.

9

When the Land Dies

It was not yet nine o'clock when I stepped out jauntily along the *ghats* heading out of Benares but already it was too hot to stand directly in the sun's blaze. I was holding up a newly bought black umbrella in my left hand and carried a two-litre water container, also newly bought, over my shoulder. This was absurdly inadequate, as I was to discover. The small blue knapsack was still strapped to my back but was now much lighter as I had mailed off many books, including my Hindi manual, having abandoned efforts to learn more of the language. I could now answer fluently the 20 questions which people asked again and again and I did not have the stamina to want to improve. I was later to regret my over-zealous desire to travel light because, as weather conditions worsened and I remained without the food for thought provided by communication with other people, my mind fixed itself on annoyances and privations which otherwise might have been taken more lightly.

Five miles from the city, the river-bed curved to the right and opened out until its brown banks were more than a mile apart, separated by the flat expanse of white sands and the slender stream of grey water. I walked along the base of a gentle, sandy slope on which tomatoes and squashes were growing. A line of wide holes had been dug 15 feet deep in the sand along the base of this slope, from which water could be fetched in plastic buckets or earthen jars to irrigate the vegetables. Sparrow-sized crested larks were running up and down the rims of the holes making their pleasing 'tee-ur, tee-ur' call, almost hidden on the sands by their dappled fawn camouflage.

I stopped to drink water from my container only once all morning and kept trudging onwards with a renewed surge of energy after being cooped up in the city. I was heading towards another bend where the river turned to the left, which I hoped to reach before lunchtime. It did not look to be far away across the hot, empty, sandy landscape in which my feet and sandals slipped. I seemed to be out there alone with the sun getting hotter and brighter hour by hour as it climbed to its noontime zenith. Suddenly, I found myself panting hard and beginning to shiver. My heart was beating fast and I felt faint. I was cold yet still sweating. I was giddy and unwell and fast becoming confused by the heat and bright light reflecting off the sands. I could not even think to drink more water from my container. I wanted to lie down but kept plodding mindlessly towards a tree on the bank where a cattle track emerged from the fields. I reached this shade with my legs shaking and my stomach ready to vomit.

I sipped water slowly for two hours and gradually began to feel comfortable again. It was marvellous to sit against the thick trunk of the banyan tree, shaded by its long branches and dangling aerial roots, listening to the soft cooing of many pigeons and reflecting on the obvious risks of heatstroke. For the first time, I allowed myself to doubt whether I would make it to the source of the Ganga. I was not yet halfway there; we were not yet properly into the hot season and already I was weakening. I could no longer be so sure that I could physically withstand the harsh conditions all the way to Gau Mukh in the Himalayas. But I still had the feeling, which had countered every difficulty I had met while planning and setting out on this journey, that all would be well. What had happened today had been a mild warning that no stupidity or miscalculations could be allowed during the next three months.

I sat under the banyan tree for several hours through the heat of the day, watching more than a hundred house swifts and dusky crag martins and a pair of resplendent small green bee-eaters sitting in long rows on electric wires leading to an irrigation pumphouse. I was becoming increasingly curious about the bird life along the river and still carried a heavy book to help me in this pursuit.

I prepared to move again when the afternoon breeze whipped up small waves on the river. The wind is called the '*loo*' (meaning 'hot wind') and I had already been warned several times about its dangers and the importance of keeping my ears and head covered and eating a raw onion each day, though no one told me the value of the onion! I set off from the banyan tree hoping to be able to refill my water bottle somewhere, and to reach the historic town of Chunar before nightfall. The banks of the river were now about 35 feet high, cut by numerous ravines surrounded by thickets of thorn bushes that provided good cover into which a colony of wild peacocks and their harems could retreat. These magnificent birds destroy crops and vegetable gardens but local religious custom now protects them. It has not always been so; peacock was Ashoka's favourite dish before he became a vegetarian.

Late in the afternoon, I came across two milkmen washing out their churns beside a big rowing boat before crossing to the village on the opposite bank. I hoped that it would be only a few miles from these to Chunar, and begged a lift. Within 20 minutes, the boat was laden with more than a dozen bicycles and their owners, numerous milk churns and passengers and we were out in mid-stream with two men rowing hard against the current. This hour before sunset was one of the best times of the day, when a breeze over the water brought relief from the heat, and the soft sunshine was reflected back by people's faces.

All too soon the sun had set, twilight faded into darkness and I was still miles from Chunar and unable to see the ruts in the cart-track as I passed through a darkened village.

'Where are you going?' asked a voice in Hindi.

'Chunar. Night halt,' I said.

'Very far. Please, you will come to my house? Night halt.'

There was nowhere else to go and I accepted this kind offer eagerly. I followed the speaker up a narrow alley and onto the verandah of a house. Five dark faces peered at me and an oil lamp was held up to my face.

'Sit down, sit down,' someone beckoned and a glass of water and two balls of *gour* were fetched. The household held a short discussion before I was introduced to each person in turn, but I caught only the name of my host, Shri Gulab Singh.

'Are you a hippie?'

It was obvious that I was not when a pipe of *ganja* was passed to me and I erupted in a fit of coughing when I took a long drag.

'Do you have revolver? Do you have transistor?'

I had neither but took out the photographs of family, friends and my home, which I had received in Benares in a letter, and for more than an hour answered all the questions that I could understand. My ignorance of Hindi and of Canadian crop yields was frustrating for all of us, and at length the group of men departed. I was taken through a low doorway into the small courtyard. Here, a piece of sacking, a glass and a bowl of water had been set out on the earth floor beside bundles of wheat. These were the first of the harvest. Two *chapatis*, each the size and weight of a dinner plate, and a bowl of extremely salty *dal* with potato slices were set before me, but I was too tired to have much of an appetite.

'He eats slowly,' said Gulab Singh, deciding after a while to eat his own meal with me.

Extra food was given to me twice, despite increasingly insistent protests that I could eat no more. 'Please,' I said in earnest, 'I am a small man. I cannot eat a big meal.'

The meal ended with a bowl of sweetened milk which I was allowed to drink without extra *chapatis*. I drank slowly because my belly was already swollen with overeating. After washing my hands and mouth, I got up slowly, hoping to be able to lie down before I was sick. However, as soon as I was on my feet I knew I was in trouble.

'One minute,' I exclaimed and dashed outside into the lane where I immediately vomited.

'Are you sick?' asked Gulab Singh when I returned.

'All day I have not eaten. Now you give me so much food.' I said loudly, hoping his wife, invisible in the dark kitchen, would hear and not think her cooking had made me ill.

'It is only too much food?'

'Yes,' I answered.

He handed me a king-size *beedi* and we sat outside on *charpoys*, face to face by the light of the oil lamp in the warm night air.

'I am a poor man,' said Gulab. 'I have only twelve bighas (four acres). I have five sons. The eldest is in Bombay. He is a mechanic. I have three daughters and my wife. She is present (i.e. alive) and healthy.'

'You are poor in money,' I said slowly in Hindi to be sure to be understood, 'but your heart is big.'

'Yes,' he said, 'my heart is big,' and smiled.

The night's sleep was much disturbed by mosquitoes and I woke several times hoping that the moon's brightness was the advent of dawn. When at last I did wake to see the glow of light opening up like a crack in the eastern horizon, Gulab was already feeding his cows by the light of the oil lamp.

'It is cool. Now is the good time to work in the field,' he said in a hushed voice, so as not to wake the three boys sleeping together on a *charpoy* nearby.

'It is also a good time to walk,' I said.

'Correct.'

He led me past the village primary school to the cart track that led to Chunar. Here at the edge of the village, the track passed two clumps of bamboo, both alive in the growing daylight with a bedlam of twittering birds.

'I am happy you have been in my house,' said Gulab solemnly.

'The blessing is mine. Thank you,' I replied.

I headed west along the track, away from the brightening, orange light flooding the eastern sky. Two hoopoes were already pecking on the path, their fan-shaped crests opening and closing as they flitted about. A few men and women were working amid the stands of wheat, cutting with their sickles before the sun should rise and the day's torrid heat begin. Other people were heading into the fields to defecate, carrying pots of water with which to clean themselves.

The sun rose an hour later, but the shadows were still long and soft when I entered Chunar through the former military cantonment (compound) that was now an overgrown village green, surrounded by the utilitarian bungalows of the British Raj. In one corner stood a three-storey brick palace, outsized and out of place. I was curious, and went to knock on the door, forgetting how early it was.

A women in her late thirties, with pale complexion and black hair, opened the door and after a few enquiries asked me to wait. Ten minutes later, having dressed, she introduced herself as Miss Marie Louise Hardless Kennedy and welcomed me into a big room to sit on a chair beside a small table covered by an Irish linen tea towel. This was the only furniture in the room, except for a mattress on the floor. The high walls were bare, the plaster cracked and the paint peeling. The marble floor was covered in dust. There were no overhead fans or light fixtures.

'Would you like some tea? Have you had breakfast?' asked Miss Hardless Kennedy, standing in the doorway, and she then moved to a small adjoining room and began making *parathas* for my breakfast.

'I've got some marmalade in my bag,' I said, removing this luxury from the knapsack. 'How does such a magnificent house come to be built in Chunar?' I asked.

'The house was built in 1901 or 1902, by my grandfather. He was a handwriting expert and it was built after he handled a case for the Nizam of Hyderabad. The Nizam told my grandfather, "You must build yourself a proper house". Poor grandfather. You see, he worked in a telegraph office until he met my mother, and he told the Nizam, "But I have no money". So the Nizam sent the blueprints of an Italian villa and so on . . .' Miss Hardless Kennedy waved both arms in an open gesture encompassing the whole, empty house.

'This used to be the cantonment here,' she said, pointing through the tall window, now opaque with dust. 'No servants were allowed to stay overnight without permission from the District Magistrate. No Indians were allowed through here after six at night. Pity it's not like that now.

'How times have changed. Of course, there's no future for Anglo-Indians here,' she said, explaining that most of her own Anglo-Indian family had already emigrated from India and thus she was left alone in the deserted palace.

'I was adopted by the family who brought me up. They were Mummy and my father.' Her real father, explained Miss Hardless Kennedy, came from a prominent American family. 'Of course, I know who they are and we have been in touch.'

Miss Hardless Kennedy gave me a letter of introduction to friends near Mirzapur, 23 miles upstream, and after breakfast took me on a grand tour of the empty house: up the shallow, marble stairway, through the echoing galleries and onto the roof to see the magnificent view of a huge rock almost 200 feet high and half a mile long, which the Ganga skirts as it flows down from the north. The modern town of Chunar lies at the base of this colossal, black rock, which rises abruptly above the brown plain and which has been used as a military fortress for almost 500 years.

I followed an old military road north from the rock beside the river, along which soldiers had marched during the British Raj and the reign of Akbar. The road was now a badly rutted track but at regular intervals I passed large, stone platforms built round open stone-lined wells. Trees were growing out of the walls of some of these, others had collapsed and the water of them all looked filthy, so I was content to sip from my own bottle. By midday I was hot and dusty and veered off the road to a strip of grass between the river and a field of ripening wheat, where I stripped off sandals, money-belt and knapsack on the bank and plunged into the water fully clothed. The Ganga was warm and dull green in colour. Several black and white kingfishers watched from the bank as I splashed about and washed myself in the weak current. My clothes took only a few minutes to dry and I sat sunbathing in underpants, happily munching a lunch of glucose biscuits, guavas and water.

That afternoon I walked contentedly under the shade of my black umbrella on the dusty track, clambering across the deep gullies eroded by rain torrents in the monsoon and twice wading through foul pools of stagnant water. In one of these a dog watched me with only its head above the water, much too comfortable in the cool to be bothered barking at a stranger. The road kept away from villages, preferring a lonely line from one derelict well to another across the empty plateau of baked earth and shallow stubble. It looked as if the land had died. Gradually, the sun sank in the sky, its white brightness shrinking into pale yellow behind the haze on the horizon.

Mirzapur was now fortunately not far away and the road was busy with clerks coming home on foot or bicycles from government offices, banks, shops and small factories. There were men toiling on cycle rickshaws, heaped with bundles of coloured wool yarns for village weavers, for this is one of India's most important carpet weaving areas, where rugs are produced to Persian designs. I reached the town after walking for an hour in the dark, and found a hotel that took me in eventually after requiring much persuasion to collect the correct forms for foreigners from the local police station, a tedious process that took hours.

After a thorough wash and a day's rest, I contacted an elderly Englishman who was living in Mirzapur and sat for afternoon tea and fruit cake from the Home Country in his spacious bungalow. Later, his driver took me 20 miles north of the Ganga over a new road bridge to visit the Seagers, the friends to whom Miss Hardless Kennedy had given me the introduction.

'We're camping at the moment. We've only one bathroom,' explained Mrs Kusum Seager heartily. The family had been waiting for months for the builders to finish their new, white home which looked like a minor palace, and meanwhile were camping out amid innumerable tin trunks on the first-floor verandah and rooms of their carpet factory. I was invited to stay and for four days enjoyed the lively banter and generous hospitality of the family and their servants, while outside the weather got ever hotter and brighter. I was also shown the family's flood album—photographs of the almost annual inundations when the Gangetic Plain becomes a muddy sea and millions of people become homeless and take refuge as best they can, many resorting to climbing into trees.

'It's interesting to see the order of priorities,' pointed out Geoffrey Seager with a mixture of humour and admiration. 'The grain store is uppermost among the branches, then comes the eldest son, the carpet—if they have one—and household items, then the father and the daughter and lastly the wife at the bottom, with the hem of her sari and sometimes her feet dangling into the muddy water.

'But you know, despite being forced from their homes which, being made of dried mud, literally melt before their eyes, and going without food for one or for several days, the villagers' humour is retained. It's rare to find anger.'

Fried bacon and eggs, home-made brown bread and thick-cut marmalade were unexpected sensual delights at the Seagers' breakfast table. The greatest pleasure came one day as I glanced through a back copy of the *Daily Telegraph*, when all of a sudden, my nose caught the aroma of freshly ground coffee. On the Gangetic Plain, at the start of the hot season, this gorgeous smell was irresistible.

'Curiously enough, coffee beans are more expensive than ground coffee. Presumably because the beans can't be adulterated,' explained Geoffrey Seager.

After breakfast on the verandah, he disappeared downstairs into his office. In 1910, his grandfather had started E. Hill & Co. which, with another British-owned firm, soon became the largest carpet exporter in India. Hill & Co. is still a household name in the town, though Geoffrey Seager left them to start a new exporting company. Carpet weaving is believed to have been imported by the Mughul emperor Jahangir 400 years ago when he brought skilled Moslems from Persia who settled around Mirzapur. Today, 40,000 of the country's 70,000 registered carpet handlooms are in Mirzapur and its surrounding villages.

Carpet weaving is still a cottage industry, employing in total about 400,000 people who receive work from the carpet companies. Though the companies' headquarters are called 'factories', each is really a warehouse with offices where orders are transcribed into designs on graph paper and bundles of coloured yarns are allotted to each weaver according to the design he is taking home. Finished carpets are then brought back to the factory for inspection, trimming and finishing, and washing with chemicals to achieve the sheen demanded by customers, before being shipped to Europe, North America or Saudi Arabia. West Germans are the biggest buyers, spending US$755 million in 1980, followed by the United States, spending nearly US$164 million. In 1980, India exported enough hand-knotted carpet to cover more than one and a quarter square miles. Even in rich countries, handmade carpets are luxuries that are vulnerable to economic recession. Exports to West Germany fell to US$450 million in 1982, leaving many weavers in India without work.

Many weavers are children aged between 10 and 14, preferred for their nimble and supple fingers and because they can work the looms while their parents labour in the fields. Anti child-labour laws are unenforceable because so many families need the income their children can earn, and although exploitation is widespread people without any work envy those who are earning. For most families, weaving is a part-time occupation bringing in 20 to 30 rupees each day to supplement the rice, wheat and vegetables grown in their fields. Weaving must therefore be fitted in around harvest and planting time and work slows during the hot season, from March to June.

On Saturday evening we dressed up smartly (in borrowed clothes if necessary) and went to the Mirzapur Club to watch a video of a Peter Sellers film that was being shown in English. The film was shown at one end of the long, white-walled room and afterwards 30 club members and their guests moved over to the mahogany bar, with its brass rail, where shop-talk among the company managers and owners has always been banned. We split into two groups, the ladies sitting down and the men crowding at the bar. I had given up alcohol for the duration of the walk, and while I was sipping my lemonade a man in a black suit stepped up close to me and asked, 'Are you the chap walking beside the Ganga?'

'Yes.'

'Well,' he said with a smile, 'you must have done something very, very bad in your previous life to deserve a penance like this.'

Before I could think of a reply, someone else added, 'Yes, but just think, at least he won't be reborn on earth.'

Later that evening I was introduced to Raj and Adarsh Dutt who invited me to spend a few days in their big house overlooking the Ganga in Mirzapur. The previous year, Raj had gone on an arduous hike with other pilgrims to Mount Kailash which, although located in Tibet, is India's holiest mountain. It is believed to be the home of Shiva and to be the actual spot where Ganga comes to earth before she emerges from the mouth of the glacier at Gau Mukh in India. Now Raj and I wanted to team up for a hike up the glacier beyond the source of the Ganga at Gau Mukh and over the 19,510-foot Kalindi Pass to Badrinath, the start of a secondary source of the Ganga. Raj had already collected a small library about the 50-mile trek, including one account of a journey made by six monks and their guide in 1945, equipped with seven pairs of improvised shoes which lasted three hours, two old ropes, one brass cooking pot, one small axe, two pairs of snow goggles and a small quantity of vegetables and dry provisions. One of the monks was naked and the others wore cotton clothes and carried two woollen blankets. We hoped to be better equipped.

Our route would take us within a few miles of the border with Tibet and we would require permission from the Defence Ministry in New Delhi to enter the restricted zone. It would be another four months before I could reach the starting point of this trek and now we could anticipate with relish the mountains and snow while we sat on this utterly flat plain at the start of the hot season.

Mirzapur had been an important trading centre during Mughul times, surpassing even Allahabad, 80 miles upstream, as the most important marketplace on the upper Ganga for cotton, silk yarns, brassware and food grains. A regular paddle-steamer service from Calcutta had been established in 1834, and the 701-mile round journey took three weeks upstream and two down, compared to the three weeks taken by sailing ships to get downstream during the monsoon, and the two months taken in the dry season. The paddle steamers were principally used for freight as passenger fares were expensive. They were much safer from pirates, and the East India Company shipped money to pay wages, government forms, cotton seeds and books (which could be kept dry) to its stations up country. Opium, cakes of indigo dye, silk and shellac were the principal commodities carried to Calcutta.

Mirzapur's merchants founded temples, built *ghats* and became patrons of sculpture to adorn their rich city. But the prosperity faded two years after the Indian Mutiny when, in 1859, the East India Railway from Calcutta reached the military cantonment at Kanpur. This was further up the Ganga, beyond the reach of steamers, and grew into a city of textile mills and tanneries which supplied the army. The steamer service continued but the advent of the railways destroyed Mirzapur's commercial importance. Many of its ornate buildings still stand, but today the town is seedy and crumbling and its atmosphere is far from healthy. At least 500 people were to die of cholera during the hot season after my visit, and thousands of others suffered gastro-enteritis. Doctors blamed the unhygienic conditions and contaminated water supply as the main causes of the outbreak.

Every year, tens of thousands of pilgrims come to Mirzapur during the nine-day festival of Navaratari, which is celebrated in north India by fasting and by visiting temples, though no one could tell me the reason for the festival and the worship was not for any particular deity. Raj, his wife Adarsh, their family priest Panditji and I went out in the car on the eve of the festival to visit several of the temples in the low hills overlooking the river.

'Don't mind if people stare,' said Raj. 'It's the first time they've seen a clean hippie.'

We reached the most important temple at midday, in the middle of the crowded alleys of the town of Vindhyachal. The temple courtyard was already congested and we moved forwards slowly.

'Tomorrow, there'll be ten times what you see here, the next day twenty times and by the end one hundred times,' said Raj, making me glad that we had come early. We pressed through the crowd to a shop where we left our sandals, washed our hands and met the guide who always attends to the Dutt family when they come to Vindhyachal. He was a tall, stout man with a large parrot-like nose who forced his way through the throng with us following close behind him. Just outside the temple doorway, he broke into the long column of other people already waiting. To my surprise men and women stood aside for us to join the line and no one objected.

A short passage, like a cattle-run, led to the temple door, and five girls and a boy sat on the wall waving small fans over our heads in return for a few coins. Adarsh stood in front of me, silent yet obviously excited. Panditji was behind and a large man with a long, white beard stood with impressive calm beside me, impervious to flies, heat and noise. We reached the small doorway after about ten minutes, to be struck in the face by a frigid blast from the air-conditioning unit inside the bare, stone cell. The little temple was divided in two by metal bars, like the turnstile gates of a football stadium. A cluster of brass bells hung from the low ceiling which everyone rang as they approached

Kali, filling the small room with loud, reverberating clangs. Adarsh rang the bell and at last we came before Kali.

The statue of Kali was the size of a large doll and was half hidden beneath red cloth and a mass of colourful flowers, with big silver eyes and a blood-red tongue. She stood in one corner protected by bars from the crush of her devotees and shared her gilt cage with two attendants who were taking worshippers' offerings through the bars as quickly as possible to keep the line of people moving. Our flowers were quickly taken and placed before the goddess, and the coconut we had brought was cracked and a little of its juice offered back to us as *prasad* (food consecrated by gods and eaten by mortals). The rest added to the sticky puddle on the floor. In less than sixty seconds we were outside amid the throng once again and pushing through to walk round the temple to complete our *puja*. Then we were led back to the shop and the *panda* tied red and yellow strings around our right wrists to signify that we had been to the temple.

To an ignorant outsider such as myself, the appearance of the temple, with its crowds, flies, soggy dirt, smells of sweat and rotting flowers and the hurried nature of the *puja* detracted from any sense of worship and holiness. I could not understand the temple worship of Hinduism and found the procedures alien and removed from the serenity of mosque or church. I was quite incapable of sharing the intensity and concentration of Adarsh, who explained to me later, 'When I go to the temple, I don't see what it looks like.'

It was in the temple in Vindhyachal that the Thugs, itinerant religious murderers, used to offer to Kali part of the booty taken from their victims. The Thugs strangled people with a knotted handkerchief and were so expert that victims were usually dead before their body reached the ground. An estimated 30,000 people were murdered each year by the Thugs by the beginning of the nineteenth century. The East India Company, concerned at the number of Indian soldiers killed while on leave, initiated an eradication campaign under William Sleeman in 1830. The Thugs were eliminated within 20 years and Sleeman's methods of rigorous interrogation and detailed intelligence gathering are still cited as examples for police work.

The Thugs' murders were not only inspired by material gain. 'Destruction of life was the first object; the booty was the devotee's earthly reward, granted him by the goddess. The Thugs told [Sleeman] how the first god had taken to himself two colleagues, one to create and one to destroy, hoping thus to maintain a balance in the population of the world. This, though crudely put, is orthodox Hinduism. But finding that the forces of destruction were losing, the goddess Kali . . . came down to earth and taught the Thugs their craft, promising them her special protection,' reported Philip Woodruff in *The Men Who Ruled India*.

Before leaving Mirzapur after a week's stay, I met an extraordinary man whose peculiar hobby was walking on the Ganga. Just before sunset one day, Shri Dwarika Prasad Chaurasia came with his equipment on a bicycle to give a demonstration. He wore white shorts and a shiny red shirt, and tied his bare feet to straps on two polystyrene-like blocks, looking like railway sleepers wrapped in red vinyl. He paused for prayer at the water's edge and stepped onto the river propelled by two bamboo poles which he used like ski sticks. Over 100 people crowded the bank and Raj and I followed him out in a rowing boat. He looked petrified, with his face cast down and legs rigid while paddling himself fifty yards out from the shore with his sticks, their pennants fluttering in the evening breeze. It had taken him nearly a year to master the balancing technique but he still looked as if he might easily fall over. After 20 minutes out on the completely calm water his confidence suddenly soared and he smiled and began riding up and down on the floats, lurching his body from side to side and creating great waves that rocked the rowing boat.

Shri Chaurasia was keen to accompany me to the source of the river but unfortunately he operated a *paan* stall in the market and could not suddenly leave the business. He asked me to visit the stall one evening before leaving, to meet some of his family and friends. When I arrived he ushered me to a specially provided chair and presented me with two apples (a fruit not yet in season), one of the pennants from his poles, with the word 'Shiva' written in gold tinsel, and a beautiful garland of orange and yellow marigolds which he hung around my neck.

'Thank you,' I responded feebly, embarrassed that an ignorant foreigner could be making a journey of such importance to Hindus, a journey which few of them are ever privileged to undertake. In poor Hindi I asked him to accompany me the mile to Raj Dutt's house. We walked through black streets, darkened by yet another power cut. When we arrived at the house I turned to him and said slowly in Hindi, 'Now you have walked with me on the pilgrimage to Gau Mukh.' This idea pleased him greatly and his eyes lit up and his face creased with a big smile.

On leaving Mirzapur, I was back on the Toilet Path, walking along the bottom of the 70-foot cliff of baked earth which martins and swifts had riddled with holes for their nests. The water level of the river was still falling, revealing mudflats and leaving small, shallow lakes which would gradually dry up in the fierce heat of summer. The small lakes attract wading birds such as red-wattled lapwings, who stand at the water's edge calling, 'Pity-to-do-it. Pity-to-do-it,' before gobbling up shellfish and frogs. The water level would continue to fall until the Himalayan snows began to melt in May. It would flood during the monsoon, and the level would steadily go down after October until it reached the low level I was now seeing in March as I walked north towards Allahabad.

By late morning the glare of sunlight and reflection from the white landscape was tiring my eyes even under the shade of the umbrella. The air was hot, dry and completely still. The river water was as smooth as glass and only the twitter of birds and buzz of insects showed that there was any life in this land. Sometimes, the surface of the river would break suddenly as a Gangetic dolphin (*Platanista gangetica*) arched through the water, taking its breath and diving again. At one point the dolphins came so close to the bank that I could hear them gasping for air as they broke the surface.

It was easy, after four months, to maintain a comfortable pace for ten hours each day, holding the umbrella over my head, pausing only to sip water from the two water bottles I now carried and to watch birds on the river. My feet were tough now and my mind dulled by the hours of rhythmic footfall, by the hot, dry air blowing through my nostrils. I walked all day from Mirzapur, wading knee-deep through the water and mud of a stream and following the base of a steep bank. As the shadows lengthened and daylight faded I asked a man in a village the way to the temple, where I intended to ask to sleep the night on the flagstones in the courtyard.

'Sleep on the stone or come to my house, with food and *charpoy*,' said my guide when we stood on the steps of the temple. I quickly accepted his kind invitation and was taken back to the village of Arjunpur.

'My name is Bhagwan Das. I am village *pradhan*—village president.' He was 30 years old and already flecks of grey showed in his close-cropped black hair. He was thin, which made him seem taller, and he liked to twirl the ends of his black moustache when he listened. He fetched water and sweets and we were still sitting on the *charpoy* outside his adobe home when night fell. Six men came to repeat the same questions he had asked me, to look at photographs of my family, friends and home and to share *beedis*.

I did not meet Bhagwan's wife that night though she sat in the shadow of the doorway listening to our conversation. Their six-year-old daughter, Santosh, had no such reservations. She stared at me for a long time when we met then climbed up and sat in my lap without saying a word. She never sat for long but ran off with each photograph to show to her mother. She had been named after one of Hinduism's newest goddesses: Mother Santosh was totally unkown in 1960 and is now said to be the bringer of good luck and material advantage.

Bhagwan asked me to stay another day and I was glad to accept. Despite the linguistic barrier we communicated easily, helped by gestures and by using our eyes.

Soon after sunrise the 'doctor *sahib*' arrived for a chat before starting his rounds and to enquire about the foreign stranger in the house. 'My brother is Doctor D.P. Singh. He lives in America,' he told me. I did not sound sufficiently enthusiastic and so he reiterated time and time again, 'My brother is Doctor D.P. Singh. He lives in America.'

A girl came for an injection and turned away her head and covered her eyes when the needle went in. A woman came next for medicine for a liver infection and she too got an injection. They each paid R5.

We were sitting in the low doorway of a small room, no larger than a double bed, covered by half a carpet and opening onto the main path out of the village. This room was where Bhagwan received visitors. It was the village equivalent of the *durbar* room where maharajahs once received petitioners and visitors amid the splendours of marbles, silks and chandeliers.

When the doctor departed, Bhagwan and I went down to the river to take our baths, joining several haggard old women and bandy-legged old men standing knee-deep in the water offering prayers and oblations to Ganga and to their ancestors alongside a young mother doing her laundry. We swam in the warm water, bathed and rinsed our clothes and then Bhagwan carried back a small pot of Ganga water to sprinkle over the family gods, and over posters of Shiva and Durga while repeating prayers. His devotions concluded with lighting sticks of incense in the visitor's room underneath the pictures of the deities.

Later, trays of *dal*, tomatoes and small balls of freshly-baked bread were served to us in the entrance room of their home by Bhagwan's wife, who hid her face from me with the veil of her orange sari. After the meal, a new audience assembled to question me and inspect my passport and photographs.

'We go on a picnic,' announced Bhagwan when the afternoon heat at last sent our visitors away. We set off on his moped for a short tour of a neighbouring village, stopping to greet the doctor *sahib* who was attending two children with scabies whose sores were a feeding ground for flies. And we stopped at the home of an old man with sons of Bhagwan's age. 'He is like my father,' explained Bhagwan when we were given glasses of sickly sweet sugar-cane juice, that tasted like honey in water.

Towards sunset the water buffaloes were brought home and tethered to pegs outside people's homes. They were given chopped green fodder and women and girls fetched them water in big, tin cans carried on their heads from a canal a quarter of a mile away. Soon it was dark; dark as it can only be miles from electric streetlights, the darkness revealing a sky full of stars crossed by a bright band of the Milky Way, which is the Ganga flowing across heaven. We were joined on the *charpoys* outside by still more questioners. They were already beginning to bore Bhagwan after one day: I told him I had endured this for three months. We sat by the glow of an oil lamp, two or three talking in Hindi and snatches of English, with others listening, smoking *beedis* or passing round a pipe of *ganja*. It was like talking to a row of dark silhouettes, with the moans of cows and water buffaloes in the background. Far above our heads, amid those bright pin-pricks of light in the heavens, India's first man in space was circling the Earth in a Soviet spacecraft. 'Indo-Soviet friendship now soars into space,' claimed Mrs Gandhi. There were no other immediate benefits to India's own space programme and no one on the *charpoys* in Arjunpur made any comment.

At dawn the next morning, Bhagwan asked me to stay longer in Arjunpur, though he had to go to a nearby town all day. I was left to spend a quiet day in the care of Santosh and a neighbouring grandfather who was threshing wheat with his son in the yard in front of their home.

Before the first rays of the morning sun spanned the river, I joined two fishermen in a rowing boat who were checking their night lines. These yellow nylon lines extended out about 100 yards from anchor points along the clay embankment. The fishermen hauled themselves out along each line, drawing it up from the depths to untangle weeds and rebait the hooks with morsels of shellfish. Four boats were out checking lines but no one had a good catch that day.

Across the river, a man was standing on a big bamboo structure built in the shallows to catch sardine-like fish in a large net spread flat across two booms. When he took his weight off the booms, the net sank into the shallow water. Fifteen minutes later, he stood back on the boom and the net lifted out of the water, trapping the small fish, which he then transferred to the beach to die and dry in the sunshine.

Fish yields are declining in the Ganga, I was told, because of increasing chemical pollution from industry and agriculture and from the practice of some villagers who dynamite the river for fish, though they collect only a small portion of their carnage. I never witnessed this last technique.

In the cool of early morning the wheat harvest was in full swing with men and women cutting the straw with hand-held sickles and bundling stooks to be taken home at nightfall. Threshing was usually done on the yard in front of each house or on the edge of villages on an area about 30 feet in diameter. This was first cleared and levelled, then plastered with a mixture of mud and cow dung which baked in the sun like concrete. The stooks were threshed on this floor by bullocks or young bulls treading round and round and breaking down the straw with their hooves. Santosh's neighbours were threshing in this way from mid-afternoon onwards, keeping their pair of young bulls tramping round and round until the straw was broken like dry noodles.

Although the use of mechanical threshing machines is increasing, no one in Arjunpur had yet bought or leased one and the harvest was gathered by people and cattle working side by side. It was no wonder, therefore, that cows were so revered. In addition to working the land and threshing grain, they gave milk and dung and transported people and produce to market. Mahatma Gandhi is reported to have commented that as soon as a tractor could do all these jobs and eat only grass he would be sympathetic to the need for tractors in the villages. Watching men and women working and living day after day with their animals, other more vicious and hurtful words of Gandhi came to mind:

> The more I penetrate the village, the greater is the shock delivered as I perceive the blank stare in the eyes of the villagers I meet. Having nothing else to do but to work as labourers side by side with their bullocks they have become almost like them.

When the cattle have trodden down the straw, the wheat must be winnowed by hand. Over and over, men and women raise up baskets of the chop, pouring it into the afternoon breeze so that the grain falls in one heap and the straw and chaff are blown into another. It is in this way that India's 1550 million bushels of wheat are harvested. The wheat harvest in March and April is sold for money for fertiliser, taxes, implements and all household spending, otherwise it is stored to feed the family or to reseed the fields next year, after the rice is harvested in October.

Fortunately, neither Santosh nor I were needed for the tedious and tiring work and we sat on a *charpoy* in the shade near where the two men were working, amicably playing a game that Santosh was trying to teach me. We chattered while playing, she in Hindi and I in English. Neither of us fully understood what the other was saying but the time passed with lots of laughter.

'Look! Look!' she would insist, her big grin revealing the two gaps in her front teeth and her eyes observing me through long, black lashes. The idea was to throw up one stone, snatch another from a small pile and catch the falling stone, and to repeat this with all the pebbles in the small pile. Santosh's hand, its fingernails decorated with red varnish, demonstrated again and again how it was done, until I eventually got it right. She would giggle, nodding her head and shaking her brass earrings. I was a slow learner and inept, and the grandfather, taking a rest from the threshing, sympathetically handed me *beedis*.

Bhagwan returned from the town late in the afternoon and we took a walk round his village. He held out his arm to hold my hand and we walked together in the warm light of evening through Arjunpur, where families lived in full view of their neighbours in contrast to the high walled yards that darken the villages of Bihar.

I cannot tell whether Bhagwan was a good or bad village president, but wherever we went he was greeted with relaxed smiles and *beedis*, suggesting at least that he was popular. No man kept four or six feet away from us, as they had in other villages when I walked with someone important. They came close and I gained the impression that they bowed to him in greeting because he held their respect. There was none of the sickening servitude and cowering which so often accompanied my walks in other villages with members of the rural elite—landlords, moneylenders, doctors and government officials. It is these people who reap the most benefits from government development projects, agricultural projects, new jobs and business opportunities and who divert improvement schemes (such as drilling tubewells) to their own use. But it was these same people—speaking a little English and holding the power in each community—who so generously offered me places to sleep, food to eat, and clean, cool water to drink.

Bhagwan led me, with considerable pride, into a long, dark barn built of adobe to show me a large flour mill, an oil press and a rice husking machine. They were all connected by drive belts to a big electric motor. A crowd of men darkened the doorway, proud of what was being shown, and eager to see my reaction. I was certainly impressed, and cursed the lack of Hindi which made me unable to understand fully what Bhagwan was telling me or to ask questions. I could not be sure whether the barn was owned by Bhagwan's family or by a village co-operative, though I believe it was the latter. It benefits the village as it means no more hauling sacks of wheat or rice or mustard seed into the nearest town to be processed, then carrying them home again. They need no longer pay another man to do work which they could easily do for themselves; nor risk being given short measures by the flour millers or the oil pressers. They could now retain the wheat germ and oil cake, previously the perquisite of the miller and oil presser, which could now be added to people's food or given to cattle in the village.

After our tour we went down to the river and were taken out in a rowing boat. A shaft of white gold sunlight stretched across the glistening water and the warm light from the declining sun transformed the river bank of clay into the richest orange. A dolphin arched through the surface of the water, took its breath and dived again, leaving ever-widening ripples breaking the calm. Flocks of green parakeets flew in lines over our heads to trees on the opposite shore. The air was cool and still. Only the water dripping from the boatman's paddle broke the silence of our journey.

I left Arjunpur soon after sunrise the next morning, after many farewells and a cup of coffee spiced with peppercorns to give it a kick against the cool air. At the next village I was stopped by a young man insisting I drink a glass of warm, sweetened milk before going on my way.

The course of the river turned sharply north after Arjunpur. I followed its route along a path at the edge of the bank through fields of *dal* bushes that were being cut down by men wielding meat cleavers, and passed the big metal pipes that raised irrigation water up the bank from the river into a new canal. I stopped several times during the day to refill my water bottles from buckets drawn up from brick-lined, open wells. I had not seen any tubewells since Benares and could only hope these open wells were not contaminated.

The lane between the brown walls of people's small homes was deserted and silent when I entered a village in the heat of the next afternoon. It was the time of day when my mouth felt full of dry grit and my mind was most dozy. I had slept the night on a stone slab outside someone's house in a small town, having walked 25 miles west and north from Arjunpur. Now, coming into a small square, partly shaded by a tree, I found a dozen children gathered round the bicycle of a man selling orange ice lollipops from a wooden box. Each lollipop cost 10 paise and eagerly I bought two. Children who had no coins brought small bowls of *dal* or mustard seed to barter, and the man would empty these into a shopping bag hung over the bicycle handlebars. Two little boys came running holding a bowl of something between them, but the man looked at their offering and shook his head. The two brothers stood dejectedly together, head down and silent.

'Go to the shop,' suggested the lollipop man.

They went off slowly, without a word, but moments later came rushing back happily, each holding out a 10-paise coin. In no time, both boys were licking big, orange lollipops and the seller seemed as delighted by the successful transaction as they were.

There were, however, two boys and a girl apparently with no money and nothing to offer in exchange for the treat which the children around them were eagerly enjoying. Their clothes were ragged and

grey and they could not hope to buy anything, but when the bugle of a
lollipop man had sounded they had come anyway and were now
standing dry-mouthed with the other children. Perhaps they hoped to
be given bits of broken lollipops from the bottom of the wooden box
on the bicycle. Perhaps they hoped a stranger also with a dry throat
would venture into their village and perhaps they hoped the stranger
would buy them each a lollipop. And when the stranger did do this,
then their wide eyes, their enormous grins and eager sucking was the
best damn sight that stranger had seen in months of walking.

Too often, I had heard people talking loosely of India's noble
poverty, her unconcern with crass material life and her superiority in
matters spiritual. Such people have never stood beside three children
who cannot buy lollipops.

Despite the steadily rising temperature and the glare of sunlight I still
found great pleasure in walking hour after hour along paths beside
swaying fields of wheat at the edge of the steep river bank, or over
beaches of white and purple sands and baked mudflats. I kept away
from villages as much as possible now, detouring around them,
preferring a route well away from habitation. I was enjoying my
solitude and was weary of answering questions, especially as people
did not always listen to the answers. However, although I enjoyed
being alone with my thoughts day after day I was aware that this
solitude could easily turn into loneliness.

I was looking forward to reaching the wild parts along the river,
away from the procession of villages and cultivated fields which I had
been following for months. I longed for the sandbanks and thickets of
tall grasses that grew further on. The impact of India's ever-increasing
population on the land has been considerable. Almost every piece of
land is cultivated, and beaches and temporary islands are marked out
and planted annually with melons and squashes when the flood waters
subside. Tigers, crocodiles and other wild animals have now almost
vanished, fish stocks are diminished and the huge flocks of geese and
ducks once said to have congregated along the Ganga have vanished.
One is left with migratory tufted pochards, a few lapwings, black
jungle crows, noisy and colourful parakeets, egrets and sparrows. My
heart soared when even a trio of white-necked storks flew leisurely
overhead, their big, black bodies and bright red legs the only colours in
an otherwise washed-out sky.

'Is it Cholera?'

I entered the grand city of Allahabad two days after leaving Bhagwan and his family. The Jumna river joins the Ganga here and I crossed the red steel bridge behind two ambling cows, passed by lines of trucks and cars while freight trains trundled overhead shaking every girder. After several attempts, I found a hotel that would take me, though it turned out to be the dirtiest place I stayed in on the journey. It took two hours just to have the room swept of debris from previous guests, the dirty bedding taken away and clean sheets provided. The floors of the communal showers were covered in gritty dirt and spat-out *paan*. The taps, at waist height, did have water but the fitting was electrified, which made taking a shower rather unpleasant. Even the basin outside the toilets gave water with a zap! And when I cleaned my teeth I discovered the basin was not connected to the drain and my spittle dripped onto my feet. Downstairs, in the expensive, air-conditioned restaurant, I ordered 'half a chicken' as a treat and was served with one dried-out wing and one dried-out leg. I did not send it back, nor call furiously for the manager, both because I was too tired and because I knew it would do no good.

One morning, as the first light was showing above the rooftops in the eastern sky I took a ride in a cycle rickshaw to the sangam, where the Ganga and Jumna rivers converge. A third river, the Saraswati, is also said to meet here but this is a spiritual flow, invisible to people with the 'vulgar' eye. Platforms of bamboo have been built in the water at the confluence so that pilgrims can bathe exactly where the emerald waters of the Jumna, coming from the right, merge with the thick, grey Ganga.

'Those who bathe at the confluence of the white and black rivers— the Ganga and Jumna—go to heaven; those of firm mind who give up their bodies here, attain immortality,' states the oldest scripture of Hinduism, the *Rig-Veda*.

Almost a million people congregate here every twelve years when Jupiter is in Taurus in late January or early February for the Kumbh

Mela. These mammoth fairs (or *melas*) are held in turn in three other cities every three years: at Hardwar (also on the Ganga), Nasik (near Bombay) and Ujjain (in central India). The four sites are said to be where drops from the pot of nectar (or *kumbh*), which gives immortality, fell when the deity carrying the pot was chased across the countryside. The self-control of the enormous crowds that gather for these festivals is astonishing and it is hard to imagine a million people camping together for several days in Europe or North America without incidents of violence and theft.

I was too sleepy, too lazy and too indifferent to be bothered bathing at the confluence of the rivers and was content with a short boat ride to the wavy line where the waters of the Ganga and the Jumna swirl together. I went back across the half-mile beach, up past the red fort that once commanded the confluence and across the open ground where people camp during the *melas*. It was here that the government of the East India Company formally ended and the British Raj began on November 1st, 1858, when Lord Canning read out the proclamation of Queen Victoria promising tolerance, justice and impartial administration by Her Majesty's Government. A commemorative stone pillar marks the site but all inscriptions have been removed.

The old family home of the Nehrus stands a mile from this site at what used to be 1, Church Road. This family of Brahmins, originally from Kashmir, was among the leaders of the Congress Party which forced the end of the British Raj in 1947. Both Jawaharlal Nehru, India's first prime minister and Gandhi's protégé, and his daughter, the late Mrs Gandhi, were brought up in this house. The big house, called Anand Bhawan (meaning Abode of Happiness), was given to the nation by Mrs Gandhi, and is now unmistakably the Nehru museum and a shrine receiving the homage of devotees. The building, of grey and cream stone, and the gardens of beautiful roses are impeccably maintained. The house has wide verandahs on both floors, reminiscent of the decks of a battleship. It was bought and renovated in 1900 by Jawaharlal's father, Motilal Nehru, with the profits from his lucrative law practice at the Allahabad High Court, being the first house in the city to have a swimming pool, electricity and piped water.

People from all over the country come to see these sacrosanct rooms, to stand behind the polished glass panel in Jawaharlal's bedroom-cum-sitting room on the first floor, where fresh flowers are put each morning on his writing desk and where a vacuum flask of water stands on the bedside table. It was as much in Anand Bhavan as in England and during years in jail while working for the Congress that he developed and expounded the philosophies and policies by which he believed his country should live and thrive.

Nehru called for India to lessen her religiosity and to break with, 'all the dust and dirt of ages that have covered her up and hidden her inner beauty and significance, the excrescences and abortions that have twisted and petrified her spirit, set it in rigid frames and stunted her growth. Today she swings between a blind adherence to her old customs and a slavish imitation of foreign ways. In neither of these can she find relief or life or growth.'

Six years before his death in 1964, Nehru wrote his testament, in which he asked that after cremation, 'a handful of my ashes be thrown into the Ganga at Allahabad to be carried to the great ocean that washes India's shore'. Nehru was an agnostic who advocated the scientific approach; 'the reliance on observed fact and not on pre-conceived theory', and he wrote that his wish had no religious significance. He stated, 'with all earnestness', that he did not want any religious ceremonies performed for him after his death, though the wish was ignored. He said his request for his ashes to be scattered on the Ganga was an expression not of piety, but of love for the river and for his motherland.

I have been attached to the Ganga and Jumna rivers in Allahabad ever since my childhood and as I have grown older, this attachment has also grown. I have watched their varying moods as the seasons changed, and have often thought of the mystery and myth and tradition and song and story that have become attached to them through the long ages and become part of their flowing waters.

The Ganga, especially, is the river of India beloved of her people, round which are intertwined her racial memories, her hopes and fears, her songs of triumph, her victories and her defeats. She has been a symbol of India's age-long culture and civilization, ever-changing, ever-flowing, and yet ever the same Ganga. She reminds me of the snow covered peaks and the deep valleys of the Himalayas, which I have loved so much, and of the rich and vast plains below, where my life and work have been cast. Smiling and dancing in the morning sunlight, and dark and gloomy and full of history as the evening shadows fall, a narrow, slow and graceful stream in winter and a vast roaring thing during the monsoon, broad-bosomed almost as the sea and with something of the sea's power to destroy, the Ganga has been to me a symbol and a memory of the past of India, running into the present and flowing on to the great ocean of the future.

The major portion of his ashes was to be sprinkled from an aeroplane, 'over the fields where the peasants of India toil, so that my ashes might mingle with the dust and soil of India and become an indistinguishable part of India.'

The gusts of dust, the enervating heat—these were increasing day by day and, frankly, I would have been happy if Allahabad had marked the end of my journey and if this had been the source of the Ganga. However, it was not. I had walked about 800 miles and was only at the halfway mark in my journey.

I intended to leave the city early on April 19th, after only a few days, so I went for a supper of Western food the night before departure as a foolish treat. I ordered fried liver and onions in a smart restaurant but forgot to ask that the spices be left out. The meal, cooked according to the Western recipe, came covered in a thick sauce of hot chillies.

Back in the hotel room, I attended to a big boil or septic insect bite on my left thigh which had swollen rapidly in the hot and sweaty conditions and was making walking uncomfortable. The swelling eventually subsided, after several days' treatment, leaving a hole in my leg the diameter of a pencil and half an inch deep. Thereafter I took particular care to keep it covered from flies.

The electricity cut out at least three times, stopping ceiling fans, during this last night in the city. Fortunately, the awful hotel did have its own generator which came noisily to life as soon as the nightwatchman could rouse himself. The night was hot and oppressive even with a ceiling fan stirring the warm breeze, and I became more and more agitated until every mosquito bite that I had ever had seemed to have come to life again across my back, shoulders and down both arms. I could not resist scratching, thus making the itching worse. After an exasperating hour of trying to sleep on the hot mattress, I went for a cold shower to chill the itching, and discovered, in the mirror of the shower room, that I had been bitten by fleas more than forty times. After a thorough wash under the cool shower, I went back to the room, threw off the 'clean' bed sheets and finally fell asleep on the bare mattress.

I was therefore happy to leave Allahabad as soon as the first crack of orange light appeared in the sky and even before the birds began their dawn chorus. The air was cool and it was, as always, the best time of the day to be walking. My knapsack was weighed down by four litres of water and seemed particularly heavy that day, and my bites still irritated. The road out of the city went past the long, sandstone pillars and wide verandahs of the Allahabad High Court where Motilal Nehru had practised so many years before. It was deserted at this early hour, when even rickshaw-*wallahs* were asleep, curled up on the benches of their rickshaws. Seven weeks later I was to read a report of the Allahabad High Court releasing a man who had been in prison for 35 years without being brought to trial. He was not the first nor the last, nor did the story rate much attention in the *Indian Express*.

By seven o'clock the sun was already strong, though it had barely risen above the horizon and my shadow stretched 20 feet across the

Grand Trunk Road. I was going to follow the road again, until I was well clear of the industries outside the city. How glad I was now to be facing north-west with the sun always at my back. It was simple walking on the main road, despite the roar and fumes of trucks, and my feet moved automatically at a gentle pace of two and a half miles per hour, which I could maintain easily for ten hours.

The sun climbed higher in the white sky, the black shadows shortened and traffic lessened until I seemed to be the only person out on the road. I halted at the roadside beneath a large tree and made myself a salad of onions, tomatoes, radishes and a carrot, and dribbled a little lemon juice over the top. I had bought four boiled eggs in Allahabad the night before and had kept them as cool as possible. Now, in the midday heat of over 110°F one of them smelt bad, but foolishly I ate the other three. It was not for another two or three hours that I began to feel sick.

In the meantime, it was swarming with flies under the shade of the roadside tree. When ants from the base of the tree began crawling over me as well, I retreated to the stone steps of a disused well that was fortunately still shaded by the overhang of the tree. The meal of salad and eggs had not been adequate, and after another hour I mixed up a bowl of cornflakes and powered milk with chopped dates, all luxury items bought in the big city. The mixture tasted awful but it was something to munch while waiting out the heat of the day and it made a change from spiced foods. In the weeks ahead, I was to become totally inured to the vile flavour of cereals and powdered milk.

I started walking again when I heard the call to prayer from the mosque of a nearby village and I walked for a few miles then sat down at the roadside to sip warm water from the bottles. As soon as I did so I knew that I did not feel well; in fact that I felt very unwell. My stomach ached and I wanted to vomit. I sat for a long time, my head between my knees, with sweat trickling down my face and back, almost oblivious to the occasional truck passing on the road. I did, however, notice a squirrel with four stripes along its back come down a tree, skip across the road and climb up another tree. A truck approached just as the squirrel came back down the trunk. They met in the middle of the road and the vehicle ran over the animal's back legs with a loud crack. The squirrel tried and failed to drag itself away. I looked round for a rock and knelt down in the middle of the road beside the struggling creature. I brought the rock down on the squirrel's head with as much force as I could, and though its left eye popped out I believe it died instantly. I struck again to be sure it was dead, then retreated to the shade and was promptly sick. I sat dazed and weak for ten minutes or half an hour, then got to my feet and paced up the hill to an open well near some houses. The water was cool and I sipped it slowly, only to be sick again, but I continued to drink in order to rinse out my stomach and to have something to retch on.

I did not get more than a few yards from the well before being brought to my knees again by the roadside and vomiting again, this time with so much pain that I thought my chest was about to split open.

'Are you sick?' asked one of four students on bicycles who stopped when they saw me kneeling by the side of the road.

I nodded. I wanted only to sip water and to sleep but was too weak to argue when the students insisted I ride on the parcel rack of one of their bicycles to the next village, where there was a rudimentary clinic.

'Have you cholera?' asked the student, pedalling hard to maintain our balance.

'No, food not good,' I whispered with my eyes closed and the wobbling bicycle making me feel giddy.

The clinic was housed in the single room of an adobe building and I was grateful to the men, women and children already filling the room who allowed me to jump the queue. The doctor felt my pulse in both wrists and I explained in English what had happened.

'Is it cholera?' asked my chauffeur eagerly. 'This is the season,' he said helpfully.

The doctor shook his head and seemed to agree with the diagnosis of food poisoning. He refused payment for his examination and I asked for somewhere to lie down and for drinking water. A *charpoy* was placed outside the clinic and the doctor sent out some glucose to mix with the glasses of cool water. I offered again to pay for the glucose and the doctor refused. 'For glucose,' I said and handed him R5.

'For glucose,' he said, and handed back R4.

I drank the glucose and water and slept until after sunset.

'What do you want?' asked the cholera enthusiast, who had been watching over me.

'Water and sleep,' I said. Fresh, cool water was fetched for me to drink and to wash my dusty feet and hands.

'You need more?'

I shook my head.

'Then I will go,' he said, having already waited several hours. He never told me his name.

It was dark when I woke again. The doctor was just finishing his clinic and the two shops next door were putting up their shutters. The doctor took me across the road to a house where I could sleep and the family set up a *charpoy* for me fifteen feet outside their front yard, although they took my bags inside.

'You are Hindu or Moslem?' asked my middle-aged host who stood surrounded by a group of his children. I believe he was confused by the green-check *lungi* I was still wearing. Green check was the sign of a Moslem, I had been told.

'Christian,' I said, adding that I had the Qu'ran in English in my home.

'What is your caste?'

'No caste. In my country, all men one man.'

He handed me a *beedi* and asked me to sleep with the men of the family within the boundary of their front yard.

I slept soundly throughout the night unmolested by mosquitoes. Could the heat have killed them, I hoped? I woke at first light to find my host already sitting cross-legged on a *charpoy* reading the Qu'ran. I explained I was making a pilgrimage by foot and that I would therefore have to go back along the road to where the students had given me the ride by bicycle the previous afternoon. It sounded daft in Hindi or English, but I was still determined to walk every inch of the way, not wanting to feel later that I had skipped even one step and thus cut the continuous thread of the pilgrimage. I walked back, cured now, the two miles to where I had been sick, while the sun rose like a big, golden medallion and the grey smoke of household fires lay like a mist across the countryside in the cool morning air.

Two days later I reached a *dhaba* at noon where I ate a delicious meal. I had left the Grand Trunk Road at dawn the day before but had not yet rejoined the river. I was not entirely sure where I was but had just kept walking. I had asked people, but the place names they gave were not marked on the map. However, I knew that if I headed north-north-west I must eventually rejoin Mother Ganga. I spent the afternoon writing letters and drinking *lassis*, the most refreshing hot weather drink made of yoghurt, water, sugar and ice. Throughout the afternoon a boy washed down the wooden tables of the *dhaba* to discourage the flies. Despite the ubiquitous clouds of them, I never once saw anyone in India kill a fly. Many times I asked the reason for this and was usually told that it was in accordance with non-violence, but I could hardly credit such an explanation. My mind was soon working out ways to rid India of this affliction and health hazard. If everyone killed ten flies every day (easily done, given the swarms) that would be seven thousand million fewer flies every day and that would surely reduce disease and sickness. Heat can do strange things to the human mind!

The *loo* winds signalled a change in the day and a decline in the ferocity of the sun. When I left the *dhaba* after another glass of *lassi* gusts of hot dust were already swirling in the air. Almost at once I was hailed by an insistent group of young men who wanted to ask me some questions. Just as I was about to leave them and was already out in the street, we saw a huge dust-storm advancing towards us.

'Here, here,' called a portly man from the compound of a flour mill across the street.

No sooner was everyone safely under the tin roof of the verandah than the fury of the wind was upon us, darkening the sky, knocking over sheets of tin, blocking out the sun and blinding us with so much dust that we might have been standing under the exhaust flue of the flour mill. These squalls pass as suddenly as they come, leaving people and animals dazed. When I went out into the street to try to leave a second time, the whirlwind returned, and before it was gone rain began to fall, gently at first, then with such violence that the ground quickly became a lake and mud splattered up the walls of the compound.

The downpour continued with thunder and lightning, clattering on the tin roof, for an hour. Afterwards the air was cool and marvellously clear but there was little time to enjoy it before it began to rain again, and lightning flashed weirdly across the brilliant orange sunset. So I was happy to accept the miller's invitation to stay the night.

I am not an early riser by inclination but during these weeks of overwhelming heat it was best to be walking during the three coolest hours of the day—from 4.30 a.m. until sunrise. After another early start from the flour miller's house I finally came to the bank of the Ganga and sat down once again among the exposed roots of a large banyan tree overlooking the water. I mixed up my breakfast of powdered milk, dates and cornflakes while listening to the cries of wild peacocks on the bank behind me. There were no people or houses in sight and I was content to be alone with the river.

People frequently thought it peculiar that I was travelling alone, though solitary *sadhus* are not uncommon. 'Are you alone? Only one?' people asked repeatedly with disbelief. 'Where is your wife? Where is your friend?' That I should want to be alone was extraordinary.

The channel of soupy, grey water was about 600 yards wide and a mile of grey sands stretched out in static waves beyond that to a blurred line of trees far away. Thick, grey clouds darkened the sky but shafts of white light glittered on the surface of the river. Long peals of thunder still growled in the eastern sky. I expected another storm and was reluctant to move from under the shelter of the banyan tree.

The storm never came and I continued along the bottom of the river bank beside the quiet water, thankful for the shade which the dark clouds provided. Later I waded a small stream and walked on the top of the bank, across undulating land of hollows and sudden ravines thick with elephant grass and, I was convinced, overpopulated with snakes. The straps of both sandals broke during the morning and I had to tie them to my feet with bandages. The dark clouds vanished after two short rain showers, revealing the sun again in all its merciless oppression.

At noon, two young men called me up the river bank to the brick verandah of their bungalow to answer questions. I resented being thus summoned to satisfy people's curiosity. However, on this particular day I later had good cause to be glad that I gave my answers cheerfully. A mile after leaving the village, while looking for a shady spot to have my lunch and take a swim, I was approached by two men who had followed me out from the village.

While one of the duo stayed silent, the other shouted questions in my face: 'Where have you come from? Where are you going?' A few minutes later his wrath turned on a boy who came along the footpath. In no time, this boy was bullied into squatting on the ground clutching his ears with his hands, doing what is called 'the chicken', imposed to humiliate. He was allowed to go only after he had started to cry. The bully then turned on me.

'Where is your revolver?' he demanded,

'I don't have a revolver,' I said quietly.

'Take a *beedi*!' His companion lit three and handed them round. 'Where is your revolver?' asked the bully, reaching out and tugging suddenly at my waist, where I wore the belt containing passport and money beneath my *lungi*. 'Let me see! Let me see!'

'No,' I said calmly and told him not to shout.

His silent companion stood up and put on his sandals to go, but the interrogation continued and he sat down again on the grass.

'Give me thousand rupees.'

'I don't have rupees.'

'Yes, yes. Give me, give me. Where is your revolver?' This tirade, punctuated by his finger prodding my shoulder, went on for about twenty minutes. An air of menace was building up, and I expected that I might soon be robbed. Every question was accompanied by the bully pointing to my knapsack, and his demands to see inside by his prodding my shoulder and staring into my eyes.

'You are my brother,' he said suddenly and gently, but I knew this gambit. It was always a preface to a demand for gifts. I remained silent.

'Give me a gift.'

I feigned not to understand.

'Give me sunglasses.'

I was wondering how best to escape this situation. The bully prodded me once more in the shoulder and my anger boiled over. I snatched up my bag and umbrella in such fury that the two men just stared. I walked away quickly shouting in Hindi and English for them both to get lost! But just at that moment two men and a boy came along the footpath from behind and called a greeting to me. Having no wish to alienate these newcomers, I stopped to greet them courteously, then burst again into an angry mixture of Hindi and English. 'You tell these men to go. No good. No good. Go away. Go away,' I shouted. It didn't work and I found myself sitting down with the whole group answering questions again. I was becoming quite desperate when ten minutes later, another man and a youth arrived and the bully cast down his eyes. I knew the cavalry had arrived. The man asked who I was and, after hearing my explanation, handed me my umbrella and told me to go. I did this willingly and swiftly.

The two men and boy were also sent on their way and caught up with me a quarter of a mile along the footpath. In a rush of Hindi, which I hardly understood, they told me how close I had come to being robbed and probably having my throat cut. They had come to protect me, they said. We walked in single file on the footpath while the saga of the afternoon was excitedly told and retold. I think I understood that the man with the youth had been a policeman who had come out from the village when he'd seen the two bad characters following me.

The heroic story was repeated during the afternoon in every village when we stopped at tubewells to drink water. All afternoon we trekked along a dusty path and I was increasingly curious about the identities of my three companions and what was inside the bundle carried by one of them on a stick over his shoulder. It was not food or firewood. They seemed to have been to every city in the country and were obviously accustomed to being away from their village. The boy was the clown of the trio; a chatterbox dressed in black bell-bottom trousers, orange shirt and black winkle-picker shoes decorated with brass studs, he would break into snatches of song then fall head over heels in the dust when he didn't look where he was going.

When the afternoon breeze was rustling through fronds of palm trees and golden stands of ripe wheat we sat in a field for a rest and a pipe of *ganja*. I was still trying to guess what was in the basket when one of the men untied the cloth covering it and took off the lid. A cobra reared its head, spreading out its hood and flicking its tongue to detect the flavour of our company. A second cobra in the basket was prodded into activity and while the boy played his flute the men posed for a photograph. It was then necessary to pay and I emptied my pocket and handed over the contents—R1-50. But my companions had their eyes on my plastic water bottles so I gave them one, pointing out that it had a leak, which they said they could repair.

In turn, the men presented me with a dried berry, dusted with red powder, wrapped in a piece of newspaper. I was unsure whether it was to prevent snakes from biting me or whether it was an antidote which I hoped I would never have to use. Though almost treading on snakes a few times I was never bitten so perhaps the preventative was effective.

After smoking more *ganja*, we continued on the path and a mile later the snake charmers were called to a home, either to perform or to remove snakes from the premises, and I walked on alone.

A golden light was shining over the wheat fields but the breeze had already petered out and soon the sun would set and it would be dark. I was between villages and did not know where I might sleep the night. I kept walking, sure that something would turn up, even if it meant sleeping in a secluded spot in a wheat field.

At length, the footpath passed in front of a small woodlot and I saw a white-bearded man in orange clothes walking among the trees. I went and asked if I could sleep the night outside the little, whitewashed temple and explained my journey. But I had a strange feeling that he already knew why I had come. He led me to a tin-roofed shed and fetched a *charpoy*, quilt and a bucket of fresh water from the well, enabling me to drink and to wash my feet.

He asked if I had food and, sitting cross-legged on a *charpoy*, in an orange jockstrap, pink pullover and scarf, watched me eat a bowl of powdered milk and puffed rice. His thick, white beard reached to his waist and his white hair spilled over his shoulders. I felt very insignificant in his presence and wished I could be more receptive to his wisdom, but I was preoccupied with the need to survive the heat and to get on with my journey.

As usual I set off early next morning, aware that I smelled bad, having not taken a bath in the river for three days, nor washed my clothes, because I had never found a quiet place at the right time of day. The shoulders and the back of the *kurta* were darkly stained with sweat and dust and I felt thoroughly grubby. It was midday before I found a secluded place to bathe, at the side of a ruined village which had probably been abandoned because the river bank had been badly eroded. I plunged into the Ganga in my blue underpants and sat alone waist deep in warm water for a long time looking across monotonous miles of beige sand.

In this part of Uttar Pradesh there is a serious shortage of wood for burning and many Hindus cannot afford to cremate their dead completely. Instead, a symbolic hot coal may be placed in the mouth of the corpse and after prayers the body pushed into the Ganga. The corpses often get stranded on sandbanks in the dry weather, when the water flows at little more than one mile per hour, and attract vultures and dogs. I had already passed a legless torso and several skulls. Now, about 200 yards from where I was enjoying my bath, I saw a dog tearing at a body while two others waited their turn and a dozen vultures waited to take over from them. The spot where I was swimming seemed quite clean although it was only about ten miles downstream of Kanpur, a big industrial city that uses the holy Ganga as a sewer.

My lunch consisted of tinned cheese, powdered milk and puffed rice. This was insufficient for serious walking but I lacked the energy to buy, carry and cook proper meals and the toleration to answer the questions encountered when I halted to buy cooked food, which was rarely available in this area.

Kanpur is a little less than 1000 miles from the Bay of Bengal, and 600 miles from the source of the Ganga. It was about 10 p.m. on April 24th when I wandered down the wide market street looking for an inexpensive hotel, exhausted after 14 hours of walking. One hotel was charging an extortionate R170 per night and the proprietors of two others glanced at my dirty, holey *kurta* and *lungi*, and told me their hotels were full. I ended up in a dingy hotel almost as dirty as myself and, after a quick meal, fell asleep the instant my body touched the bed.

It was very late the next morning when I woke and peeled off my filthy clothes. Then I washed myself twice. I carried a white *kurta* and pyjama trousers to wear as 'Sunday Best' clothes and though they were creased from the bottom of my knapsack I changed into them and went out for breakfast.

Geoffrey Seager had kindly given me an introduction to the Dutta family who lived in the Kanpur civil lines, where the British had lived in big bungalows amid wide, lush lawns. Dr Dutta was superintendent of the MacRobert Hospital and Mrs Dutta was the representative to British residents in Uttar Pradesh of the British High Commissioner. Shortly before lunch, with my hair washed and neatly combed, and wearing my smartest clothes, I walked up the drive and entered the MacRobert Hospital.

Mrs Marjorie Dutta was sitting at a desk in the wide entrance hall and immediately invited me to stay.

'We'll get you settled in before lunch,' she said. 'You can have a bath and change into some clean clothes.'

I nodded my head and smiled, for I was wearing my only clean clothes. 'Yes, of course.'

11

Burden of Heat

The quiet seclusion of the Dutta household was wonderful, and my only forays out into the heat were to walk to the post office to collect my mail or to go on outings by car with Mrs Dutta. Kanpur is unremarkable but we visited All Souls Church, built in Romanesque style in pink stone to commemorate the Europeans killed during the Mutiny of 1857. According to Mrs Dutta, the church was originally intended for a site in Tuscany but had been built in this city of textile mills and stinking leather tanneries because of bureaucratic error.

The Duttas provided western delicacies such as fish and chips, cold, purified water and luxurious cigars, which I smoked on the verandah with Dr Dutta, revelling in the first stimulating conversations I had had for months. Unfortunately, I contracted amoebic dysentery, which was not at all uncommon in the hot season. There were already reports of cholera and hepatitis outbreaks in Kanpur, and Dr Dutta sent me back to bed with a course of tablets and a flask of cold water. The course of drugs was to last five days but I felt better almost immediately. The terrific heat outside was increasing every day and I was eager therefore to keep moving, so Mrs Dutta and her son Robin flagged me off from the garden gate after breakfast of cornflakes with sliced banana, boiled egg, toast with strawberry jam and coffee. It was 8.30 a.m. but already so hot and bright that it felt like noon.

I knew that the next 350 miles up to Hardwar would be the most gruelling and difficult of the whole journey; it was now the heart of the dry season with its searing, lifeless heat and blinding light. It was, of course, wanton madness to think of walking across a dead land of abandoned fields and silent villages, but I wanted to get on with this journey and was now eager for it to be over.

I walked north from Kanpur along a narrow road near the river bank and stopped for lunch when my feet were walking on the shadow of my neck. My appetite was small but I munched through the *parathas* and potato *subzee* which the Duttas had generously provided and drank the last of the filtered, boiled water from their household.

It was unpleasant to sit in silence in the shade of a tree with ants crawling up my arms and legs, and flies always buzzing round my feet and face. It was no respite to sit for two hours or more without ever a whisper of a breeze, surrounded by motionless shadows of yellow grass, waiting for the passage of the sun overhead. I would have much preferred to have walked on without stopping, but to have been out in this midday sun, even under an umbrella, would have required more lunacy than even I possessed.

I had emptied both my water bottles before the hour when it was safe to move again into the open, so I sat, half-asleep, thinking longingly of the cold water so freely available from the Dutta's refrigerator. The *loo* wind in the afternoon was much too strong for the umbrella so I wrapped my towel around my head like a turban and was careful to cover both ears, as Professor Varma my Hindi tutor in far-away Calcutta had warned me. The towel was lime-yellow with two bright bands of orange and I was an odd spectacle. One man even saluted me when we met on the footpath and I could only presume he was mistaking me for a holy man or member of some Sikh sect. Perhaps he wasn't sure what I was, but thought it best to show respect. I had no idea where I might sleep that night, but kept walking and towards sunset a group of men weighing mustard seed called me from the footpath.

I was welcomed by Noushad Ali, a Moslem in his early thirties with shoulder length hair, cheering smile and discoloured teeth. He was overseeing the weighing and division of the tiny purplish seeds between himself, as landowner, and two cultivators, after a day of cutting and threshing. A haggard woman, with legs like brown sticks, came begging for the sweepings and they gave her three handfuls of dirt and seeds which she took with a grin and wrapped carefully in a fold of her threadbare sari.

The sun was setting as we entered the village. A table was fetched out into the public square of baked, manila-brown earth, which was surrounded by the brown walls and small doorways of several adobe houses and cattle stalls. Noushad took a handful of fresh *chena* from a passing boy and someone else fetched a pitcher of cool water. Later, sweet, milky tea was served in a cup and saucer for my benefit. Word of the arrival of a foreigner soon spread and children and men gathered for the interrogation session.

One teenager nudged me again and again and asked the perennial question 'What is your caste? What is your caste?' My response met with the usual incredulity, and it was well after dark when eventually one of the old men told him that it was true that I had no caste. The boy didn't believe either of us.

Two of the children in the group that had gathered round the table on which we were sitting were markedly different in colour to the other children. One child was very pale, the other very dark.

'He's black,' said a man, much to the boy's embarrassment. 'But you are correct,' he said, holding the pale brown boy by his shoulders. This boy was a polio victim with thin, useless legs. Two more children, both mentally retarded, came to view the stranger in their village but stood at a distance, wary both of myself and of the boisterous confidence of the other children.

Some months earlier a young man working as a prison warder had said to me, 'Now they have a drug to make brown people white, isn't it so?'

'Do you want to be white?' I had asked.

'Oh certainly. White is much better.'

Advertisements in the newspapers for brides and grooms often state the desired colour of the spouse, among other conditions such as caste requirements. 'Pale' or 'fair' is the most popular prerequisite. Occasionally, advertisements state, 'Caste no bar. No dowry,' but usually, illegal references to caste and dowry are made obliquely:

WANTED extremely sweet, beautiful, fair, smart, slim, homely, educated girl, around 22 for Gursikh, handsome, graduate, 25/169, business only son, property in South Delhi, respectable family girl main consideration. Box—*Hindustan Times*.

The preference for pale skin dates back to the arrival of the Aryans who, like the British in India, drew a colour bar between themselves and outsiders. It was the Aryans who labelled the darkest peoples as 'untouchable', though they still required them to do menial tasks. In time, it was the association with these very tasks—such as cleaning latrines—which made people Untouchable, according to those who said they kept their own hands clean.

There was no obvious track to follow from Noushad's village so I followed the boundary ridges round empty fields, zig-zagging towards the north-west across the hard earth. I stopped once in the bottom of a badly eroded ravine to defecate and I stopped suddenly a second time just before treading on a two-foot-long red and orange snake. I walked closed up like a clam against the fierce light and heat, my mouth shut, drawing the hot, dry air deeply through both nostrils to avoid cracked lips and sore throat, my eyes screwed up against the glare of bright, cloudless sky, my thoughts inconsequential.

By zig-zagging across the fields, I kept parallel to the river bank.

Thick haze veiled the far shore, though I decided the faint line on the horizon was a blur of trees miles away across white sands and far beyond the trickle of the river. There were also trees where I walked, scattered in the empty fields or standing in clumps amid isolated homes or hamlets. There were no villages here, only occasional clusters of homes, built of baked mud and thatched with grasses. The crops had all been cut from the land, leaving barren pavements of cracked earth and dry stubble. The soil was so hard that the fields were like a succession of concrete playgrounds.

I stopped again at midday under a large mango tree near a small, white-washed temple dedicated to the monkey-god Hanuman. I enjoyed a cool swim in the river and then had to go hurriedly to the latrine again. I was disconcerted to see a streak of blood in my faeces, and although I felt no pains or grumbling in my stomach or intestines, blood in the stool can be a symptom of amoebic dysentery. Perhaps I was not cured, or maybe I was already reinfected within just one day of concluding my cure. Every day I was drinking more than 10 litres of water from open village wells and eating foods prepared by other hands.

The risks of infection were great but I had already decided that I would have to accept them. I did not want to sterilise drinking water with chemicals (in themselves harmful in large quantities), because to treat water offered to me in people's homes would have given offence. Moreover, the same water I was offered to drink would be used for washing foods, dishes and the hands preparing the meals, and contaminated water was only one of many sources of infection. I might become diseased just as easily by wiping my mouth with a cloth that had been soiled by flies. I realised that it could only be a matter of time before I became seriously ill and unable to carry on. I had therefore to cover as many miles as possible before this happened.

Late that afternoon, I headed inland, not knowing precisely where I was, hoping to reach a village or small town. A boy was selling thick slices of water melon for 20 paise in a village and I ate two, the sweet, pink juices dribbling down my hot, dry chin. I refilled both water bottles from a tubewell and continued inland, heading towards the setting sun. I eventually emerged onto the Grand Trunk Road and turned north to reach a small town in the last light of day. I immediately looked for the red ice-boxes of the lemonade and cola drink-sellers and sat for ten minutes sipping two ice-cold Limcas. There was nowhere remotely suitable to sleep in the congested and noisy market-place but another mile up the road in the dark I found a line-hotel, where I could both eat and sleep.

To my relief there was no one there to ask me questions, so I watched the crescent of a new moon setting beyond the black horizon and drank about three litres of cool water. After serving me a large meal of *dal*, two fluffy *chapatis*, *chena* and tomato *subzee*, the owner of the line-hotel put away my belongings in the strongroom and I fell asleep stretched out on a *charpoy* by the side of the road.

It was easy walking along the same Grand Trunk Road that I had travelled when leaving Calcutta four months earlier. I walked for hours, my mind blank, holding up the umbrella with my right hand and resting my left on the strap of one of the water bottles. By midday I had walked 16 miles and stopped for a big meal, lots of water and a two-hour sleep in another line-hotel on the outskirts of Kannauj. This town had once been the capital of northern India but now it is known chiefly for the production of *attar*, perfumed oil.

It takes between five and ten thousand flowers to make two pounds of pure *attar* and though little bottles sell for R15 one pound of the best can cost nearly R100,000. It is the perfume of both rich merchants and rickshaw-*wallahs*. About 100 small factories make *attar* in Kannauj by boiling the petals in water and collecting the steam in a container of sandalwood oil. The oil absorbs the fragrance of the flowers and loses its own smell in the process.

The following day at lunchtime, a middle-aged man in a white *dhoti* and *kurta* appeared beside me with the words, 'My great curiosity makes me very attracted to you.' We were two miles from the large town of Farrukhabad and he declared his great desire to accompany me.

'And why does God allow so much suffering?' I asked, to get the conversation going.

He turned to me declaring, 'Only Hinduism can answer that. You see, in this life we pay for our deeds from the previous life. It is not God who allows this suffering but we bring it to ourselves.'

I had already heard and read similar sentiments over and over again. The most outspoken came from Swami Vivekananda of the Ramakrishna Mission in Calcutta, 'We, we and no one else, are responsible for what we suffer. We are the effects and we are the causes. We are free therefore.'

After 1030 miles and many months I was still battling with this Law of Karma. It was all too neat. For example, according to the *Karmavipka*, 'The stealer of rice will first sink into hell, live 18 years as a crow, twelve years as a heron, and then regain his human form, but always be afflicted. He who slays an animal not intended as a sacrifice will, in the form of a turtle, suffer in hell, then appear on earth as a bull, and then again as a man with an incurable distemper.

According to the *Agni Purana*, something not born as a human lives eight million lives as an inferior creature. 'Of these he remains 2,100,000 among the immovable parts of creation, as stones, trees etc.; 900,000 amongst the watery tribes; 1,000,000 amongst insects, worms etc.; 1,000,000 amongst birds; and 3,000,000 amongst the beasts.'

Many contemporary Indians would scoff at these calculations, but the belief that people have earned their conditions on earth today in previous lives remains. Wealthy people, healthy people deserve their positions and the poor, the sick and the low caste have earned their misfortunes. We help them in order to improve our own karma.

I asked my companion about the fate of peasants in Bihar. 'What have they done to deserve corrupt police, perverted politicians, worms and meagre food?' I asked.

'Their time will come,' he replied placidly.

We parted with a handshake on the outskirts of Farrukhabad and I went to seek out the house of a family to whom I had an introduction through the Duttas. Unfortunately they were all away in Kanpur, so I booked a clean, quiet and inexpensive room in a hotel run by an obese man, who smiled constantly. He led me to a nearby, open-air restaurant at lunchtime and patted his vast belly to prove that the food was good.

I awoke from my afternoon sleep with one thought in my mind. I lay naked on the bed with the breeze from the ceiling fan blowing over my chest and legs, and the bedsheet damp with sweat from my sticky back. My eyes were wide open and I could see only one certainty—I was not going to last much longer. Physical and mental stamina were being worn down quickly each day. The four days walking from Kanpur had used up energy and spirit which I knew even two days' complete rest could not replenish. I felt like a small, clay figure gradually drying out, hardening and about to crack in the scorching heat. Before I became irrational, as I thought I surely must if I continued much longer, I wanted to think out my situation calmly.

I had three choices.

The first was to continue at the pace I had maintained successfully so far, but I would have to accept the increasing risk of a sudden mental or physical breakdown. Could I risk failing to complete the walk? It was not just for myself. The Save the Children Fund was treating my journey as a sponsored walk and the money raised was to be spent in India.

The second choice was to slow down, to walk as little as four hours each day and to stop as soon as the temperature reached 100°F—at ten o'clock in the morning, by which time I could have walked ten miles. Then I could take cover for twelve hours and sleep through the heat, like everyone else. I was 250 miles from Hardwar, at the end of the Gangetic Plain, a month away. Could I go on for a month? Would my health survive the extra days on the Gangetic Plain? There would be much more time in the villages if I walked only ten miles daily and I was confident people would welcome a stranger, if only as a diversion and something to gossip about. But could I withstand this verbal assault much longer? Meeting people had been one of the main attractions of the walk beside the river, but now I wondered whether my increasing agitation and desire to be left alone did not, at least partially, spring from being completely fed up with five and a half months of repeating answers to the same questions. There was an additional danger, if I travelled more slowly, of reaching the Himalayas in the monsoon and risking landslides and road closures.

The third option was to speed up the pace, to cover more miles each day, and thus to reduce the number of days I was exposed to the dangers of heat, disease and exhaustion.

None of these possibilities appealed to me. I was unsure what to do but knew that the wrong decision would prematurely end my pilgrimage and also put me in physical and mental danger. My physical condition was deteriorating daily. I was losing weight quickly because of the heat and because I was no longer eating properly. I had no appetite for spiced foods after so many months of the monotonous diet, but was learning the extent to which my sense of well-being is rooted in my stomach. It did no good to deny this, especially in the difficult conditions in which I now found myself. Yet, of course, *mori* and powdered milk were totally inadequate for a body sweating ten litres of water and walking up to 20 miles every day.

What would happen if I became ill again? It would be easy to get heatstroke; many people suffered or died from it every hot season. No one was immune and no one knew when it might strike. People took precautions such as staying out of the sun for the six most scorching hours of the day and exerting themselves as little as possible; sleeping, basket-making, knitting, or gossiping with family and neighbours. But even in the shade the danger was not removed. Sunstroke had proved to be a misnomer as the danger came from heat, not direct sunlight. And no one could escape the weeks of heat. However thick the walls of a house, however small the doorway, however few or tiny the windows and dark the interior, the heat always got inside eventually. It would always be cooler inside than out in the glare but when the temperature in the shade reached over 110°F it didn't make much difference where one chose to suffer.

Heatstroke was only one of the dangers in this hot, dry weather. My helpful medical book also listed salt depletion exhaustion (though I

carried salt tablets), water depletion exhaustion, prickly heat, heat
hyperpyrexia and heat cramps as the most serious disorders which
would quickly endanger a person's life. I am not a hypochondriac but it
was sobering to think of the hazards. The greatest danger was in being
alone and then not noticing the symptoms because of drowsiness and
the inability of the brain to function coherently. I dismissed these
potential problems, trusting myself to prudence and common sense. If I
could remain mentally stable I was confident I could survive the
conditions.

And what of my mental condition? This was the most dangerous
area, where perception and existence merge to form what the mind
perceives as reality. It was easy, being alone, to create a monster in
one's mind by distorting the seriousness or levity of one's situation. If I
came to believe that I could not withstand the conditions much longer,
then I probably wouldn't. I already felt oppressed by the heat and the
dust. I wondered how long I could last before withdrawing into my
own silence and becoming incapable of continuing. I tried therefore to
think of the future, of the days and weeks ahead, of the paths ahead, of
the balance of risks, and of my own mental and physical stamina before
deciding whether to slow down, maintain or speed up the pace of the
journey.

It was evening by the time I had sorted through all this and I returned
to the open-air restaurant for another substantial meal of rice, *dal*,
vegetable *subzee* and a crispy *popadom*. Then I went back to the hotel
to sleep it off. When I awoke, my mind was clear and the decision
made: I would execute Plan Three—convert the walk into a route
march, walk as hard and as fast as possible to a town called Bijnor 203
miles upstream. At most, it would take eleven days and I could hope to
do it in less. I would walk without rest days, setting off before first light
in the morning and walking until midday, and again from mid-
afternoon to sunset. I would walk and walk and walk to get off the
Gangetic Plain. I would concentrate solely on reaching Bijnor, where I
had been invited to stay by the Bishop of Bijnor. At most, it would only
be three days' walk from there to Hardwar. Then I could climb into the
foothills of the Himalayas and there would be gushing streams of water
and cool breezes. Although I expected to arrive in Hardwar worn-out,
the plan seemed to give the best chance of completing the walk for my
own satisfaction and for the people in India who would receive the
money donated to Save the Children Fund.

I spent most of the next day sleeping, resting my feet, both of which
were slightly swollen, and buying food for the journey. I was annoyed
at how difficult and time-consuming living in India was. It took hours
in the noisy, smelly lanes of the market to buy fruits and vegetables or

to accomplish simple errands such as buying stamps and two dozen Band-Aids for the minor cuts on my feet and ankles. It took me an hour to find a man who sold dried fruits as I wanted a pound of sultanas, to mix with the *mori* and powdered milk. The man did not even get up from sitting cross-legged on a mat but took a piece of paper and wrote down the price: R40. They were a luxury I could not afford, although I later found out that his price was not excessive. No wonder they were offered in minute quantities to the gods in the temples. Instead of sultanas, I went to a drug store and bought a box of glucose (including a free stainless steel teaspoon!). In retrospect, I have no idea why I didn't just buy sugar.

I left the town at 5 a.m. under a grey sky and a warm drizzle, humming a tune down the almost empty street, where the shutters of every shop were still pulled down and padlocked. By lunchtime, I had covered 18 miles of the 203 miles to Bijnor at a brisk pace, and was so pleased with myself that I stopped for two teas and two *samosas*. By early evening I'd walked 25 miles of my mad dash north and felt very pleased with myself. I strutted off the Grand Trunk Road, which continued to Delhi, and slept the night on the concrete roof of a Jain temple in a filthy village. I woke as soon as there was daylight and was well on my way, with both water bottles full, by the time the yellow sun rose like a dull moon above the haze across the flat horizon.

A sandy cart track led north-west, with the river lying somewhere to the east. I had that familiar feeling of being now alone in a wilderness of abandoned fields, tramping over hard, baked earth and hot sands beneath a faded blue sky that reached from horizon to horizon. The country was wild and open where I rejoined the Ganga, what I can only describe as moorland desert—with sand dunes in every direction, covered by meagre clumps of dead grass or patches of chest-high *kars* grasses. I walked by the narrow, grey river with giddy spirits, despite the breeze of enervating air and gusts of hot dust blowing in the face, listening to the calls of lapwings. I was lunatic enough to enjoy for a time the miles of sands, the heat, the glaring light and the harsh landscape that surrounded me.

One of the straps of my knapsack and both straps of the sandals snapped during the afternoon. It took several minutes staring blankly at the damage for me to work out how to make temporary repairs. Several hours later, I stopped for a swim in the warm river, as much to relieve the pain in my shoulder from the knot of the shawl in which I was carrying the knapsack as to wash and to cool down.

The sun was shrinking now into an impotent disc beyond the haze, and I contemplated sleeping out among the dunes, but decided to head inland towards a village of small, brown houses two miles away in the trees and to impose on its hospitality. The *pradhan* was not at home but I was told to put down my belongings and after a while a man came and led me off to eat, which I found strange because the village was too small to have a tea-stall. We arrived in a yard in front of a house. It was about forty feet square and six men were already gathered round two *charpoys*. I sat down and passed round a packet of *beedis* and explained how I came to be in their village. Cows were brought into the yard and tethered at feeding troughs. Leaf plates were set out on the earth floor in two rows, and when more than a dozen men and children had arrived in the warm, dusty gloom of nightfall we were called to eat. As I got to my feet I noticed a young man taking money and entering names in a book. I didn't know what this was for but gave two rupees which was received with a smile and a murmur and my name was entered in the book.

A small, clay cup was placed in front of us and hot *puris* and *karela* (a sour-tasting vegetable) and potato *subzee* were served onto the leaf plates. Everyone was hungry and the conversation died as we feasted. An unidentified spicy, whitish drink was poured into each cup, fermented sugar-cane juice perhaps. We were attended by two men and a boy who exhorted us to eat more and more.

Eventually I offered my thanks and returned to the *charpoy* outside the *pradhan*'s house, wanting only to sleep after such a big meal and 15 hours of walking. I lay on the *charpoy*, feeling so worn out that I was already beginning to doubt the sanity of this dash to Bijnor. Soon a group of men came offering *beedis* and asking lots of questions. I was very tired but answered as cheerfully as possible. Only now did I discover that the meal had been a wedding feast. As the bright half-moon rose higher in the blue-black sky, the bridegroom arrived out of the dark, wearing a tall crown of coloured papers and tinsel on top of his white turban and standing on a bullock cart. Drums, bugles and bells heralded his arrival and a crowd gathered to welcome him in procession to the bride's house. I settled back on the *charpoy*, wanting only to curl up in sleep. Hands offering *beedis* and men asking questions woke me twice more, but at length the conversation turned to other matters and I was able to fall asleep and hope not to be missed. I was woken a third time by an old woman haranguing the *pradhan*. She kept pointing at me:

'And he ... ' she was shouting. 'And he ... ' But I could not understand what she was saying, and no one could explain.

Half an hour later, I had to get up and we were led back to the threshing floor where we had feasted, to squat on the ground by the light of a hurricane lamp while six women ate a meal. It was now after ten o'clock, I estimated, and I was aching with fatigue, shifting my weight from one weary buttock to the other on the hard, earthen floor and trying to smile for my generous hosts. When the women finished their meal the men were told to line up again. I now understood what the old woman had been saying: not enough food had been served at the wedding feast! It had been a poor meal, by her account, to offer a guest in their village. We had therefore to eat the meal all over again. Nothing could have been less welcome but it was impossible to refuse, especially when everyone else was tucking into this unexpected double helping with such zeal. A dessert in a small, clay bowl was brought to me as a special treat. It was yoghurt sweetened with molasses, which I loathed and on which I always gagged, but I could not refuse this generosity, so I swallowed it quickly and hoped not to be immediately sick.

A young man woke me some time later with an invitation to the wedding ceremony, but fortunately he did not press the request on his stupefied guest.

I was out of the village before sunrise next morning and heading towards the river again, watched for a little way by an inquisitive but shy jackal. The river was a narrow serpentine channel, twisting between distant permanent banks, and I walked in a straight line towards the north-west, aiming a little to the right of a clump of trees blurred in the haze ahead. It was impossible to know precisely where I was on this vast plain, but I touched the river about four times during the morning as the Ganga meandered back and forth across its floodplain. This route took me up soft sand dunes, along animal tracks crossing wild pastures of dead grasses and skirting herds of cattle that were being driven to the river in clouds of dust to drink and cool off by boys with sticks. Even from the highest dunes, I could see only wave upon wave of sands and grasses as if some demon had suddenly turned a raging, yellow ocean into sand.

The outline of a big bridge miles away had shimmered in the haze all morning and at midday I was climbing its approach road. There was a tea-stall and police checkpost where the road and rail tracks combined to cross the long bridge and I sat with relief under a little mango tree, sipping sweet, milky tea, eating juicy slices of water melon and plates of *chena*, and smoking *beedis* with the men as they waited for customers. The gates on the road were closed four times during the afternoon when trains trundled across the bridge and it was then that these vendors got their business. Trucks, tractors and crowded trailers, bullock carts, cyclists, motor-cyclists, overloaded local buses and a few Ambassador cars with silent passengers secluded in the back lined up as if at the starting post of a bizarre race.

One of the plainclothed policemen at the checkpost interrogated me politely and seemed quite happy, even pleased, when he heard where I was heading and where I had come from. Despite turning up in places where foreigners were almost unknown, I had been stopped by police only three times and had always been allowed to go freely. Even so, I felt nervous near the police knowing their reputation for extortion and violence, and fearing that one of them might decide to prohibit my journey.

At about 4 p.m., when the afternoon breeze began to rustle the leaves of the mango tree, I embarked on what I knew would be the most difficult section of the whole walk. According to the map, the Ganga flowed underground for the next 35 miles leaving quicksands on the surface. However, a channel of water about 400 feet wide flowed under the rail bridge. This was the mighty Ganga in the hot season.

Once more I was out on that desolate plain of moorland desert, heading towards the smudge of trees on the horizon, tramping up and over sand dunes, shaking out the hot sand from my sandals and sipping warm water from the water bottles. The sun was now too low in the sky for the umbrella to give any protection and I walked with sweat and dust trickling down my face and stinging my eyes. Flies buzzed around my nose and ears and the sleeves of my *kurta* were soon soaked with gritty sweat wiped from my forehead.

I was at least two miles across the sands from the village along the river's permanent banks and I decided that I would sleep out in this empty wilderness under the stars. I doubted anyone would come here at night. Even in daylight, the villagers feared robbers and only ventured out in groups to cut grass or graze cattle. No one but a fool would wish to be out here alone at night, so, paradoxically, I considered myself safe. I selected level, grassy ground near a dry channel of the river and collected dry grasses and cow dung to make a fire to brew the tea and a bowl of Marmite soup (another generous gift from the Duttas) which would be my supper.

The water was longer heating than I had expected, having never used cow dung before for a fire. The sun had set and its orange light turned to the palest pink all across the western sky before the sweet, black tea was made. I sat with the shawl spread out like a picnic rug, glad to be truly alone at night for the first time in 1150 miles. I sipped the Marmite soup and munched glucose biscuits, watching the stars and a satellite far above in the bright sky. The half-moon was so bright that the warm night shone with a blue light. I had walked 20 miles on the third day of my dash to Bijnor and, after packing away all my equipment, lay down on the shawl using my towel as a pillow for a very early night's sleep. I was undisturbed apart from a chilly wind which gave me a temporary sore throat, but three wild *sambur* (Indian elk) watched from 100 yards away when I set out in the first grey light of the next morning. Already the stars had hidden themselves and the moon had been gone for many hours, but there were still a few more hours to go before sunrise and I was eager to make the most of the cool air, when not a reed was in motion nor a bird flying in the air.

Even with the protection of an umbrella, the sun's heat soon gripped my shoulders and arms like an ox's heavy yoke. By late morning both water bottles were empty and I was becoming badly dehydrated. My urine was a dribble of dark yellow. In an emergency I would have to drink from the river, after boiling the water as there were too many sewer pipes and corpses to drink the holy water untreated. I carried a small aluminium pot, the size of a soup bowl, but I calculated that, in the heat, I would need to drink as much water per hour as could be boiled. I kept walking.

At midday I reached a village where the Ganga flowed along the base of the 30-foot escarpment of the permanent river bank. I was already feeling slightly sick, and I filled my belly with water and refilled both water bottles at the village handpump. I did not return to the baking heat of the river plain. Instead, I lured myself along a cart track on the top of the bank hoping to meet a lollipop man.

I never found the lollipop man and made do with two bits of dry bread, similar to baby rusks, bought from a village store, and warm water from my bottles.

There was little breeze. It was hotter than hell, hot enough to bake meringues. They could then be filled with fresh cream and served with a big pot of tea! I tried to banish such thoughts from my imagination while I sat out the worst of the heat beneath a few meagre thorn bushes, panting and half asleep, until shadows began stretching out from clumps of grasses and I started walking again.

'Do you have food?' I asked at a tea-stall on the outskirts of a village beside the Lower Ganga Canal, half a mile inland from the river.

'Yes,' said the fresh-faced man, after peering into a pot to count his *chapatis*. He bade me sit down and poured a glass of tea from one of the blackened kettles on the hearth. 'Today, you stay here,' he said.

So I did, enjoying tea and sticky, sweet pastries called *ladoos* and later a meal of *dal* and *chapatis*. The stall-holder eventually packed up his kettles, pans, cups and glasses into the big wooden chest at the back of the stall, wished me a good night and went home to his wife and two-year-old daughter. I lay down on top of the table with my knapsack beside me and immediately fell asleep.

These nights were never long enough and Day Four began all too soon. I was awake even before the man came back to relight the fire in the hearth and open up his stall for business. I brushed my teeth and refilled one of the water bottles at the handpump, and set out beside the Lower Ganga Canal, where drinking water would be available.

This canal, built in 1878 to connect Narora and Allahabad, is one of the routes popular with *sadhus* walking from Hardwar, Rishikesh and the temples in the mountains down to Benares, Vindhyachal and beyond, but this was not the season to meet anyone walking on the plain. Even the officers of the British Raj had had enough sense in the hot season to evacuate to towns in the hills until the monsoon. The tow-paths of the Upper and the Lower Ganga Canals and, lower down, the Grand Trunk Road itself are popular with *sadhus* because they are safer and more direct; and begging is easier than out in the wastelands beside the river. The two canals irrigate an area exceeding five million acres between the Ganga and Jumna rivers, which previously had been near desert outside the monsoon season.

I was now walking in the shadow of the twin cooling towers of the Narora Atomic Power plant, which is currently being built beside the canal and is scheduled to open in 1988. It stood on the other side of the 150-foot wide canal, across from the rutted and dusty track which served as the main road for carts with creaking, wooden wheels and groaning axles pulled by hapless bullocks, all skin and skeletons, straining forward.

It was a shock to realise when I sat down in the evening outside an *ashram* on Day Five that the end of my pilgrimage was in sight. The miles and months of walking had seemed to stretch out from Ganga Sagar in the Bay of Bengal to infinity but all of a sudden both miles and days were countable. It was simultaneously reassuring and saddening.

Water was available from wells at villages beside the canal, though I declined water from one well when the bucket came up full of transparent, wriggling things. I plodded along the sandy road and at midday retreated behind bushes hoping that no one would see me and intrude with their questions as, having rejoined the road, I was once again easy prey. During these days, I growled my way north like an ill-tempered animal; unsmiling, teeth clenched, walking with determination and no compassion, a sad turnabout from the enthusiasm with which I had set out from the Bay of Bengal six months before. I could only hope that a less daunting climate in the hills would revive my humanity.

I made a small fire behind the screen of bushes, shaded by a wide mango tree. Six boys who were herding goats along the canal bank appeared and stood about 40 feet away watching what I was doing. I ignored them and hoped they would go away. They were silent until the tea was brewed and then they came forward.

'Where are you from?' asked the tallest boy, who was dressed, like his companions, in ragged and dusty shorts and shirt. I answered and sipped my tea.

'No milk?' exclaimed the boy when he saw what I was drinking. 'You must have milk,' said the anxious lad in Hindi. 'Milk is good,' he repeated.

I said that I did not want milk, but no one listened. The boys fetched up one of their goats and took off the little cloth bag which guarded her teats from thirsty kids in the flock. One boy took the plastic cup from my hand and two others held the goat steady at my feet while he milked her directly into the teacup. The goat stared as blankly as myself. The cup of milky tea was handed back with a smile. Then they noticed I was sitting on the bare ground, and offered a piece of sackcloth which one of them was carrying on his shoulder. I declined, so two boys shook the cloth, laid it behind my back and rejoined their four friends sitting staring in a row in front of me. They all smiled and chattered when, with a shrug of shoulders and a smile, I sat back on the sacking.

'Do you eat mangoes?' asked one of them.

I nodded my head and two boys went off to collect fallen green mangoes. I had nothing to offer them, so I showed them my five photographs of family and home.

'I want to keep this,' said one of the boys.

'Sure, one for each,' I said and they shared them out, though I don't know what the sixth boy did. The mango collectors returned with enough mangoes to give bellyache for months, and invited me to their village of Jatpura for tea, but the afternoon breeze was already blowing and it was time to be moving again. We exchanged addresses and parted. Many months later, I received a postcard from Shri Vijai Singh Balwan, who lives in Jatpura and had evidently heard about me from the boys.

I regretted my forced march, but was still sure it was best in the circumstances. I walked beside the canal until lunchtime the next day (Day Seven), then turned right along the road to Garmukteswar in order to get back to the river. This was one of the most unpleasant days of the walk. The *loo* winds started soon after sunrise, swirling round dust in blinding, hot gusts and making me perpetually uncomfortable, fretful and irritated. The hot dust stung my ears and made both nostrils ache. My mind was dulled, my body listless, as I tramped on, half asleep mostly, sipping warm water from the bottles and cowering under the hot shade of the umbrella; humourless, eyes screwed up and mouth shut, leaning forwards into the miles ahead. I was withdrawn, anti-social, short-tempered and worn-out. I hardly spoke all day. I never smiled. I was infuriated every time someone came close and I detested those endless stupid questions.

Once the Ganga flowed past Garmukteswar, my next stop, but it abandoned the town years ago and now flowed to the east. I slept the night on a hot stone bench outside a temple and was woken by the priest's pre-dawn prayers and the jangling of bells close to my head. I bought a miniature packet of tea from the first shopkeeper to fold back the wooden shutters of his shop and left the town along a wide track of deep, floury sand. The sun rose all too soon on the eighth day, ruining the early morning, and I followed the track towards this dirty, yellow disc that was half-hidden by the brown haze. I was soon out beyond the melon fields and was once again into the wilderness, alone with my thoughts, the swish of my *lungi* through dry grasses and the odd alarm calls of birds.

I never expected to see Indian Army tanks encamped amid trees near the track and I passed by quickly, hoping not to be stopped by officials. A tank lurched past me within six feet later in the morning but didn't stop, and roared away in a fog of dust.

I tramped north-west across the empty sands, scrubby bushes and dead grasses of a region called the Kabir. It is a dull, grey, flat landscape. It is here that what is probably the last pig-sticking in the world takes place. This traditional sport was inherited from the British, and every April Indian officers compete for the Kabir Cup in this fast, dangerous and gruesome sport of pursuing wild boars on horseback and trying to stick the animals with sharpened lances. The Kabir is the last wild region along the Ganga plain, and was the only stretch of the river where I might still see crocodiles.

'Course, crocodile was the poor man's tiger,' the ruddy-faced, octogenarian Englishman with whom I had tea in Mirzapur had explained. 'You could hire a boat and go out and get yourself a decent trophy. There were lots of crocodiles then, but it was not easy to shoot, you know. Tricky. One never could get within 150 yards before the buggers dived and they were gone and you were left looking pretty silly in your rowing boat,' said this *burra sahib* (big chief).

The slim *gavial* crocodile (*Gavialis gangeticus*) has a long, narrow snout with about 100 teeth that is ideal for seizing fish and frogs under water. The reptile lives almost all the time in the water, with the female emerging to lay eggs at night in pits dug in the river bank. Poaching has been illegal since 1972 but enforcement of the law is impossible and *gavial* numbers have declined as the burgeoning population has encroached further and further onto the marginal lands beside the river. The *gavial* is now an endangered species, and although I looked carefully along the river in many remote places I never saw one. Later I found out that there are now only an estimated seven *gavials* along the entire length of the Ganga.

The Kabir and the forested slopes north of the river towards the mountains have been settled by thousands of refugees who fled the slaughter that accompanied the Partition of India in 1947, and by refugees from East Pakistan (now Bangladesh).

Despite arriving as refugees, or perhaps because of it, they have prospered and the hamlets I walked through were the most prosperous since West Bengal. Tractors were out disking the brown soil, driven by Sikhs in yellow or blue turbans, and I passed a line of concrete poles for electricity although as yet there were no wires. Homes were still built of baked mud and thatched with grasses, but I saw petrol engines which are used for driving threshing machines, fodder cutters and irrigation pumps. In one of these hamlets I was invited to stay with a family. The wife lit the fire outside the front doorway and boiled water in a brass pot for tea while she listened to her husband asking the questions.

The family had abandoned the Punjab after Partition and settled in the Kabir. Their home was a long room made of mud walls almost two feet thick, windowless, with a low doorway, and thatched with grasses on which pumpkins were growing. They had their own handpump, two cattle sheds made of plaited reeds, and fencing round their compound to keep dogs out. The family was obviously thriving; not rich but full of hope and having confidence in the future, eager therefore to work hard, to take modest risks with new seeds and to invest in machinery. This was in striking contrast to the despondent sloth in which many millions of the country's peasants exist—too poor to be able to afford to take risks and too frightened to show initiative.

After tea I was taken round to be shown off in the hamlet, calling first at a home where two wizened and very dark women were sitting in the last, soft light of the day smoking *ganja* in a hookah pipe. One woman squatted on the ground and the other, the thinner of the pair, sat on the edge of a *charpoy*. The hookah stood between them and they passed the mouthpiece back and forth. When told of my journey the woman on the *charpoy* put out her bony arm and pulled me to sit down beside her. She offered the pipe to me but I was content to smoke a *beedi*. She chattered all the time and gripped my hand with her own trembling fingers. Presently, she put her hand to my face and felt over the hollows of my eyes, the line and length of my nose, my lips and chin and the length and thickness of my hair. Her other tiny hand kept hold of mine, squeezing gently with affection. It was only now that I realised her dull eyes were blind and her lungs probably deeply scarred with tuberculosis. Her touch was maternal and soothing, but my host whisked me away to visit other friends.

We returned home in the dark to see flames leaping from the top of the *tandoori* oven. My host's wife was standing beside this orange demon holding sticks in one hand, ready to drop them in the top of the barrel-shaped oven built with thick walls of baked mud. When the fire had quietened to red embers, she slapped *chapatis* against the hot walls to bake in the dry heat, then served them with *dal*, vegetable *subzee*, pickles and relish. The meal was delicious and reviving. I looked round at the five members of the family also busy eating and felt again that pleasure I had found in Indian hospitality at the beginning of my trek, so that I began to be sad that what had recently become such an ordeal was almost over.

I left Mirzapur before sunrise next morning (Day Nine) after two cups of sweet, milky tea and many good wishes, heading north, hoping to find the ruins of Hastinapur. I did not. Hastinapur had been yet another mighty city beside the Ganga but historians are not even certain of its exact location, since it was washed away by the Ganga in 1000 BC.

Nervous energy alone was keeping me going as long day followed long day in the never-ending heat and dust. Farrukhabad was now 175 miles behind me and with luck and hard walking I might reach Bijnor, on the opposite side of the river, that night, and enjoy the comforts of a bishop's residence.

The road across the dry floodplain was silent, except for occasional motorcycles and local buses. I counted down each kilometre-post, had glucose biscuits and tea for lunch, and refilled the water bottles at two handpumps. Gradually, the heat of the day passed and shadows lengthened again. I was still seven miles from Bijnor and knew I could not reach the town on foot before dark. However, I could not bear to stop for the night when the comforts of Bijnor were so near, so I decided to take the bus into the town and return next morning to complete the journey on foot. From Bijnor it was only two or three days to Hardwar. I had almost made it. Finally I would be across the Gangetic Plain and 1400 miles of the journey would be accomplished.

But compared to walking at two and half miles an hour for so many months, it was no pleasure at all to rush in a bus past ponds and marshes of reeds, and lurch suddenly round bends. The bus reached the end of the road several miles short of Bijnor, amid sand dunes and dry grasses where a group of horse-drawn tongas (two-wheeled open carriages) were waiting. We transferred to those with everyone's bundles and set off at a slow pace on the sand track towards another enormous, grey barrage being built across the Ganga more than a mile away. It was several hours and utterly dark before we eventually reached Bijnor. I was thin and exhausted but I had arrived.

I asked three students at the bus stand how to get to the Bishop's house. The news was bad: the Bishop of Bijnor did not live in Bijnor, and the place that I had assumed was a suburb of the town was in fact 37 miles to the north. Suddenly, I felt terribly weary.

I slept most of the next day, hoping that a groin swelling would subside and that infected cuts and insect bites on feet and ankles would form healthy scabs. At dawn the following day I walked back to the barrage, along the sand track and the asphalt road to the village where I had boarded the bus. Then I took the bus and tonga ride back to town.

The tea-*wallahs* of Bijnor had not yet served their first customers when I left the town, on the asphalt road that headed for the foothills of the Himalayas. These low hills, of white boulders and pebbles with dwarf green trees, emerged from the haze late on the second afternoon, and I reached Hardwar at teatime, taking an instant dislike to the holy city, which reminded me in its tawdriness of Blackpool. It was May 19th, 25 weeks since I had set out from the Bay of Bengal and also my 28th birthday, a fitting day to complete the walk across the monotonous bleached landscape.

Half a million people come every year to Hardwar to bathe, to make *puja* and to receive *darshan*, in addition to the million who attend the Kumbh Mela every twelve years. Streets were noisy and congested with holiday-makers hunting for bargain silks and other fabrics, shoes and bangles, and streetside photographers crowding husband and wife, four children, grandmother, grandson, son-in-law and his mother into studios for family portraits. The women would stand perfectly still, as if not breathing, and the men would take themselves seriously and stand rigid, not smiling, as if preparing to withstand a tidal wave.

The city really was a Blackpool-by-the-River. In addition to all the temples and the bells and chanting, and the holy men (and occasionally holy women) dressed in orange or red, there was a fairground with coconut shies, ferris wheel and dodgem cars. A cable car up the hill behind the city offers a panoramic view of the foothills and the grey river and, for the pious, there's a temple beside the funicular station in which to make *puja*. In Hardwar, as everywhere else, there is no distinction between holiday and holiness, pilgrim and tourist.

12

Tiger! Tiger!

I woke in a dingy hotel in Ramnagar in a foul mood and weary of India. I recognised that much of my antipathy derived from fatigue and I was hoping to lighten my foul humour by a week's tiger hunting in Corbett National Park, which lies between the Ganga and the foothills of the Himalayas. I believe it is evidence of the odd kinship of affection and disaffection between Indians and the British that the country's first national park should be renamed after Jim Corbett, one of the world's foremost naturalists and big-game hunters, ten years after he had abandoned the country. In the 14th week of India's independence, at the age of 73, he sailed with his sister Maggie to Kenya where White Man's supremacy was still recognised.

Ramnagar was just outside the park, and I had come by bus from Hardwar to New Delhi to do a telephone interview with a radio station to help the fund-raising of Save the Children Fund, and to collect cold weather clothing for the trek over the Kalindi Pass. I had been unable to find out in New Delhi whether permission for the journey from Gau Makh to Badrinath was required or not, or from whom, and was trusting Raj Dutt and myself to good luck. From New Delhi I had come by an early, and much-delayed, bus to Ramnagar, where it proved necessary to book accommodation before continuing into Corbett National Park.

'It is not possible to go today. There is no accommodation,' the officer in Ramnagar had said the previous afternoon. 'You must go on the bus tomorrow. It is the end of the season. There is a rush,' he'd explained, directly contradicting the advice of the government tourist offices I'd visited in New Delhi.

'Can I camp in my own tent?'

'It is not allowed.'

It took two hours to obtain from the officer a single piece of paper, which reserved one bunk bed for four nights in the park. He was as full of enthusiasm and usefulness as flat tonic water is of bubbles. I would have to stay overnight in Ramnagar, with other would-be visitors. I was tired and so annoyed that it was little wonder I had woken now after a fitful night's sleep in such a foul mood.

According to the officer, the bus was scheduled to leave at two in the afternoon. 'But sometimes it is late. It may leave at three o'clock.' Both times were wildly inaccurate. The daily bus left from down the street at 5.10 p.m., not long after its actual scheduled time, and pulled up at the park gates at sunset, when the gates were due to be locked for the night. The bus finally reached Dhikala, the main centre in the park, which had a restaurant, and the forty-hour journey, which takes no more than six hours by car, was over. Contrary to the insistence of the officer in Ramnagar, there was plenty of accommodation at Dhikala. There had been for days and I can only hope that someone gets good bonuses from hotels and restaurants in Ramnagar for telling visitors they are stranded there.

I was booked into the Log Hut because I had been told in Ramnagar that there was no other accommodation available except for R100 per night rooms with air conditioning, which I did not need. In fact there was an ample variety of accommodation available, from campsites to small marquees, but it was impossible to switch. I asked but encountered that intellectual fog that obscures so much of the country:

'You wish other accommodation, you must go to Ramnagar,' said the officer at Dhikala.

'They say everything is full—which it isn't.'

'You must go to Ramnagar for registration of accommodation.'

The argument was circular and futile. One young English couple on a fishing expedition had a letter from Ramnagar stating that they should be given a R100 room if available or, if not, a large tent. Rooms were available but they were put into a tent.

I wondered at the justice, or even the good sense of charging non-Indians 60 per cent higher prices for entry into the park and accommodation and giving such shoddy service. The incessant claims of poverty by the Government of India looked less credible when at the same time so many opportunities for development, employment and prosperity were missed altogether or thoroughly messed up.

Apart from foreigners willing to put up with any conditions, the park seemed to be visited only by rich Indians in their own or government cars. A glance through the Entry Book at the park gate showed that, with the exception of foreigners coming by bus, almost all other visitors came by car. It was difficult to see how people could learn about wildlife conservation if national parks were accessible only to India's governing class and not the millions of middle-class office and factory workers. There were no scheduled bus tours from New Delhi and the only day tour, from nearby Naini Tal, often came too late in the day to be allowed entry into the park.

The Log Hut where I was sleeping had 12 bunks, one light bulb and six lockers, one of them broken. Someone had scribbled a note above one bunk, 'A snake was found here 17 May 84'. There were toilet blocks nearby with washbasins without taps and electric switches with bare wires. It was servants' accommodation, though that seemed an inadequate excuse for the poor maintenance. The dormitory had no fan and even with all the windows open it was stifling at night, so I slept outside in pyjamas on a blanket on the concrete verandah. It was quiet for an hour and then a furious row erupted filling the camp with rabid shouting, whining and weeping. After an hour I fell asleep thinking about seeing a tiger. I was told in the morning that a tiger had wandered through the camp at four in the morning.

Two warthogs and a thin jackal looked up from the camp garbage pit when I rode past high on the back of an elephant. It was just after sunrise and we were crossing a meadow of lime-green grass behind Dhikala. The camp was in the middle of the flat grassland and stood on the edge of a 100-foot cliff overlooking the mile-wide floodplain of the Ramganga river and the backdrop of green hills beyond. A small herd of chital (white-spotted deer) had been grazing in the meadow but they had now all gone. We entered the forest, under the canopy of *sal* trees, and the elephant paced slowly along the dew-damp trail, her four passengers swaying from side to side on the wooden *howdah* on her back. The *mahout* sat astride the animal's neck, with his bare feet tickling and kicking her flapping ears and his hands ready to strike her big, grey head with a sharp gaff if she misbehaved.

We turned off the dirt road after half a mile and followed a footpath through matted undergrowth. It was dim and silent inside the forest, beneath the green sky of treetops held aloft by trunks like an orchard of telegraph poles. We travelled in silence, looking down from the elephant's back, peering, watching, waiting, hoping for movement in the bushes and a split-second glimpse of a tiger, though it did seem far-fetched to imagine that we might see one of the 90 tigers in a park of 203 square miles. But the tiny chance kept us all quiet and watchful.

The upper branches of undergrowth snagged our feet as we moved forward. Then the elephant stopped. The *mahout* motioned for complete silence. There was a tiger somewhere near us. A second elephant carrying visitors closed up behind. We waited and moved forward a few paces and waited again, our breath held, our eyes straining. We moved forward again and saw on the ground beside the elephant's big feet, four dismembered legs of a sambur, the remains of a recent kill. Our elephant moved silently forward. We peered into every hiding hole, every shadow and dappled pattern of twigs and grasses in the morning light. Twice we circled through the undergrowth, pausing to listen, watching and waiting. We found the remains of another kill. We went further along a path into the forest. Then one *mahout* called in a whisper to the other and the suspense was broken. This tiger was not going to show itself.

Jim Corbett could attract a tiger by imitating its mating call. His knowledge of the jungle telegraph was wide and included leopard, barking and spotted deers, sambur, monkey and many birds including peacocks. A hunter almost killed Corbett one day, when he mistook Corbett's calls and shot what he thought was a leopard. Corbett gained his adeptness and knowledge of calls during a lifetime spent among jungle folk, as he called the animals; shooting with a double-barrelled muzzle loader at the age of eight, poaching in the forests of the foothills of the Himalayas with Uncle Kunwar Singh in his teens and spending many years tracking animals.

In the thirties, Corbett organised elaborate tiger shoots for the viceroy, Lord Linlithgow, and thus made the acquaintance of many of the British élite. He is now known internationally as a killer of man-eating tigers and leopards, and his fame spread largely as a result of his writings. Corbett's first book, *Man-Eaters of Kumaon* was a best-seller in India, England and America, and was translated into 16 languages, six of them Indian, and made into a film. Corbett wrote seven books in total. Most of them were of tracking and stalking man-eaters in the forests of the foothills of the Himalayas, exactly the type of country now preserved in Corbett National Park. He tracked man-eaters alone, on foot and armed only with a rifle. He killed a total of 12 man-eaters responsible for the deaths of almost 2000 people and killed his last animal when he was aged 71.

Shortly after five o'clock that evening, we were riding an elephant again, heading east from the camp along the edge of the cliff into the forest. Rain showers in the early afternoon had cooled the air and cleaned it of dust and haze. Now in the late afternoon light the strands of lime-green grass shone with refreshed glory. The rains had extinguished flames from several forest fires on the hillsides across the river from Dhikala, though blue smoke was still rising above the green canopy. These fires had been deliberately started by the forest department, I was told, in order to burn off undergrowth before the rainy season started, when the forest floor would otherwise become a tangle of new growth too thick for animals to penetrate.

Our elephant walked with lolling gait, reaching out with her trunk and clasping the grass, then tearing each clump with a casual swing of her front leg as she stepped forwards and popping the grass into her mouth. We visited a water pool in the forest but found no tracks in the soft mud and moved through the trees towards the river. We had to cling tightly to the *howdah* as the elephant stepped down the steep sandy banks. Three samburs waited without alarm on the pebble beach when we emerged from the forest cover, and waded through the water until it reached their knees, where they stopped and turned their heads to watch us.

We were now on the floodplain of the Ramganga, having safely crossed the 100-foot river; amid tall reeds, uneven sand banks, dry channels and marshy creeks half-hidden by overhanging grasses, any of which might conceal a tiger. We were hushed and alert, peering into the shaded gloom. It was too much to expect to see more than a tiger's tail swishing in the grass. And even then we would be lucky. The five skilful *mahouts* brought up their elephants, steadily closing a circle about 100 feet in diameter. Our elephant stepped three feet down into a dry channel, with all of us holding on tightly, and we jumped suddenly as a bird flew out. We gripped the posts of the *howdah* and all of our eyes were fixed on the grass and shadows around us, while everyone waited for a sign and the sudden call of a sighting. All the elephants stopped. They moved in, closing the circle further and stopped again. We were still looking. One elephant, ahead of us and to our left, stepped forward eight paces through the tall grass. Suddenly, a tiger leapt out in clear view, springing high above the grass with paws outstretched against the sky. In one magnificent leap, the animal bounded 20 feet into the centre of our circle and crouched in the grass 30 feet away facing us with white teeth and wide eyes. It growled, warning us repeatedly not to come closer. It was unafraid of elephants and angry at the intrusion.

'Let us go,' murmured one nervous tourist but the *mahout* smiled and took no notice.

'Let us go.'

We stayed for several minutes, then backed off and turned to go, stopping at the river to let the elephants drink the clear water and for our own exuberance to cool. I had never seen a more magnificent creature and understood what had inspired William Blake to write his famous poem.

Tyger! Tyger! burning bright
In the forests of the night,
What immortal hand or eye
Could frame thy fearful symmetry?

Next morning we returned to the Ramganga floodplain at sunrise, to the same dry channel half-hidden by overhanging grasses. Incredibly, the tiger was still there, better camouflaged in the grass and his growls louder than before. Again we formed a loose circle around the animal.

One elephant went one pace too close to the tiger. It pounced forward, charging with a roar yet stopping short as abruptly as it had moved, and crouched in the grass: it was only warning us. Meanwhile, the attacked elephant had backed off, its trunk in the air for protection, and the four other elephants rocked from side to side uncomfortably and swung their trunks back and forth. We stayed a few minutes longer and then withdrew, leaving the tiger still growling.

The tiger is now a protected animal. Shooting has been banned since 1971 and with US$1 million aid from the World Wildlife Fund for Project Tiger and US$7 million from the Indian Government, a total of 15 reserves have been established and the tiger saved from extermination in India.

Corbett National Park became the first Project Tiger reserve in 1973, when the total tiger population in India was estimated at 1827 and declining by 100 animals every year. Jim Corbett had reckoned there were 3–4,000 tigers in 1947, down from about 40,000 at the end of the nineteenth century.

There were many reasons for the decline; mass slaughter by British viceroys, lesser dignitaries and Indian maharajahs, poaching (a skin can fetch up to US$20,000 on the black market) and the continuing destruction of the forests where tigers live. India has lost about 17,000 square miles of forest, an area larger than Switzerland, in the 37 years since Independence.

I counted myself especially fortunate to have seen a tiger on two occasions, and decided not to go out again on an elephant ride. Back at Dhikala, and dismounted from the elephant via a concrete platform like a two-storey bus shelter, we were told four tigers walked through the compound the night before between 10 p.m. and 1 a.m. This rumour gave myself and a young man from New Zealand a fright because we had been out on the terrace overlooking the Ramganga by starlight and had heard sounds and seen shadows. The compound had been dark and silent when we had hurriedly crossed to the Log Hut, aware that something was watching us and following.

We calmed down and still slept on the verandah, with the moon and the bright stars above and shadows on the ground. I lay awake, thinking of Subedar Ali, one of the *mahouts* in the park, who was still in hospital three months after being mauled by a tiger called Sheroo. Subedar, aged 26, had been out chopping branches in the forest for his elephant. The elephant had warned him with her trunk just before the tiger sprang ten feet up into the tree and wrenched Subedar to the ground. In a final struggle, convinced he was about to die, he had plunged his hand inside the tiger's mouth and twisted its tongue. The tiger had almost chewed off his hand when Subedar was saved by rolling away down a slope while a second *mahout* and two elephants drove off the tiger. He had crawled towards his own elephant, who had wrapped her trunk round his mutilated body and lifted him onto her back, according to the newspaper report. The tiger was captured two weeks later and crated off to a cage in Kanpur Zoo.

Humans are not fodder for either tigers or leopards and few animals become man-eaters. This usually occurs in old age or if they are wounded so that they are unable to kill their usual prey. The animals may also acquire a taste for human flesh by eating an uncremated body and adopting this new and easy food supply.

There was little to do in camp at Dhikala during the day but the breakfast in the restaurant was so good that half a dozen young foreigners and myself made the meal last several hours. We swapped tiger stories, commiserated with those who had not had a sighting, ordered more coffee and more buttered toast (made in a real toaster and not just singed bread) and feasted on my pot of marmalade. Boiled eggs and toast were the only foods I could eat with enthusiasm because my stomach was still delicate and my appetite jaded after the months of monotonous spiced foods in the villages.

The restaurant served full Indian meals for R10 or a Western meal of powdered soup and appalling mutton goulash with half-warm, half-cooked potatoes for R25. Dessert consisted of one mashed banana spread with churned, condensed milk and priced at R7, which we found out only after it had been served. I complained to the manager but it did no good. He had already decided that we were hippies because we did not change into Western clothes for dinner, unlike the Indian visitors, and because I wore a *lungi*, and treated us according to our lowly status. On the last evening we did dress in our *sahib* and *memsahib* uniforms (smart, uncomfortable Western clothes) and were greeted with civil words and a notional bow at the restaurant door.

After breakfast on the second day, I went to the small library of tiger and wildlife books in a cabinet in the park office. My hopes of finding a quiet read to pass the warm day were dashed. The cabinet was locked and the man with the key was away.

'He is on leave.'

'How long?'

'Two weeks.' The park officer was unconcerned and sat back comfortably in his armchair.

'Why on earth don't you keep the key here in the office?'

I didn't understand what the man muttered in Hindi, but could easily guess.

I had been disappointed not to see any crocodiles earlier. Corbett Park, however, boasted both *gavial* and *mugger* (estuarine) crocodiles and I was keen to see both. The crocodile pool on the Ramganga river was seven miles from the camp at Dhikala. There was no vehicle to hire. The transport that tourist officials in New Delhi had promised proved to be 'not possible'. Likewise, the armed guides to accompany visitors outside the camp were 'not possible' when I explained where I wanted to go. Instead, the guides spend the day smoking *beedis* in the compound and I never got out to the crocodile pool.

I did walk out of the camp on my own, half a mile away to a watch-tower on the edge of the forest and overlooking the Ramganga. I was still approaching the tower when I heard bushes rustling just ahead and saw the tall, dry grasses moving. I stopped dead and watched, not knowing whether the animal was a warthog, deer, baby elephant with its mother watching me, python, leopard or tiger. My heart was in my mouth and I backed off one pace at a time. I made a detour then ran up the ladder of the watch-tower. Just at that moment, the rustler emerged—a big mongoose and quite uninterested.

If I ignored the locked book cabinet, the high-priced dessert and the apathy of most of the staff, and cooked fish caught by the English couple on the fishing expedition, the quiet life at Dhikala could be thoroughly enjoyable. It made a complete change from the previous months of incessant questioning though I missed the Ganga. Dhikala was poorly organised but I found it restful, so I showered, shaved, and dressed neatly in shirt and trousers to go to the park office to ask for an extension to my four-day stay without having to return to the officer in Ramnagar. The chances were slim, I knew, but it was worth at least asking.

'How long do you wish to stay?' asked the park official.

'Four nights.'

'Then you stay in the Log Hut,' he said smiling.

I was forced to laugh. There are many days when this country totally baffles the outsider. There are days when one curses and others when one cannot contemplate ever leaving, when one is embarrassed ever to have fretted.

For all the infuriating inefficiencies and unfulfilled assurances, when urgent help was needed, the park officials did all they could. That evening, Kevin, the young Englishman on the fishing expedition, was suddenly taken sick with what he thought were angina pains. A jeep and driver were provided without delay, or charge, to take Kevin and his girlfriend to Ramnagar. The public hospital in the town was clean, efficient and equipped with an ECG machine in working order. The attack passed off and doctors declared him healthy.

Earlier that same evening, the restaurant manager announced that the public bus would be finishing the next morning because of the imminent arrival of the monsoon. After nine o'clock one could only leave by hitch-hiking or taking a taxi and paying whatever price was demanded. There was no choice but to leave and six of us departed on the scarred bus, leaving behind two others who were confident they could hitch a ride out somehow before the park closed as soon as the rains began. These were expected within 14 days.

Eight hours after leaving the park, I was in the railway station at Moradabad buying a first class ticket to Hardwar where I would resume the walk. Reservations on the train were 'not possible' but I hoped to find somewhere to crouch down in first class. At least in India there is no such thing as a full train.

The train was not due until 1.15 a.m. and I sat for nine hours in a brown, padded armchair in the sultry First Class Waiting Room reading a book and watching rats scramble quietly from chair-leg to table-leg and into holes in the walls without anyone giving a second glance. I had not bathed all day but there were showers in the waiting room and a notice in English and Hindi saying soap and towels were available from the attendant at a charge of R1-50.

'It is not possible,' the attendant told me.

'Why not?'

'It is not possible.'

'The sign says towel and soap—ask you.'

'No, no.'

'Yes, yes. Where is the complaints book?'

He waved his arm vaguely down the platform crowded with people and suitcases.

'Which place?' I demanded.

'Give me one rupee and fifty paise for towel and soap.'

I did this and he produced the items from a black trunk at his side.

The train to Hardwar arrived an hour late, after a train bound for the much-troubled Punjab had arrived so crowded that men sat three deep on the roof, boys rode on the buffers between carriages and tired faces with bright turbans were peering out from all windows and doorways, but as always in India there would be room for a few more. My train came in at 2.15 a.m. and sleepy bodies along the platform came to life in a hectic scramble to board before the guard blew his whistle. I tried to enter three First Class carriages, each time being told by the attendant that they were full.

'This is First Class,' announced the black-jacketed train conductor with clipboard in hand. He looked me up and down and saw the blue backpack, *lungi* and worn-down sandals.

'Yes,' I said. 'And I have a first class ticket.'

He was surprised. 'Let me see,' he said and inspected it closely and handed it back. 'It is not possible. The train is full.'

'The train is not full,' I said. 'There's no such thing.'

'You must get your ticket refunded and go second class.'

'And will you keep the train? No, you will not!'

'I cannot help. You must go in the morning.'

'It's already the morning and I'm bloody well going.'

The conductor was unconcerned and turned away. I walked briskly down the train trying the doors, but they were all locked. I attempted to climb onto the buffers between the carriages but decided that this was too dangerous. The door of the next carriage was open.

'You cannot go there,' called the conductor coming up quickly behind me.

I turned round. 'Too bad. I've a ticket to go to Hardwar. I've waited nine hours and I bloody well will go to Hardwar!' I was now shouting, ranting in the middle of the night. A small crowd gathered on the platform.

'You must come off,' repeated the conductor.

'No! I won't get off. I'm going to sit here,' I declared and promptly squatted on the floor in one corner of the corridor to await the arrival of the armed police to throw me out. I was left alone for a few minutes, except for the crowd staring in through the door who eyed me with a mixture of curiosity and amusement.

'Your ticket please,' said a new man quietly. 'You may sit up there,' he said, pointing to a conductor's seat at the other end of the corridor. Two officials of the railway joined me, declining my offer of the seat and spreading a cloth on the floor, taking off their shoes and settling down to their places for their journey.

'I heard your discussion with the conductor,' said one of the men.

'I was not very polite.'

'No matter. Cigarette?'

13

Up the Mountain Road

The train pulled into the congested station at Hardwar at 6.15 am on June 2nd and after several cups of tea I set out towards Rishikesh, 15 miles away. I now carried a large blue backpack bought in New Delhi and though the gradient of the road through the *sal* forest was gentle I did not get more than a few miles before sitting down in the shade with back, hips and shoulders aching. I realised that I was still too weary and too thin to carry this heavy load up to the source of the Ganga.

I had climbed only 930 feet in the 1380 miles from Bengal but had now to climb 12,500 feet in 175 miles to Gau Mukh. My body and mind were so drained of energy that I wondered if I could make it even without the baggage. I would certainly not reach my destination if I tried to carry the heavy backpack crammed with a thousand essential items for the two-man mountaineering expedition up the Gangotri glacier, over the Kalindi Pass and down to Badrinath. It was already digging into my shoulder blades and hip bones. My feet also were rebelling against the weight and several septic sores were still unhealed. In Rishikesh, I would have to decide what to do, and hoped to find a letter from Raj Dutt. Meanwhile I plodded on, halting frequently for tea at roadside stalls or just to take the weight off my back and feet by sitting in the shade.

It was after teatime before I reached Rishikesh, a congested town that is the staging post for pilgrims going into the mountains and a town of many *ashrams* and holy men. Hills rise up on three sides of the town and the fourth is open down to Hardwar and beyond onto the Gangetic Plain. Now, in June, the summer sun was melting the snows and glaciers far away and releasing a torrent of swirling, grey water that flowed through Rishikesh in a stream nearly half-a-mile wide. The river had been clear and much narrower three weeks earlier than I had last seen it.

In the peak season of May and June tens of thousands of people throng the town, filling every street and alley, every bench and bus-stand. The town becomes very dirty, smelly and noisy; yet the busloads of pilgrims seem to be oblivious to all this.

Thirty men and women from a village far away walked in a line through the jostling crowd. The women were small, clad in scarlet and orange saris and wearing heavy silver bracelets around their bony wrists. All of them were silent, their mouths closed and brown eyes fixed ahead, unmoved by the commotion and their unfamiliar surroundings as they marched through the streets barefoot, with their grey-haired husbands in a line behind them. The men, too, were silent, dressed in clean, white *dhotis* of rough, homespun cloth, with coils of white cloth wrapped round their heads. They were all going to the temples to make *puja* and to receive *darshan* beside Mother Ganga.

Much later in the day, I saw them coming back excitedly along the main street, everyone chattering at once, looking round at the pots and pans, the clothes, cloths and cool drinks and the stalls of hot and cold snacks.

I walked through the town and a mile upstream to the government-run Tourist Bungalow, where *ashrams* line the banks of the river. A group of men were gathered outside the main gate. They were all on strike. Despite asssurances from the manager that there were no telegrams, I marched inside to collect the telegram addressed to me that lay on the counter. It was from Raj Dutt:

'Deeply regret unable join trip. Will try meet you Gangotri.'

Short of a miracle, there was now no way I could make the trek from Gangotri to Badrinath, the second main headwater of the Ganges. I felt very relieved to be spared the additional strain and physical exhaustion that the hike up over 19,510 feet would have demanded. The heavy trekking equipment was no longer required, and I could unload most of the big, new backpack and leave the extra equipment here in Rishikesh. For the first time for days, I whistled as I returned to the town and I bought a celebratory slice of water melon from a stall—but it was rotten.

Perhaps because of my appearance—*lungi* and *kurta* with a back-pack—the manager of the Tourist Bungalow sent me to the Swiss Cottage where many low-budget Westerners and the newly-mobile young Japanese camp in little chalets in the garden for R5 per night. It was run by a quiet, middle-aged *swami* who watched over his heterogeneous flock with humour and grandfatherly indulgence.

I met a second *swami* as I took my bath standing in my underpants on a concrete platform in the middle of the garden. He was a gaunt man in khaki shorts and shirt who came to refill the water bucket at my feet. Again and again he refilled it from the handpump close by, while I enjoyed the cool shower. Never once did he utter a syllable or respond to my greeting.

Thousands of young Westerners come to the *ashrams* of Rishikesh every year to join Hindus seeking peace and instruction in meditation or yoga. Their money has built several big *ashrams*, concrete palaces with spires and a peculiar mixture of Hindu teachings and Western business methods.

The Maharishi Mahesh Yogi's palace, made famous by the Beatles, is now closed to foreigners and the Mahesh Yogi has gone to Switzerland following his devotees. Transcendental Meditation remains a thriving multinational corporation but the influx of Westerners with money, eager to support their *gurus*, has caused local alarm and pushed up land prices.

'It is dangerous to allow such elements to operate freely in the country. The practices of these cults are not religious at all. It is a hocus-pocus of magic, fancy ritual and group frenzy. There is no sanction in the scriptures for this parody of Hinduism,' according to an editorial in *The Hindustan Times*.

The editorial continued, 'It is not unlikely that these so-called "*ashrams*" are espionage centres. The suspicion is that amongst the gadgets they bring to the country, there are wireless transmitters also.'

The Divine Life Society, founded by the late Swami Sivananada in 1936, is one of the best-known and most popular with Westerners seeking Truth and organised calm. In the main courtyard of the large *ashram* complex, there is a tall, marble obelisk setting out the *swamiji*'s 20 instructions outlining the essence of yoga and the philosophies of the Vedanta scriptures:

> Get up at 4 a.m.; do not overload the stomach; preserve *Virva* (vital force); sleep separately; speak the truth at any cost; speak a little, sweetly; reduce your wants; never hurt; do not depend upon your servants; always have a *japa-mala* (beads) on your neck; serve the sadhus, sannyasins and the poor, the sick and the suffering; do not be lenient to your mind.

In addition to the pilgrims who stay in Rishikesh and the *ashrams*, many thousands pass through the town on their way to the holy places up in the mountains. Today, the increasing affluence of many people is enabling Hindus from all over India to make the journey their parents only dreamt about. Hardwar and Rishikesh are therefore thriving on this new business. Buses, chauffeured cars, clothes, bedding, fruits, walking sticks, cakes and breads and much more are available to the pilgrim tourist. Only 20 years ago pilgrims went up to Gangotri, Kedarnath or Badrinath on foot or on horseback along a narrow bridlepath, sleeping in lodges spaced every few miles. Military roads were built up the valleys following India's defeat in the war with China in 1962, and the old bridlepaths and pilgrim lodges have now almost completely vanished.

I left the tent, cooker, kerosene, utensils, extra clothing and surplus books behind at the Swiss Cottage in Rishikesh before I started up the steep hill out of the town, passed by crowded buses that belched fumes and by packed government and private cars with rolls of bedding strapped to the roof-racks. Most of these turned left, along the direct road to Tehri, while I continued beside the river and would reach Tehri by the longer route.

After walking three miles, I stopped to make tea and toast on a fire of sticks and dry leaves at the roadside. I sat for a while looking over the edge of the road, 250 feet down to the river and then out across the plain that stretched all the way back to the Bay of Bengal. I was now among the foothills of the Himalayas, walking on the left side of the V-shaped valley through which gushed the turbulent Ganga. The valley walls rose steeply all round so that the sky seemed to be shut out, and only a little blue crack could be seen overhead. The *sal* trees and dense underbrush grew all the way up the slope, above my head and beneath my feet, and the women slash branches from the top of these precipitous trees for animal fodder.

The road cut across this greenery like a slit from a sharp knife, exposing rock and gravel like a bleeding gash. It clung to the contours of the hillside, curving out around promontories and bluffs, then swinging back round in bends wherever a stream had cut a gully. Down below, the Ganga snaked through the valley as if resisting the confinement of the mountains and eager to be released. It is no wonder the mythology said she had been an impetuous goddess when young. Around one of these sweeping bends, I came in sight of the first tumbling brook of clear water cascading down the hillside, its bubbling, white energy refreshing to behold after months of the plain's stagnant water, and its chilly water invigorating to drink.

I plodded on all morning as the road cut first diagonally up the hillside then wound down, and then climbed up again. By lunchtime, the Ganga was far below, hidden by green slopes, and it was too hot for me to continue walking, so I stopped to boil up a packet of tomato soup in the shade of a mango tree beside the dry bed of a stream. Two men and a boy came with two cows and showed me a pool of water hidden away behind bushes full of noisy birds. The pool was alive with little fish. Beyond sharing its location with me, the trio made no conversation and I was left alone. How marvellous, I thought, not to be molested by questions.

After lunch, I sat back to idle away the hottest two hours of the day and another man came to join me under the cool canopy of the mango tree. He was not a holy man but wore white clothes, white plastic slippers and carried a shawl and a little bag like a man's purse. He slept for a short time, then he opened his eyes, sat up and announced in Hindi, 'I am going to Shri Badrinath. I have no money.'

It was a straight statement of fact and after a moment I gave him R5. I could not assess the truth of what he was saying, but I could not refuse a man who *might* need the money to continue his pilgrimage on foot. In the same way, villagers give food to *sadhus* and other holy men, content if only one among a group of frauds is genuine.

'Will you drink tea?' I asked.

'No, no.' But he got up and took the water bottle to fill it, while I cleaned out the soup pan and relit the little campfire.

'My country is Rajasthan, far away,' he said, when we were both resettled under the dark shade of the tree. 'I am going to Shri Badrinath. I came with two hundred rupees in my pocket. When I was sleeping in the temple in Rishikesh, I woke and the money was gone from my pocket. I have eaten no food but now I shall eat, thanks to you.' He saluted me with the palms of his hands held together against his chest but he refused to stay for some tea and went off up the road before the water boiled. I stayed to enjoy five little cups of lemon tea listening to the chatter of birds and watching the antics of a black-faced monkey who scurried along the cliff dislodging rocks that fell with a clatter into the ravine 50 yards from where I was sitting.

I stopped again for a rest later in the afternoon at a stall built on stilts over the edge of the hillside. Inside, there was a man dressed in white with his back towards me who was asking, 'How much is *dal*? How big is the *chapati*?' He ate his meal and when he stood up to buy a bundle of *beedis* I realised that he was the pilgrim from Rajasthan.

We walked together along the road, which now led steeply down to the river and along what was signposted as 'Marine Drive'. The afternoon's sunlight made the river appear as a gurgling, swirling torrent of milk chocolate, spewing up over rocks and cascading down in foaming waves. Here was no goddess. This was brute force and anger, all brawn and no grace. The sun sank until hidden by hills in the west, and in an instant the colour of the water changed to concrete grey.

Whenever I stopped, my companion stopped just as months before the stray dog had. I did not want company, nor did I want someone to feel indebted to me. 'How much money do you have?' I asked. He took out R2; what was left from the five rupees after his meal and *beedis*. I gave him another R10 but was unable to explain adequately in Hindi that he need not wait for me, so I told him to go. He went off reluctantly, but I soon caught up with him and we walked together as grey storm clouds gathered overhead.

When it was almost night, and with no idea of where to sleep, we reached a clearing in the forest where a dozen *dhabas* lined the road. Only one place, at the far end of the line, would serve us food this late. A bare-chested man was sitting on a chair out in the road sipping tea from a saucer, while a youth squatted on the kitchen counter talking to a friend holding a transistor radio and hens strutted freely on the empty table tops. There were no other customers. I ordered lemon water, rice and fried *dal*. But when the food came, Gars, the man from Rajasthan, refused everything though he must have been hungry.

An hour later we settled down to sleep on the narrow benches beside the tables. The expected storm never came and it was a warm, humid night, relieved by a slight breeze. A couple of *beedis* inhaled deeply into my lungs dulled the mind sufficiently to sleep, but during the night I had to rub mosquito repellent over my hands and face.

We awoke to the clatter of pots being cleaned and people clearing their throats. When I got up buses were already passing through with their horns blaring. They halted, disgorging plump, middle-aged travellers eager to eat. It was 6 a.m., too early for me to eat spiced foods, so I consumed two *parathas* and a cold bottle of Limca and bought lemons for tea-making along the road.

Gars said he wanted to come with me to Gangotri, but this I could not countenance. I badly wanted to be alone, to be unobserved and unquestioned. Only by being alone during the day could I continue to cope with the crowds, noise and questions encountered every evening. So I set off alone down the winding road towards the river and halted after a few hours to make a second breakfast of lemon tea and reheated *parathas* with a tin of sardines.

The broad road now turned sharply left round a bend and began a five-mile climb up 2400 feet. The Ganga was left, a silent, khaki ribbon far below. Up and up, the road curved round wide bends, each like the waistline of a sumo wrestler, reaching higher and higher up the hillside. The ground fell away suddenly from the edge of the road, down arid slopes of cactus and dwarf bushes. At one time cultivated terraces covered much of the hillsides, but the soil is stony and poor and today many of the terraces are abandoned and their retaining walls have collapsed. I could find no reason for this and could only surmise that streams had dried up after the trees on the tops of the hills had been cut down, or that the people preferred the physically less demanding work of cracking rocks in road gangs or serving busloads of pilgrims. Despite climbing higher and higher, and although the valley was now several miles wide, the view was disappointing. A haze thickened throughout the morning until the undulating ridges of the surrounding peaks became only wavy lines in an opaque, white sauce. At midday I reached the summit of the hill, to be greeted by children filling water pots at the mouth of a white, marble lion. Then the road started down the hillside again and by evening I would be beside the Ganga once again.

My lunchtime fire was not a success. I halted under the shade of a solitary mango tree at the roadside and built a small fire to make soup and textured vegetable protein (TVP), a dried, vegetarian convenience food. But the fire refused to burn with any vigour. Five girls and two boys, who were herding sheep and goats along the road, decided to stop to watch my dismal performance and contrived to keep their animals surrounding me under the mango tree while they sat in a group 30 yards away. I frantically fanned my little camp fire, trying to bring it to life while the goats were pushing in to have a look. Several times I struck out at the blank-eyed nuisances incessantly nosing at my backpack and the pan of tomato soup on the fire.

The soup finally boiled, simmered and was at last ready. I poured a little into my plastic cup and sat back with the cup and soup pan beside me to relax over the meal. The next moment, the cup was spilled and a goat's greedy tongue was lapping up the soup left in the pan beside me. My patience snapped; my umbrella became a weapon and I struck out wildly at the stupid animals. None of them moved away with any haste whatever, which only enraged me more, and delighted the tittering children.

It was after sunset when I rejoined the river just beyond a deep gorge of purplish rock, 43 miles from Rishikesh. I could see Devprayag, that day's destination, several miles away, perched at the bottom of the hillside between two rivers cutting violently through the rock. This confluence of her two headwaters, the Bhagirathi and the Alakananda, is the true birthplace of the Ganga. The narrow Bhagirathi, running from the left, was the sacred thread which I aimed to follow.

I walked briskly as daylight gave way to misty twilight and heavy, brooding clouds gathered all around. It was eerie walking alone on the empty, windswept road with the wind whistling through the telephone wires and lightning flashing suddenly behind black mountains in the distance. I hurried along making mental preparations to use one of my new supply of metallic 'space blankets' as a poncho when the storm broke and the heavens should open. It grew dark and silent. The wind stilled. I expected to be drenched at any moment. Already a wall of heavy rain was advancing down the valley towards Devprayag from the north, and there was lightning but no thunder. I was now not far from the town and could see pin-pricks of light shining, but these blacked out when the electricity was suddenly cut.

Big rain drops were falling when I reached the outskirts of the town and the downpour began in earnest just as I stepped up into one of the *dhabas*. I ate the welcome hot meal of *chapatis, dal* and *subzee* with the rain clattering on the tin roof, combining with the roar of the river to make conversation impossible.

I did not want to sleep a second sweaty night in dirty clothes on a narrow bench in a *dhaba* and so I decided to go the the Tourist Bungalow when the rain stopped. The town was black and I had to rely on flashes of lightning to see my way across the swaying suspension bridge above the torrent of the Bhagirathi and up through the empty, narrow lanes of the town. I began to worry that the bungalow would be full. But I went anyway and was greeted by a young, cheerful manager who was unabashed by my unprepossessing appearance, and put me in a double room with its own clean bathroom. Within half an hour, the electricity came on and I congratulated myself on finding such luxury. I stripped off the grimy, sweaty clothes and looked into the mirror before taking my first shower for two days. I knew I had become thin, but the pale skin over my bones seemed to be transparent, and hip bones, collar bones and shoulder blades were all protruding. My arms were thin and shapeless, like tubes with bony elbows. Both legs were gaunt with knee-caps several sizes too big. Even my buttocks had shrunk and the skin was loose which made it uncomfortable to sit for long in a chair. This was not helped by a big pimple on one buttock.

The three-day hike up from Hardwar had tired me out more than I supposed and I slept twelve hours and then went back to bed in the morning after a brief trip to the market to be shaved, to have my sandals repaired yet again, and to search for eggs for breakfast and buy bananas and lychees which were currently in season.

Hindus say the junction of the Bhagirathi and Alakananda rivers is second only to Allahabad in importance. The double-storey houses of the medieval town stand in neat rows, one above another, up the hillside in five rows separated by narrow lanes and steep steps. Each house is painted brown on the lower half, then white up to the grey, slate roofs which look like big fish-scales. Windows are small and every house is fronted by a narrow wooden balcony with a few potted flowers. There are no vehicles and everything must be carried into the town by stocky porters with thick, muscular legs who haul 200-pound sacks of rice and wheat, boxes of fruit and vegetables and household furniture across the suspension bridge from the road, along lanes and up the steps and through the narrow doorways into people's homes, shops, or dark warehouses.

Today, few pilgrims stay in Devprayag, and it is only a ten-minute halt for weary passengers in cars and buses who look across to the pretty houses from tea-stalls on the opposite bank. Then the horns blare and it's all aboard again and off up the valley road in swirls of dust and fumes.

Sixty years ago, before there was a road, 60,000 pilgrims used to trek from Devprayag every year up the right-hand river, beside the Alakananda, heading for the temples at Kedarnath or Badrinath. The trail was also an ancient route for traders going to Tibet. In 1918, travellers and villagers living in the valley faced the additional danger of a man-eating leopard that killed over 125 people and many domestic animals in an eight-year reign of terror.

This was not the first man-eater in the valley around the town of Rudraprayag. There was a centuries-old tradition that tigers and leopards killed unworthy pilgrims who travelled up the valley. The Man-eater of Rudraprayag became the most famous of these, and many people believed the leopard was no mere animal but an evil spirit or a *sadhu* and that only fire could destroy the evil. Eventually Jim Corbett was summoned, for his longest and most exhausting hunt.

When, eventually, the man-eating leopard was killed, news of Corbett's success spread quickly and thousands of people came to see the dead animal for themselves, bringing roses, marigolds or a few petals with them to be poured as tokens of thanks at Corbett's feet. An annual fair commemorating the killing of the leopard was held in Rudraprayag for many years and it is still celebrated in local folk songs. A memorial stone stands at the roadside where the leopard was killed and a graffiti writer has added to the inscription '10 p.m.'—the time of death.

After two days of rest in Devprayag I plodded up a long road winding diagonally up the side of the mountain in the valley behind the town. I had been told this was the road to Tehri, and I walked holding up the front of my *lungi* to cool my thin legs. All the streams were dry, and I passed many brass pots and large, square tins set out by the road for a water truck that later came crawling up the road.

I reached the top of the hill after five hours only to realise that I was at the head of the wrong valley and therefore on the wrong road. I shrugged my shoulders and kept walking. I would eventually reach Tehri.

Under the strong sun of the afternoon, I walked along a level road just below the crown of the hill, somewhere between the Bhagirathi and the Alakananda which were both several miles away. The road soon deteriorated into a gravel track used by flocks of goats and sheep, by people walking to village markets or out collecting firewood or fodder, and by the one single-decker bus that lurched along between communities. It was a marvellous walk, even if it was along the wrong road, with a panoramic view to my left of a vast, bowl-shaped valley stretching out below into distant haze and sillhouettes of row upon row of rounded hills. All the hillsides were cultivated in narrow terraces, held up by brown, drystone walls. These had been built over generations, tier upon tier, along the contours of the hills and looked like giant heaps of salami slices, peppered by clusters of brown and white houses. Scattered plots of lime-green were luxuriant beds of rice seedlings soon to be transplanted when monsoon rains appeared. Then the streams would become gurgling cascades flooding the terraces and there would be field work for all family members and for the landless labourers. This was still three weeks away and, until then, the women were out in twos and threes fetching large pots of water from springs half a mile from their homes or climbing trees to cut fodder to be carried home in big baskets on their backs. These chattering groups always fell silent when I passed and never replied to the greeting of a strange man.

I halted to make lemon tea and mashed bananas on toast on a little fire of sticks and grass, and got wet when it began drizzling. I was walking between villages and wondering where I might sleep the night when I came to a small freshly-painted, cream-coloured bungalow set back a short way up the hillside in an orchard.

'Is this your house?' I asked a sun-tanned man in purple shirt and khaki shorts who came down the steps as I approached.

'Nope. It's an *ashram*,' he replied with the drawl of an American Southerner.

'It is possible to stay the night?'

'I dunno. You'll have to ask Cyril.'

I found the decision-making Cyril and asked him. After a glass of water I was led up to the bungalow and shown a bed in the ante-room to the kitchen.

'Hello, I'm Jennie,' said a smiling young Englishwoman, dressed in plain blouse and ankle-length skirt. 'I'll make some tea.'

Jennie was an English teacher on a quick visit to the *ashram* from a hill station about 45 miles away by road. She and James (from Louisiana) were to leave early the next morning after omelettes and hurried goodbyes to catch the bus to Tehri.

While Jennie made tea, I took a shower; the first with shocking cold water for six months. It was a welcome tonic, once I got used to it, washing off the dirt and fatigue of the day and the months of heat and dust. I began to understand why in the wintertime I had seen Bengalis taking cold showers enthusiastically.

Cyril came to sit with us on the verandah after dark while we waited for supper to cook on the kerosene stove, but Swami Manwathan, head of the *ashram*, was unfortunately in bed with a stomach upset.

'He gets like that. He doesn't sleep. He says people sleep too much. And then these things happen. He gets sick or he falls off a bus,' explained Cyril, sitting back comfortably with his legs sprawled. Wearing blue denim jeans, hiking boots and a T-shirt he looked younger than his 39 years. Cyril had been born in India but his family had emigrated and he had spent 15 years in the film industry in England and Canada before returning to India for longer and longer holidays. He had met Swami Manwathan on one of these visits and eventually reached this remote *ashram* to collaborate with *swamiji* (who was a year younger) in building their joint dream of serving the people by setting them an example. They were building up the eight-and-a-half acre *ashram* slowly, and had already established a weaving hut and planted fruit trees with the teamwork of a handful of youths and widows. Sale of apricots, apples, peaches and pears would eventually provide a steady income and also demonstrate to people in the valley that they could do the same for themselves. This is the slow and stony road to rural development—filling out forms, writing letters, and visiting bureaucrats to squeeze out the money that politicians say is so easily available to villagers.

'We've resisted the temptation for me to call up my rich foreign friends or for *swamiji* to go off and pull some stunt. We haven't brought in lakhs and lakhs (hundreds of thousands) of rupees. What would be the point of that? We want to set up a sprinkle irrigation system, for example, in such a way that the people here can also do it.'

For ten years before someone donated the land for an *ashram*, Swami Manwathan had walked the roads and paths of the Garhwal hills campaigning against animal sacrifices in the temples, which he abhorred for their senseless violence and because the cost of a goat could burden a family for years.

A large temple stands on the summit of the hill behind the *ashram* and on one particular day animals, people and priests were lined up while *swamiji* was speaking out against the bloodletting. 'These animals should not die,' he said and stretched out his hand to touch one of them. The animal fell dead at the swami's feet, according to the story. After this sign from God, animal sacrifices in that temple ended and soon afterwards land for an *ashram* was donated.

'Does *swamiji* meditate?' asked Jennie, after our meal of rice and stewed vegetables.

Cyril thought for a moment. 'Oh, I don't think so. No, I don't think he ever does. Oh, perhaps when he puts his head on the pillow.'

Electricity (when there is current in the power lines dangling across the valleys) and roads already reach many communities in the valleys containing 450 villages and 100,000 people within a 10-mile radius of the *ashram*. Pipes running down the hills bring water from springs to many communal taps, eliminating one of the women's chores. The families remain poor, subsisting on whatever they grow if they have land, and what they can earn locally or receive from family members working in Delhi or other cities on the plain. People call it a Money-order economy: local opportunities and markets for local produce are expanding but the centuries-old attitudes of the stocky, stalwart people seem to change slowly.

'People here live in the thirteenth century, the pre-industrial age,' Cyril explained. 'That's what we want here, with a few modern conveniences such as electricity, a road with a bus service, piped water and a kerosene stove in the kitchen.

'Everything, everything is possession. Every single thing, every ailment and sickness, everything that happens is said to be possession by some spirit. Personally, I think it's a way for the women to let their hair down and let it all hang out. They're repressed so much. Such behaviour wouldn't be tolerated, but then they become possessed by some spirit. And wow! They can scream and dance around and let it all hang out,' commented Cyril.

I reached Tehri, 20 miles from the *ashram* and 8300 feet above sea level, late the next afternoon, my legs trembling as I descended the hillside towards the town of 7,000 people. It looked a tidy place with green, bushy trees and tin-roofed houses arranged neatly on a flat peninsula between the junction of the Bhagirathi and one of its tributaries at the head of a relatively flat valley. However, up close, the streets of Tehri were dirty, the drains stagnant and infested with mosquitoes and the town is in fact built over many small hills, dominated by the cream-coloured palace of the former Maharajah of Tehri-Garwhal.

I was tired and went directly to the home of Shri Prem Singh, a Sikh friend of Cyril's, who lives alone in rooms overlooking a clean street near a small clock-tower looking like Big Ben, which had been built for Queen-Empress Victoria's Diamond Jubilee in 1897 but no longer worked. After a shower and a simple supper, Prem told me about the Tehri dam project which he strongly opposes.

The 832-foot dam is being built across the narrow Bhagirathi one mile downstream of Tehri and will be the fifth-highest rock-filled dam in the world. Work on the dam began in 1970 and is due to be completed by 1992. However, the four tunnels being dug to divert the river through the side of the mountain while the dam is being built are four years behind schedule. The lake behind the dam will flood Tehri and much of the valley, submerging 10,500 acres of land, 4000 of which are currently arable. At least 24,000 people will have to be resettled and already several thousand acres of forests have been cut down to make room for them in another valley.

Opponents of the project say the weight of the 575,000 million gallons of water in the lake will trigger earthquakes or other seismic activity. Prem Singh believes water will leak through the soft shale valley walls, or even cause the structure to collapse.

The cost of the project has risen from R180 crore in 1968 to R1090 crore in 1984. It is planned eventually to produce 2000 megawatts of hydro-electricity and to store enough water to irrigate 667,000 acres, an area larger than Luxembourg. The planned lifespan of the dam is 100 years but opponents claim that the accumulation of silt washed down after deforestation upstream will reduce this by one-third. They are angry that hill people will have to lose their homes and land while the benefits will flow to people living on the plain. There is a strong suspicion that contractors pay bribes to politicians and bureaucrats to approve the project and thus keep it funded, no matter how ill-chosen the site or ill-conceived the project.

I stayed with Prem Singh for two days, sleeping for much of the time, regaining energy and allowing the infected sores on my ankles and feet to heal. On the third morning, just before leaving Tehri, I stopped in the market at a small shop for two 'full-fry eggs' (cooked on both sides rather than burnt on the bottom and raw on top) and buttered toast with marmalade from a pot I was carrying—a morale-boosting breakfast.

Both sandals and feet were in good repair, though nine plasters still covered infected cuts and insect bites. I was pleased to be moving once again in the soft rain and clean air, and was delighted when at mid-morning I passed a kilometre-stone by the side of the road. 'Gangotri 163 km'—101 miles to go.

Five miles beyond Tehri, the valley ended and the hills came together once again. River and road converged through a narrow, V-shaped valley of black rock and grey slate, draped with dangling vegetation. Streams came cascading down narrow gullies, and disappeared into the brown river at the bottom. Lonely pine trees stood along the windswept ridges above the road and mist drifted through the tangle of vegetation on the lower slopes. A telephone lineman, in blue trousers and barefoot, dangled precariously over the cliff edge on a rope hanging from a telephone pole beside the road, while he and a second man strung up a wire.

I bought two pounds of fresh apricots for R4 in the next village and ate them all at once. The grim clouds of the morning finally cleared, leaving a sky of intense blue, almost turquoise, and a bright sun highlighting every shade of green. Families of monkeys came out to sit munching berries in the branches of the *sal* trees.

I expected to reach the next town, Uttarkashi, the following morning and after that there would be organised places to stay. This would therefore be my last opportunity to sleep out alone beside the Ganga. It was well after sunset when I left the road along a path leading down 250 feet to an isolated place beside the rushing river. There was a small village near the path and in no time, 13 boys came running, whistling and waving their arms to discover the identity of the stranger.

'You are going to Gangotri?' asked the biggest boy, repeating what I had just told him. 'Where are you going?'

I pointed to the river. 'Bhagirathi.'

We went down together in silence to the flat strip of grass and sand beside the grey, roaring river. I put down my backpack against a flat-topped rock which was about the size of a double bed.

'Are you going to sleep on this?'

'No, no,' I said, smiling and pointing to the earth, 'Here.'

The last of the daylight was fading fast, so without explanation I began hunting for twigs and dry grasses for a campfire. The boys immediately joined in, all the time telling me to stop and let them do it.

'No, no, *swamiji*. We will do it.'

We all collected firewood and there was soon enough driftwood for a dozen fires.

'Are you a *sannyasin*?'

'I am on a pilgrimage,' I said, looking at the pairs of wide eyes so eagerly observing me as we crouched on the ground opposite one another in the gathering gloom.

'Come to the village to sleep.'

'Thank you. No. I will sleep beside Gangaji.'

'You have food?'

I nodded and pointed to the backpack.

'Come to our village.'

'Thank you, no,' I repeated quietly. 'I have come from Calcutta, on a foot march, by the bank of Gangaji. So I shall sleep here.'

'Is it so!' exclaimed a voice, whose face was by now invisible in the dark.

I laid out a fire between two flat-topped rocks but hesitated to light it in front of these experts. The fire lit with the first match, then struggled with lots of smoke and little melodrama.

'We will go now.'

We all got up to say farewell to one another with small bows and the boys marched off in a line back to their village. I was alone in the dark beside the flicker of the campfire and the roar of the river. I put a pan of packet soup fortified with TVP on the fire. Then I took off my sandals and paddled in the river. The water was far colder than I expected. My feet were quickly numb but it was a glorious sensation to ache with cold, to feel the chill rising up my legs and to splash the water over my face and neck. It was good too to step out of the water and to feel the warmth returning to my limbs.

I stirred the soup and sat in the dark watching the fast flow of the river, silver by moonlight. I was now within 100 miles of my destination and almost 1500 miles from the start at Ganga Sagar. What did the river mean to me now, after so many miles and so much anger and pleasure?

The river had become very special to me. Mine was a personal reverence for the river, and although I understood little of how Hindus regard the Ganga I had gained her for myself as a symbol of something far greater than mere human endeavour.

I could not name the river as a goddess. I doubted there could be any connection between spiritual and temporal, except for a Great Spirit in the Sky in which all Creation exists. Worship and personal petitions and the law of karma could bring no changes; there could be no thunderbolts of vengeance. If personal gods do exist, Ganga and the others must be deaf, blind and cold. It had been a long way to walk just to come to this.

After the soup and a pan of lemon tea, it was time for bed. I put on the new thermal underwear my father had sent from England under pyjamas and *kurta*, spread the shawl on the ground and wrapped myself and the backpack in a 'space blanket'. Lightning and thunder closed in soon afterwards and heavy rain came pouring down, striking the metallic sheet like the timpani of a symphony orchestra. I closed my eyes and was soon asleep. It would be just bad luck if the metallic blanket attracted a bolt of lightning.

I pulled back the blanket with a loud crinkling next morning and peered out with sleepy eyes at the world. Rain was still falling and brown mist hung over the fast-flowing river. The day looked no brighter when I woke again later. The ground was sodden and there was no chance of my making a fire and enjoying a cup of hot tea. After pouring off rainwater from pockets in the 'space blanket' and carefully wiping off a cluster of large, black ants who were sheltering under the backpack, I climbed the path and crossed through the village towards the road. It was still drizzling and I was thankful to be protected by my faithful umbrella. Men and boys watched my passing from the shelter of covered verandahs while women and girls worked out in the wet, fetching drinking water in brass pots.

My sandals soon became soaked on the water-logged road. When one strap snapped, I took off the sandal and walked with one bare foot for five miles before stopping for a breakfast of tea and five *puris* spread with marmalade. Eggs were not available and I could not bring myself to eat more spiced *chena*. There was no one to repair the broken strap so I tied the sandal to my foot with a bandage and did the same with the other sandal when another strap broke later in the day.

The solitude of these days, as I steadily approached the source of the Ganga, was so comfortable and enjoyable that I hardly noticed my increasing weariness. I climbed through gorges of purple rocks, up sudden, steep rises and long inclines for most of every day. Yet I halted often amid tall cedar trees with giant cones, to make tea and to watch the hills all around and the waters far below. These were still the foothills and merely a preparation for what lay ahead. Halts to make tea and bowls of soup fortified with TVP became longer and longer as I became gradually overcome by mingled contentment and exhaustion.

Every day, I passed a dozen *sadhus*, also walking alone or in pairs, up or down the valley, wrapped in orange robes or wearing only a loin cloth. They travelled much lighter than I, usually with only one blanket, a begging bowl and a staff. Three miles from Uttarkashi, as I approached in the early evening, I saw a man lying face down in the middle of the road. He was marking a line ahead of himself with a stick, then standing up and pacing to the line, pausing to pray, then lying down again in the dust. I was amazed and stood watching at the side of the road as he approached slowly by body-lengths.

'Where are you going?' I asked when he stopped and greeted me.

'Madras,' he said.

'Madras!' I exclaimed. 'But that's over a thousand miles away.'

'You are coming from?'

'Ganga Sagar. Calcutta.'

'Is it so? Very far.'

I was so astonished to meet someone performing a pilgrimage by lying down in the road for the whole distance that I forgot to ask him where he was coming from. White dust covered his shirt, his knee-length *lungi* and the fronts of his dark, brown legs like bizarre make-up. He carried nothing with him, not even a blanket or a begging bowl. His eyes were bright, yet calm with quiet confidence, and he was perhaps 40 years old. I stood in silence smiling and watching, then we wished each other well and went our separate ways.

14

Bathing at the Cow's Mouth

I stayed in the Tourist Bungalow in Uttarkashi for nearly a week, mostly sleeping, eating and reading. My sandals were now so dilapidated that a cobbler had already asked me, '*Sahib*, why don't you buy yourself a new pair?' I had been unable to explain to him that I wanted to wear them for the whole walk, and found a cobbler in Uttarkashi able and willing to repair all the straps of both sandals. Unfortunately, my green-check *lungi*, that had lasted more than six months was now in shreds so I bought a pair of pyjama trousers several sizes too short and brown in colour with purple and yellow stripes. They were a marvellous sight, but the colours unfortunately faded with each washing.

I still had no stomach for spiced food so I ate mostly fried eggs, buttered toast with marmalade, tins of baked beans and processed cheese, crackers and pounds of lychees and bananas and drank coffee. This bland diet was expensive, and I had soon consumed every tin of baked beans in Uttarkashi.

I slept most of each day alone in a four-bed dormitory at the Tourist Bungalow, enjoying the rest and allowing the sores on my ankles and feet to heal. Every day, after five o'clock, the tour buses and cars would arrive on the front lawn and boxes, bags and metal trunks would be hauled by porters and the bungalow was invaded.

I bought several English-language newspapers every day and was shocked one morning to read a report that the Government of India was suddenly requiring visas from all Commonwealth citizens because of the civil unrest in the Punjab. Foreigners' Registration Offices were reported to be in chaos, many of them completely ignorant of any new regulations. No one seemed to know the correct deadline or procedures for applying for a visa, a situation encouraging India's petty-fogging bureaucrats and policemen to exercise their administrative power. I decided to ignore the visa requirement until after I had completed the walk. I could always plead ignorance of the new regulation. I was now within 70 miles of Gau Mukh, and was much too close to risk being sent back to New Delhi by an assertive policeman or official.

It rained hard for two hours on the morning of my departure from Uttarkashi so I set out late huddled under my umbrella. This was not the rainy season, I was told, only pre-monsoon showers. *Sadhus* were also out in the rain, with umbrellas and wet feet, coming into town with their begging bowls. I was soon away up the misty valley and when the drizzle stopped after an hour the clouds slowly broke up and vanished. Bright sunshine transformed the river from grey to white and brought the greens of trees and grasses to resplendent life. Far beyond the bends in the river, where massive cliffs constricted the gorge, and above the undulating ridges of the hills, I at last glimpsed a few jagged Himalayan peaks. The violent, narrow river seemed to be drawing me up through gorges beside miles of cataracts where the constant hissing of cold spray echoed on the valley walls and where the Ganga flowed in a boiling torrent, seething and rushing, hostile and arrogant, with a fury as if falling from heaven.

Further upriver the next day, the water was calm, moving with the speed and stealth of a fat alligator several miles long. Beyond this, the river channel reverted to its thundering, pounding cataract with boulders the size of houses and a constant throbbing that echoed on the valley walls. I stopped to make tea in the mid-afternoon and was aware of a dramatic change in my surroundings as I looked up the sides of the gorge to the forests and the grass slopes above. The foothills had been abruptly left behind. I was no longer cocooned in a valley between hills whose proportions were human. The summits in these new surroundings reached into the highest clouds. Naked, jagged rock was thrusting above the hillsides close at hand. Somewhere there, yet more remote, the Ganga had her source.

I sipped my sweet lemon tea daunted by the vastness and distance and revitalised by the new challenge. I felt like a little boy wearing his first pair of long trousers; not wholly sure of himself but happy to cast aside the short pants of yesterday. I finished the tea, put away the pan and put out the campfire. A bus rushed by with horn blaring and big wheels swirling up dust. I congratulated myself on not being cooped inside one of those lurching, tin boxes with sick people vomiting from the windows, ate a chocolate bar and set off up the road.

At once, the noise of the water abated. The valley widened and while the river flowed through the gorge, the road began a steep climb, swinging back and forth in hairpin bends up and up the mountainside. I followed the footpath that climbed up the mountain in a long straight line but it was slow going. My legs would stiffen up then relax suddenly and I would walk quickly until the stiffening recurred. I was inhaling hard and holding my dry mouth open to be able to breathe. I frowned and clenched my teeth. I was worn out but had to keep going and paused only briefly.

The path ran through a small army fuel storage area and up through a village of grey houses with narrow balconies and roofs of broad planks. Children were playing and singing in the small village square and we waved to one another as I walked by. The footpath was also the bed of a trickling stream, strewn with garbage and excreta. It took more than two hours to reach the top and I emerged onto the road hot, weary and surrounded by flies. I had not reached the top of the mountain but this was the end of the climb, and the road ran level now. I started walking after a ten-minute rest but was disappointed to see the road descending round another set of hairpin bends until it recrossed the Ganga at the bottom of the valley.

'Oh God,' I muttered to myself and sat down on a rock to munch another chocolate bar.

Chill winds were bringing storm clouds up the valley and the afternoon sunshine had vanished. The path dropped precipitously through a forest of cedar trees and grey boulders and I stepped cautiously, fearful of slipping or having both weary legs fold up underneath me.

The rain held off for several hours, enabling me to reach shelter for the night in the village of Hirsil and to eat a meal of scrambled eggs with tomatoes and onions fried in a pan laced with chilli powder. Heavy rain came when it was dark but by then the little village was deserted, and the shutters of the grey stone houses tightly closed. I shared a room over a *dhaba* with two boys, but I was much too tired to strip off and stand out in the rain for a wash though I knew I smelt bad. I sat instead on the edge of my bed smoking *beedis* until sufficiently relaxed to allow myself to sleep.

I woke next morning to the sound of heavy rain pounding on the roof and I went back to sleep, happy to remain snugly under a quilt for a little longer. But when at last I did rouse myself and look outside, there was not a cloud in the blue sky nor any sign of rain. The sound of the downpour was coming from the village tap, squirting water onto a concrete pad in the gravel lane below. The shutters of a dozen shops were already up and there were a few people in the street but I felt no guilt at having stayed in bed as it was not yet seven o'clock.

By daylight, the teahouse where I had eaten the night before looked like a gloomy, stone-built barn. The tea-*wallah* was sitting cross-legged on the low, earthen hearth behind the stove, surrounded by tins, pans and his money box. There was a large hole in one side for the draught and firewood to enter and two round holes in the top for kettles and pans, from which flames emerged and smoke escaped up to the roof. Hospitably, the tea-*wallah* made two 'full-fry eggs' and tomatoes, this time without the chilli powder.

Another man was sitting in a dark corner, spinning wool with what looked like a builder's plumb line. He looked up as each newcomer entered but never spoke, and he kept his right hand pulling strands of wool from a ball in his left hand while his fingers kept the line and the small weight at the bottom perpetually spinning and dangling near the ground.

Outside in the sunshine, a boy played with his toy motor car, made from a tin can wired to a long stick, the steering wheel being made of wire and silver paper.

By 8.30 a.m., I was once again walking amid the songs of birds and the scent of the pine forest. Gangotri was just 16 miles away and I expected to reach the end of the motor road at Lanka by lunchtime and Gangotri by evening. Though weakened by fatigue and feeling almost as tired as the night before, I could not permit myself a day's rest now I was so close to Gangotri. After Hirsil, the road gave up all pretence of being properly surfaced and became a regular forestry road of sand and gravel, though this did not seem to slow down the buses of pilgrims heading for Ganga's temple in Gangotri.

The road ran along the bottom of a half-mile wide valley to the right of the river, which was now flowing modestly over pebbles and boulders. Though grey in colour, the water looked inviting. I paused to watch a man standing ankle deep in the frigid river, holding a jug in both hands and pouring out the water as an offering. He was standing erect, wrapped in a brown blanket with ragged hem and half turned away from me so that I could not see his face. This hermit's cave was a short distance along the road, up the bank on the right under an overhanging rock. It looked to be a dark and dry shelter. When the man came back to the road he saw me watching but without speaking, smiling or showing any reaction whatever, he went up the bank to the cave. What a contrast to the superior and self-conscious pose of many *sadhus* in orange garb who loiter at the holy places.

I did indeed reach Lanka by late lunchtime and sat eating a little meal in one of the 30 *dhabas* built in rows under smoke-stained tarpaulins. Lanka was the end of the road and the terminus of the bus route from Rishikesh, a distance of two twelve-hour bus rides or nine days of walking. Here the hundreds of pilgrims emerged dazed and tired on shaky legs to eat in the *dhabas* or to cook their own food on small fires. From here, all pilgrims had to walk down several hundred feet into a gorge where the Bhagirathi thunders through a 150-foot channel. A second chasm was crossed by a small, wooden bridge and everyone had then to climb up the side of the gorge to the road. A box-girder bridge is being built across the chasm to link the road from Rishikesh with the existing ten-mile road to Gangotri and all too soon the buses will drive from the doors of Delhi to the gate of Ganga's temple in Gangotri. The only remaining experience of the hardships faced by pilgrims for centuries, slogging up the footpaths before the road made it easy, will be gone.

It was an arduous trek along the gorge even for someone used to walking, but gruelling for people from the plains who had never in their lives climbed higher than the roofs of their single-storey homes. Porters were available to carry small or frail people or bags or bedding, in baskets strapped to their backs. The social matrons from New Delhi, Madras, Bombay and Calcutta, with folds of fat bulging over the thick wraps of their silk saris, could be transported in coffin-shaped chairs carried on poles by four grunting, sweating porters.

Once again the stitching of both sandals was broken but I could not find anyone to repair them. The soles were now worn almost flat and the uppers had been patched with many small, square pieces of leather. There was no option, even if I'd wanted it, but to continue walking in worn-out sandals tied to my feet with bandages torn from the green-check *lungi*.

The warm evening light shone on the faces of the mountains rising above the forest in which Gangotri is situated, when at long, long last I entered the large village and stopped to stare at a kilometre-stone:

'Gangotri 0 km.'

It was June 21st. I was here at last; still twelve miles from the true source of the Ganga but so close now that I could not suppress a feeling of having made it! Few venture beyond Gangotri to the glacier at Gau Mukh, and it is to the small *ashrams*, isolated caves and the temple of Gangotri that the pilgrims and holy men have journeyed from the plain. The glacier once actually reached Gangotri, but is retreating.

The temple is not open all year round, opening when the snows melt at the beginning of May. It closes again in November when the silver doors of the squat, grey-washed building, about the size of a rich man's house, with a central dome and four corner turrets, is sealed for the winter.

This year the temple had opened on May 4th and in the weeks since then hundreds of worshippers had been arriving every day. They are pious people with petitions or prayers to the Mother, or are fulfilling vows to give thanks in Gangotri, perhaps for the recovery of a sick eldest son. Coming to Gangotri is also a holiday in exotic scenery and clean air, a break with domestic chores or field or factory work; a holy holiday and no less of a pilgrimage for being so. Making *puja* in the temple remains the most important duty and the people come forward barefoot with trays of assorted offerings. Pilgrims bow in the doorway, their foreheads touching the threshold, and with palms pressed together, prayers are made in a mumble or in silence as the *pujari* takes the tray to the gods. Worshippers are forbidden to enter the temple.

There stands Ganga, set on high and dressed in rich clothes that almost obscure her face. The lesser gods in this temple stand below her, likewise overdressed. A silver canopy decorated with silver paisleys stands over them all, but the interior of the temple is otherwise dark, with black walls and a black flagstone floor. The *pujari* puts the offerings before the deities with apparent indifference induced, perhaps, by the repetition of a task as monotonous as any assembly line work in a factory. Perhaps he was thinking it was all futile, but maybe it only seemed like this to an outsider and he acted with apparent unconcern because he was merely the messenger and intermediary between worshipper and the gods.

The *pujari* cracks each coconut against the canopy and offers the trays with sweets to the gods. The pilgrim waits, blocking light from the door and gazing eagerly at the deities, recognising the familiar faces yet not seeing them, as a person might look through, but not see, the glass pane in a window. Prayers are directed *beyond* what is seen. And how effective those prayers can be! A verse in the *Padma Purana* declares:

What need of expensive sacrifices, or of difficult penances?
Worship Ganga, asking for happiness and good fortune,
and she will bring you heaven and salvation.

A spoonful of sweetened water is poured onto the outstretched palm of each right hand, to be drunk and the hand wiped over the head. Then the *pujari* dabs a finger mark of red powder on each forehead. He hands back the tray with the sweets as *prasad*, food consecrated by the gods to be consumed by mortals.

It was the end of the day when I approached barefoot to the temple door where the white-clad *pujari* was standing. An attendant came with a brass tray four feet in diameter, carrying the paraphernalia of his trade—three conches, hand-bells and stainless steel plates. The tray was taken into the temple and a moment later the attendant came back with a tumbler of hot tea for the *pujari* at the end of another busy day. I put a few coins in the box and in return received the holy water and the mark of red powder on my forehead.

'Where will you stay? You will stay here?' asked the *pujari*, offering to let me sleep in one of the pilgrim hostels. But I had already made arrangements and I was staying at the Yoga Niketan, a branch of the main *ashram* in Rishikesh popular with young Westerners. It was run by a tall young man called Bhim, who was always immaculately dressed in white clothes which contrasted dramatically with his curly black beard and deep-tanned face.

Instruction in yoga and meditation are provided at the *ashram* for R20 per day but I could not pretend to have come for tuition so I explained how and why I was in Gangotri.

'How long will you stay?' asked Bhim, surprised at my story. 'After five days, it is my birthday. You have come by foot beside Gangaji. It is a great thing if you will stay for my birthday.' He perceived the moment's doubt on my face and added quickly, 'It is six nights' stay but you pay only five nights.'

The *ashram* was built on four wide terraces surrounded by a dry-stone wall beside the gushing, noisy Bhagirathi. I was shown to a room in a small, barn-like building, below the room where meditation and yoga were conducted. There were quilts on the carpeted floor and no furniture. I dumped the backpack and sat down in the doorway.

Two Australian women, an Englishman and a Swiss man were sitting near the cookhouse waiting for a VIP visitor who was expected to arrive in time for supper. Twice, word came that he was on his way but he didn't appear. Darkness was falling fast, appetites were whetted and the night was cold so it was decided we should eat. For the first time in months I was sitting wrapped in my shawl and still feeling cold.

'It's bedtime now. We get up rather early,' explained one of the Australian women after we'd washed our trays with ash and cold water. No sooner had we retired to our separate chalets than the gong sounded. The VIP *swami* from an *ashram* in Rishikesh had arrived and we were summoned for an audience on the cold verandah of Bhim's chalet.

'The greatest sin,' explained the *swami* when we were all assembled wrapped in two or three blankets, 'is thinking that this body is all; that I am so tall, that I am male, I am female. This is the greatest sin.

'When Adam and Eve were in the Garden, when they had eaten the fruit, what was the first thing they became aware of? Their nakedness!' exclaimed this elderly man, dressed in bright orange, from his woollen hat to his thick woollen socks.

'The greatest merit is to know that all is Brahman. That you are placeless, all pervading, all one in the supreme spirit.' For a few minutes the *swami* spoke in Hindi for the benefit of the five Indians in his audience, and then returned to his theme in English. 'Thinking only of here and now. This is the greatest darkness,' he said.

'*Swamiji*, how can we remove this darkness?' asked one of the Australian women.

The *swami* nodded, rubbing together his hands. 'Buddha said, "It does no good to beat a drum, to sweep the floor or to bring in a bulldozer. To end darkness you must bring in light". So you must attain knowledge.' He paused and looked at the group of foreigners. 'Not the knowledge of the intellect, but what Western philosophies call intuition. We call it special knowledge, divine knowledge.'

After this we were allowed to return to bed.

The gong for meditation the next morning sounded at 5 a.m. I did not get up but was woken again by a knock at the door at 6.15 a.m. and got up to drink hot tea outside the cookhouse with a dozen other cold people wrapped in blankets.

My planned days of rest at the *ashram* were cut short by the arrival of a tall, bearded, young Londoner called Joe Collins. He arrived by bus and was eager to get to Gau Mukh and if possible beyond to a place called Topoban. He asked if we could go together and though I wanted a few more days of sleep and rest, Joe was impatient to go on. He was convinced that within days the monsoon clouds would cover the mountain peaks for the season and that the torrential rain might also cause landslides that would block the footpath to the glacier.

Our indecision was resolved when we woke to see a cloudless, blue sky and bright sunshine the next morning. I awoke with considerable pain down both thighs and hamstrings but by now I would have crawled to Gau Mukh if necessary. We explained the change of plans to Bhim, who was annoyed that I might miss his 35th birthday. In the event, I did miss it. I returned to the *ashram* at lunchtime after all the celebrations had passed.

Joe and I stopped for a breakfast of mashed bananas and fresh *parathas* and tea, sold at exorbitant prices, before leaving Gangotri. Within half a mile of the village we met a young, fresh-faced Englishman wearing baggy Kashmir trousers and a long, green shirt.

'Come and have a coffee,' he said. 'I'm living in a cave just up here.'

We followed him up the path to an overhanging slab of rock surrounded by a stone wall that formed the cave. Our host pulled back a plastic sheet revealing a gap in the wall and led us inside.

'It's a bit dark, till your eyes get used to it.'

He was barefoot and I bent down to take off my sandals at the door to the cave.

'No need to stand on ceremony here,' he said, cheerfully settling down beside the open hearth and in no time having three small branches blazing brightly and smoke rising to the already soot-blackened rock just above our heads.

'Where you from then?'

'Brixton,' said Joe.

'I'm from Crystal Palace myself. Been here in India four years. Most of it's been up in Kashmir. I stayed up there two years. Lovely place is Kashmir. They're very clean up there,' he said rubbing his clipped, blond beard and busying himself rinsing out a pan and throwing the dirty water out through a gap in the wall.

'I've been here 20 days this year. Last year we had a stream just here,' he said, pointing up the valley. 'You could have yourself a good wash. This year there's no water, nothing. Lack of snow in the winter, they said. I've to fetch my drinking water from Gangotri.

'I was up here last year with my girlfriend for a couple of months. We went down to Rishikesh. That's where we started fighting. We took a kilo of marijuana with us—it grows wild round here, but it's too early yet. It's no good—and she was selling it and hiding the money away in her pocket and I was selling it and hiding the money in my pocket. We ended up with no grass and it seemed like no money.'

The pan of water boiled and he mixed in milk and coffee-chicory powders and stirred it round. We were one cup short so our host drank from the pan in between telling us more about his dwelling place.

'Seen the little guinea pigs? Lovely little creatures—they get into everything. See that bag there, hanging on the pole. They can even get into that. Little bastards. They're worse than the rats. They're even eating my clothes. And they took the last of my sugar last night. I had it in a bag there, by my head. Even then they'd come and had it.'

Four young men from Gangotri, in ragged and much patched jackets and jodhpur-like trousers, were outside crouching against a rock in the sunshine and looking through the opening in the wall.

'They'll be off soon. They're wood cutters, getting eight rupees a day. They're just curious. They come round often enough, scrounging cigarettes. But they're good lads and they sometimes bring me *ganja*.'

The cave was bare, except for one bag and a change of clothes hanging from the pole, the pan and a few tins of food, a blanket and a plastic bag with a couple of books and some papers.

'I can go away for four or five days and nothing here'll be touched. If I have to go down to Rishikesh I have to stash everything away. Last time I put away a pair of—what d'you call them?—tongs, like, for handling the fire. I hid them away and I still haven't found them. I just have to think. It'll come to me. Maybe I'll have a look today—been saying that for the last two days.'

Joe and I were soon on our way again but it was now too late for us to reach Gau Mukh in the remaining daylight. I wanted to savour the last miles and was becoming strangely afraid to end my journey, perhaps because, after seven months of walking, I couldn't imagine what else to do!

We were walking on a well-constructed path up the left-hand side of the V-shaped valley with the grey river to our right, passing among the last cedar trees, too scattered to be called a forest. The season for flowers was only just starting but wild rose bushes bore cream-coloured or red-violet flowers. Unfortunately, the handful of pilgrims and trekkers going up to Gau Mukh each day during the summer seemed unable to resist picking the wild flowers, which soon wilted and were thrown away.

Late in the afternoon, Joe and I reached the Lal Bab Ashram at Bhojbasa on a windswept, gravel plain ten miles beyond Gangotri. We were both extremely weary and grateful for the hot, sweet tea given to us as soon as we sat down. The energy that had powered us up from Gangotri was suddenly expended. This was partly due to the altitude as we had climbed another 2400 feet and were now at 12,500 feet. This final trek was fast draining my last reserves. I was tense, quiet and aware I was getting agitated at the least disturbance. Joe went to ask Lal Baba (meaning red father) if we could stay the night and, thankfully, he was told we were welcome.

'He knows he's running a hotel and provided you put money in the box, you can stay as long as you want,' explained Eric, a cheery South African who was travelling with his girlfriend Kim from Australia. 'He's turned out two *sadhus* because they didn't have money.'

We rested and chatted and within an hour of the sun sinking behind the high ridges the air became cold. This was both a welcome and uncomfortable sensation after so much heat. The absence of flies was certainly a blessing. Cold, opaque mist was already closing like a wall down the valley and round the mountain peaks. Soon it would be drifting through the *bhojbasa* trees just ahead of the *ashram* and creeping over the grey boulders that were strewn over the flat-bottomed valley like a giant's marbles. Soon we would be completely engulfed by the icy mists and the roar of the river would be muffled by the hush.

We were shown to a dark, empty room where we could sleep on the carpet with three other foreign guests: an Italian dressed like a *sadhu* and even more bony and emaciated than myself, and two well-fed, confident American scholars who were fluent in Hindi. Joe crawled into his sleeping bag and I changed into the thermal underwear and wrapped myself up in my shawl. Blankets would be available only after supper, which was currently being boiled in the kitchen, and the thick woodsmoke drifted through the room to the window. I lay flat on my back on the floor, with eyes closed and my mind withdrawn, focusing on Grieg's Piano Concerto and the four beavers on the bank across the river at home. I did not know whether this mental withdrawal was good or bad, only that it was essential for my survival. I had come to the end of a long mental and physical rope: I was still holding on, but only just.

Though conscious of the cold all night, I was warm enough in four blankets provided I remained still. It was so warm in this cocoon that the flea bites around my waist began to itch. By morning I felt so snug that I couldn't bear to get up. Joe urged me to rise because one of the Americans was offering to take us up the hillside to a magnificent view of the valley and of Gau Mukh.

It was hard work hiking up the steep hillside so early in the morning through the coarse grass. We reached a flat-topped rock below the bare cliffs and sat to watch the mist clearing off and unveiling the vast and grotesque snow-capped peaks all around us. The valley was several miles wide and smoothed out to a U-shape up towards the glacier. Trees and grasses gave way to a stark landscape of boulders and gravel which quarter-filled the valley with rubble. This was the Gangotri glacier, a barren creature of greys and browns, with a rough back like a crocodile slumping down the valley. Though we were more than two miles away we could pick out the Cow's Mouth, Gau Mukh, as a black spot on the end wall of the glacier. It is here that the Ganga is born.

One massive block of rock with three peaks stands on the left side of the glacier and we sat for a long time watching the light of the rising sun jumping from behind these peaks over the dark glacier and striking the snow-covered face of Mount Shivling on the right-hand side. The yellow light crept down from the 21,460-foot peak, over the knife-edge ridges of the solitary mountain and across the back of the glacier into the bottom of the valley.

At length, we returned to the *ashram* to find Lal Baba's appearance had been utterly transformed since the previous evening. Now this middle-aged, rather flabby man wearing thick, black spectacles was naked except for a patch of cloth over his genitals, a gold watch strap and a single string of prayer beads around his neck. He was a devotee of Vishnu and had painted three thick, vertical lines in red and white on both biceps, across his chest and across his forehead. He was sitting in the sun writing in a book and arranged for tea to be brought to us by one of his followers. The two mugs were brought after 20 minutes by an ageing man wearing shabby clothes who had come from Agra to serve his *guru*, along with a teenager who was also serving Lal Baba for the summer. Lala Baba's own *guru* had died a few years before. This guru had lived for more than 30 winters at Bhojbasa and spent the summers up the side of Shivling in a cave at Topoban where Joe and I hoped to go. He is said to have eaten only potatoes and to have died by falling into a crevasse at the age of 139. It was in his honour, and following his example that Lal Baba went naked as often as the weather would allow. We put ten rupees in the box and set out on the final three-mile hike to Gau Mukh which would take us about two hours. We passed through the grove of short, bushy *bhojbasa* trees which are valued for their honey-yellow bark which peels off in sheets like parchment. It was on these sheets that India's holy books were first written about 3000 years ago. The trees only grow in the inaccessible upper valleys of the Himalayas and inevitably have become especially holy.

Falling rocks have flattened the guide rails along several of the cliff ledges on the path and in one half-mile stretch sand and gravel continually trickled down. The weather remained fine and therefore the path was easy but during a rain rocks might easily tumble across the path and landslides are common.

Beyond the tree-line, the path narrowed until it was no more than a line of whitewashed marker stones spaced six feet apart, stretching across a moraine of loose rocks and gravel. A tingling excitement was growing within me as we picked our way forward, round boulders the size of big white cannonballs, giant speckled dumplings, over white sand as fine as flour, ample evidence of the glacier's colossal power to tear away and grind down mountains.

Suddenly, just ahead, came the echoing roar of boulders and blocks of ice tumbling from the glacier into the river. We quickened our pace across the jumble of rocks and soon reached the edge of the moraine. Here at last we came face to face with the archway of green ice called Gau Mukh.

The colossal glacier itself was still a quarter of a mile away but it did not take long to walk the remaining distance and thus to arrive, finally, at Gau Mukh.

'Well, congratulations,' said Joe, shaking my hand.

'Ah yes,' I mumbled. Could it really be over? Was all the struggling and the passion of seven months completed? Not wanting my enthusiasm to turn cold, I did not delay taking my bath in the river. I stripped to my underpants and stepped quickly over the boulders and ice at the water's edge and entered the Ganga for the last time. The water was not deep but it was icy cold. I waded out towards the main current where blocks of ice were rolling over, bouncing, floating and breaking up in the current. Then I sat down. The cold shock emptied my lungs with a sudden exhalation. I could not believe I was actually bathing in the melt-water of the glacier. Already my legs were numb, though in the glorious sunshine I did not feel cold.

I scooped up the sandy, grey water in my hands and splashed it over my head, chest and arms. This was such a physical shock that I was paralysed for several moments, my mouth hanging open, my breathing stopped and my mind gone blank. I washed my hair then continued splashing the water about in my cupped hands. Unconsciously, this action became an offering and libation to the Ganga and to the goddess. It was an acknowledgement of her presence and a moment of thanks for my safe arrival at this holy of holies. It was also an act on behalf of the many hundreds of people whose prayers and good wishes and hopes I had carried with me throughout my journey from the Bay of Bengal.

I had even carried a poem written in Hindi by Shri Raghunath Prasad Vikal, a retired postal worker in Patna, who had heard of my walk and dedicated a poem about the river to me:

> Chuckling, overflowing! Full to the brim
> Foamy, Bright! the Ganga from the hair of the Rishi (Shiva),
> Beautifying the dry sand
> Oh how beautiful is the sight!

I sat in stunned silence, but moments later I was unable to endure the cold any longer and got up out of the water. I soon dried off in the sunshine and felt tired and somewhat dazed. I sat slowly chewing raisins, peanuts and cashews, while Joe cooked up chicken soup over a fire of dry roots and twigs he had carried up from Bhojbasa. We drank the soup with processed cheese, crackers, tins of fish and cold *chapatis*. Our celebration luncheon was followed by lemon tea and glucose biscuits. The melting of the ice reaches its height soon after midday and we sat in the sunshine with the crashes of falling ice and rocks echoing round the canyon.

This was my journey's end, 1557 miles from the Bay of Bengal, and with a total of £24,000 raised for the Save the Children Fund in India. Yet I could not end the walk. I wanted to keep going, to walk beyond the finishing line, to be sure that the journey was absolutely over, and that I could therefore let it go.

Puffball white clouds were already gathering round the peaks so we did not linger before setting off towards Topoban up a trail of loose pebbles and sand on the left side of the glacier. We slipped and sank up to our knees in the cold rubble again and again as we climbed up about 400 feet. My umbrella became a crutch, and grit and little stones got caught painfully between my toes.

We lost the trail of footprints when we reached the top of the glacier and had to pick our way slowly as best we could over the ridges and small crevasses. It was like trying to walk across a storm-whipped sea that had been suddenly frozen, allowing us to climb jagged waves and cross deep troughs. It was a desolate place, not altogether silent, for there was always the wind and the small clatter of stones falling as the whole glacier shifted. I fell once and winded myself but we crossed the glacier safely and started up a wall of loose, yellow rocks to the left of three streams cascading onto the glacier. This was where we had been told to go and we were aiming for an orange flag at the top of a ridge above our heads.

Joe's long legs took him confidently up the near-vertical cliff while I plodded on behind with knees and legs aching from the strain and my mouth wide open to suck in the air in loud gulps. The way was clearly marked by small cairns of stones and we reached a row of orange flags about half a mile above the tiny river. We sat for a rest sucking cough drops to relieve our raw throats, but it began to drizzle and a cold wind was blowing up the valley. We were both tired and eager to reach the encampment of Simla Baba. The afternoon passed, the temperature dropped and the rain fell more heavily but we were kept warm by our exertions up a long, grass bank, the way still marked by stone cairns. We reached the top of this climb to discover that we had made it. We had now only to cross a meadow of green grass, flowers and a small stream to reach our destination.

We had expected Simla Baba's camp to be austere: his tent was made of plastic bags, pieces of tarpaulin, plastic sheeting from a Japanese mountaineering expedition and sheets of tin, held together with ropes and built on a low wall of rocks and sods of earth. The tent measured about five feet by ten feet and was about five feet high.

We entered through a low, wooden door, then sat cross-legged on sacking spread on the right-hand side of a hearth in the centre of the tent. Simla Baba was stretched out on the other side of the fire, wearing only a cloth over his genitals, numerous necklaces, two silver rings on his right hand and a red headcloth with gold thread. He was a muscular young man, probably in his late thirties, with dark, pitted face, wrinkles round his eyes and a few strands of grey in his bushy, black beard. He chain-smoked either cigarettes or *ganja*.

We were welcome to stay one night and after half an hour's rest on the floor of the stone-built guest hut next door we were called into the smoky tent to eat rice, stewed kidney beans and hot tea.

He spoke a little English, when he felt so inclined, and with a mish-mash of sign language, good humour, English and Hindi, he asked us where we were from and what we were doing. When I told him about my journey from Ganga Sagar he at once broke into laughter, lit himself another cigarette and declared with enthusiasm, 'Your name is

India Baba. Yes yes. India Baba. You sleep here,' he said, pointing to the ground where I was sitting. 'One blanket. He is holy man.' Simla Baba knew that I had no sleeping bag and for one moment I thought the man was sufficiently crazy to give me only one blanket from his ample supply.

Joe said he felt very light-headed, which was not surprising at 14,600 feet. I was subdued and silent. Those reserves of energy which had powered my climb from Gau Mukh were now exhausted. Mid-way through the meal I let out a long, silent sigh. 'I feel out of it,' I murmured to Joe.

But I was not so far out that I did not join Joe, Eric and Kim (who had arrived earlier in the day) and Ram Baba in a disused cave in the encampment which was surrounded by tin cans of marigolds. Ram Baba was a self-effacing young man and Simla Baba's disciple. It was he who carried firewood on his back from Bhojbasa across the glacier and up to Topoban for his *guru*. Outside the cave, the day was ending and mists closing in. We sat in candlelight, smoking, chatting and drinking the tea which Ram Baba made and fetched for us.

All of a sudden Simla Baba appeared in the low doorway, furious and raving at us in Hindi. Ram Baba refused to translate, taking the brunt of the attack upon himself and ushering us out of the cave. This was the first sign of Simla Baba's volatile and violent temper, which was perhaps induced by drugs. The next day Joe and I were to be angrily accused of taking all his food and firewood and of not going when we said we would. We were grateful for the hot food and tea but did donate rice, *dal*, peas, milk powder and half a dozen giant pine cones as firewood. In addition, we had planned to leave money but we were discouraged by his tantrums.

By suppertime, Simla Baba was once again the genial host, serving big portions of *dal* and *chapatis* in the hot, smoke-filled tent. There was a small hole in the roof to let out the smoke but this seemed to be blocked. Simla Baba sat on his mat in front of two shelves where he kept his possessions; a dozen tins of provisions, several large tins beside a framed picture of Durga riding a tiger, his wrist-watch, his packet of cigarettes, a large container of kerosene, his flashlight, candles, oil lamp and a transistor radio.

We washed our plates outside with ash from the hearth and a little cold water, then sat in the tent again because Joe wanted to hear the nine o'clock news in English. The day's events of a world far away were brought inside our camp by the monotonous voice of All India Radio:

> . . . The situation in the Punjab is returning to normal . . . There has been widespread flooding in Calcutta . . . Wimbledon begins tomorrow. . .

Simla Baba clicked off the radio and the intrusion was banished. Dense mist surrounded the camp and nothing existed in the chilly, damp night beyond the tent, the marigolds and the stone guest hut. I went inside and lay down on the floor near the door, wrapping myself in three blankets. I closed my eyes. Soon I was almost asleep, aware only that someone was spreading another blanket over my shoulders. It was now all over.

Appendix: Equipment List

1 umbrella (carried from Benares)
1 knapsack (from Canadian Mountaineering Equipment Ltd.)
1 pair Bata sandals
2 *kurtas* (thigh-length shirt)
1 *lungi* (ankle-length cotton skirt)
1 pair pyjama trousers
1 pair underpants
1 money belt
1 towel
1 mosquito net
1 shawl
1 woven shoulder bag
1 emergency 'space blanket'
1 blanket (in cold season)
1 bottle ink
1 fountain pen
2 pencils
1 flashlight
1 notebook
1 compendium of notes from Indian guidebooks
3 1:1,000,000 maps from Defense Mapping Agency Aerospace Center, Missouri, USA
2 books, bought to read on journey
1 Hindi self-teacher book
1 tube toothpaste
1 toothbrush
1 comb
1 bar of soap for laundry and washing (replaced as needed)
70 Fansidar anti-mosquito tablets
25 aspirin tablets
1 snake bite kit

1   tube antiseptic cream
30 Band-aids (several hundred throughout journey)
1   packet gauze
1   roll sticky tape
1   small bottle antiseptic wash
1   camera
1   wide angle lens
1   70–150 mm zoom lens
1   lens cleaning kit
    supply of film
1   close-up ring
1   2×converter

Selected Bibliography

Basham, A. L., *The Wonder That Was India,* Fontana Ancient History, London, 1967.

Bernstein, Henry, T., *Steamboats On The Ganges,* Orient Longman, Bombay, India, 1960.

Bhagavad-Gita, trans. by Swami Prabhavananda and Christopher Isherwood, Sri Ramakrishna Math, Madras, 1982.

Bhattacharyya, Taundeb, *Ganga Sagar Mela,* Govt. of West Bengal, Calcutta, 1976.

Carvalho, S. A., *The Bandel Church and Hooghly,* St. Joseph's Press, Krishnagar, West Bengal, 1972.

Chaudhuri, Nirad, C., *The Continent of Circe,* Jaico Publishing House, Bombay, 1983.

Chaudhuri, Nirad, C., *Hinduism,* Oxford University Press, Oxford, 1979.

Corbett, Jim, *The Man-Eating Leopard of Rudraprayag,* Oxford University Press, Madras, 1957.

— *Man-Eaters of Kumaon,* Penguin Books, Middlesex, 1970.

Crooke, William, *Religion & Folklore Of Northern India,* S. Chand & Co., New Delhi, 1925.

Darian, Steven G., *The Ganges in Myth and History,* University Press of Hawaii, Honolulu, 1978.

Dave, J. H., *Immortal India* Vol. I–IV, Bharatiya Vidya Bhavan, Bombay, 1970.

Dowson, John, *A Classical Dictionary of Hindu Mythology and Religion,* Routledge & Kegan Paul, London, reprinted 1979.

Eck, Diana L., *Banaras: City of Light,* Routledge & Kegan Paul, London, 1983.

Etienne, Gilbert, *India's Changing Rural Scene 1963–1979,* Oxford University Press, Delhi, 1982.

Fischer, Louis, *The Life of Mahatma Gandhi,* Harper & Row, New York, 1983.

Fishlock, Trevor, *India File: Inside the Subcontinent,* John Murray, London, 1983.

The Ganga Basin, Basin Sub-Basin Inventory of Water Pollution, Central Board for the Prevention and Control of Water Pollution, New Delhi, 1984.

Ghosh, Sachindra Lal, *West Bengal,* National Book Trust, New Delhi, 1976.

Growth And Potential of Tea Industry In India, Economic And Scientific Research Association, Calcutta, 1983.

Handbook of the Bengal Presidency, John Murray, London, 1882.

Hiro, Dilip, *Inside India Today,* Routledge & Kegan Paul, London, 1976.

Hunter, W. W., *Annals of Rural Bengal,* London, 1897.

India, A Travel Survival Kit, Lonely Planet Publications, Victoria, Australia, 1981.

Kala, D. C., *Jim Corbett of Kumaon,* Ankur Publishing House, New Delhi, 1979.

Mathur, M. B., *Uttar Pradesh,* National Book Trust, New Delhi, 1976.

Moorhouse, Geoffrey, *Calcutta,* Penguin Books, Middlesex, 1971.

— *India Britannica,* Paladin Books, London, 1984.

Naipaul, V. S., *India: A Wounded Civilization,* Penguin Books, Middlesex, 1979.

Nehru, Jawaharlal, *The Discovery of India,* Oxford University Press, New Delhi, 1946.

Newby, Eric, *Slowly Down The Ganges,* Picador, London, 1983.

Prabodhanand, Swami & Anand, Swami, *Across Gangotri Glaciers,* Popular Book Depot, Bombay, 1961.

Prasad, Ram Chandra, *Bihar,* National Book Trust, New Delhi, 1983.

Randhawa, M. S., *A History Of Agriculture in India,* Vols. II & III, Indian Council of Agricultural Research, New Delhi, 1982 and 1983.

Rennell, James, *An Account of the Ganges & Burrumpooter Rivers.* London, 1781.

Rushbrook, L. F. (ed.), *A Handbook for Travellers in India, Pakistan, Nepal, Bangladesh & Sri Lanka,* John Murray, London, 1982.

Schulberg, Lucille, *Historic India* (Great Ages of Man), Time-Life Books, New York, 1969.

Sen, K. M., *Hinduism,* Penguin Books, Middlesex, 1961.

Sivaramamurti, C., *Ganga,* Orient Longman, New Delhi, India, 1976.

Spear, Percival, *A History of India,* Vol. 2, Penguin Books, Middlesex, 1965.

Spear, Percival, *The Oxford History of Modern India 1740–1947,* Clarendon Press, Oxford, 1965.

Statistical Outline of India 1984, Tata Services Ltd, Bombay.

Strickland, Cyril, *Deltaic Formation with Special Reference to the Hydrographic Processes of the Ganges and the Brahmaputra,* Longmans, Green & Co., 1960.

Tagore, Rabindranath, *Gitanjali,* Macmillan India Ltd, Delhi, 1981.

Thapar, Romilia, *A History of India,* Vol. 1, Penguin Books, Middlesex, 1966.

Woodruff, Philip, *The Men Who Ruled India: The Founders,* Jonathan Cape, 1953.

Index